The authors wish to thank the following for permission to reproduce copyrighted material: The Viking Press, Inc., Jonathan Cape Ltd., and The Executors of the James Joyce Estate for an excerpt from *A Portrait of the Artist as a Young Man* by James Joyce, Copyright © 1916 by B. W. Huebsch, Inc., 1944 by Nora Joyce, Copyright © 1964 by the Estate of James Joyce, all rights reserved; Doubleday & Company, Inc., and Darton, Longman & Todd Ltd. for excerpts from *The Jerusalem Bible,* Copyright © 1966 by Darton, Longman & Todd Ltd. and Doubleday & Company, Inc.; Holt, Rinehart & Winston, Inc., and The New American Library, Inc., for excerpts from *Varieties of Mystic Experience* by Elmer O'Brien, S.J., Copyright © 1964 by Elmer O'Brien.

Library of Congress Cataloging in Publication Data

Gannon, Thomas M.
   The desert and the city.

   Reprint. Originally published: New York: Macmillan, 1969.
   Includes bibliographical references and index.
   1. Spirituality—History.   I. Traub, George W.
II. Title.
BV4490.G26   1984   248'.09   83-24898
ISBN 0-8294-0452-X

Library of Congress Catalog Card Number: 69-10502

SECOND PRINTING

Loyola University Press
Chicago, Illinois

Printed in the United States of America

THE DESERT AND THE CITY

An Interpretation of the

History of Christian Spirituality

BY

Thomas M. Gannon, S.J.

AND

George W. Traub, S.J.

Loyola University Press, Chicago

The Desert and the City

Contents

Preface

MAN TODAY IS INVOLVED as never before in a quest for his own identity. He seeks above all to know who he is—and why he is. In reality, he has always sought such knowledge, but rarely with such urgency or with so tormenting a sense of loss—lost meaning, lost identity. At the same time man also searches—often secretly, often unconsciously—for the identity of God. He wants to know who God is, dimly aware that only by such knowledge will the meaning of his own life manifest itself. Here too he struggles with a numbing sense of lost awareness: he has no personal experience of divine reality, and the God of religion often seems to him a sentimental father figure or a vague hypothesis. So he gropes in the darkness for a God beyond the God of religion, fighting the feeling of a world lost to irredeemable secularity.

The Christian believes that these two identities, man's and God's, are found together or not at all: that only in knowing God can man come to know himself. To say what man is, I must start from God. But, paradoxically, the reverse is equally true: I can start from man, true man, to say what God is.

This book is a study in the history of spirituality, an attempt to realize how man has pursued this double quest. In undertaking such a task our own approach has worked along socio-cultural and theological lines, conceiving spirituality as something brought to the surface by the deep underground currents which are fed by the gospel and which successively give birth to new ideas and new foundations of the sacred in society. We reject at the outset any conception of spirituality as a search for religiosity lived for its own sake or as a set of doctrines which may be correct in theory but which, when uncritically transposed to the present without regard for their cultural context, divert us from an integral Christian life and distort history and genuine personal commitment. True spirituality is lived in a most personal, serious way; it is the integral life that faith in Jesus Christ gives us as we live in this century, among these men, in this world. It is only in this sense that spirituality can have any meaning and that we can take an interest in its historical development.

A word is required about the purpose and method of this book. Our purpose is neither apologetic nor polemic, though some controversial statements will doubtless be made. Nor do we undertake a compact one-volume history of spirituality touching on all the major figures and movements within two millennia of Christianity. Although writing from a basic acquaintance with the whole history, we are frankly selective and interpretative in our presentation. We begin, for example, not with the New Testament, the basic source of inspiration for all forms of Christian life, but with writings of the third century. We have little to say about Teresa of Avila and John of the Cross, two towering figures in spirituality; and little mention is made of Protestant piety. As a result, this book offers no more than a preliminary meeting or encounter with what we consider to be certain crucial currents in traditional and contemporary spirituality. Our overall question is simply this: if every age must rewrite its own history, where are we to find an authentically Christian spirituality for our time?

It seems hardly necessary to add that, given the breadth of our canvas, we should not be expected to play the "scholarly mandarin," drawing delicately with an exquisitely fine brush. Considerable research into the writers, the ideals, and the institutions of spirituality is already available; without it the present interpretative study could not have been written. Nevertheless, there is need to put the results of this scholarship together. To do so in any definitive way would clearly require many volumes. The originality of the present work derives not so much from our own treatment of any specific topic, but in the way we conceive the development of spirituality and the particular problems on which we dwell in more detail. In choosing to call this book an "interpretation," then, we mean to suggest something of this methodology. While aware of the strictures regarding the use of the "big brush" in historical matters, we have decided to proceed, hoping at least to be careful in its use.

It will soon be obvious that this book is written primarily for people with an apostolic vocation in the world (whether laymen, religious, or clergy). This fact accounts for the more detailed attention given to the ways of discerning God's will while little space is devoted to the ways of discerning the different stages of mystical prayer. Obviously, this choice is not a disparagement of the contemplative way of life, but merely a recognition that most people are not called to it.

Among our canons of selection and interpretation, however, one seems to have been basic: We have sought to address the questions of our Christian present to the sources of our Christian past. How can modern men and women be guided into more creative spiritual lives while accepting, even rejoicing in, the fact that they are, and must remain, modern people? Our answer to this question remains rooted in an attempt to come to terms with the authentic tradition of spirituality as developed within the Church, since we do not think that there is any other basis which offers the slightest hope for success. Only the man who truly possesses the past can earn his own present.

But as a safeguard against the degeneration of the Church's living tradition into dead convention we have sought inspiration for our interpretation from our present problematic. It is mainly because of the questions which stir our own lives and the lives of our contemporaries that the history of spirituality has genuine meaning. Certainly we do not believe that there are any good old days to which Christian spirituality should return, any old cultural forms that *a priori* must be retained. Rather, it is our hope that an encounter between currents of modern thought and past streams of spirituality may prove to be constructive. In seeking to understand ourselves in the present, we believe that only the basic ascetical theology and the solid spiritual experience of the past contain the necessary apparatus. Such an encounter, however, must begin with clearing up misunderstanding about what "traditional" spirituality is and with apprehending precisely the values and interests we have—often unconsciously—inherited from our predecessors and which some people today have assumed to be beyond question. For this reason we may be accused of lacking sympathy for certain spiritual concepts and practices that have nourished the life of the Church in the past. But every writer of history possesses his own canons of interpretation. He brings his own questions to bear on the data at hand; in fact, even his selection of data is determined by these questions. We hope, therefore, that those who may be inclined to disagree with some of our interpretations will at least become more aware of the antecedent suppositions that lie behind their own reading of history.

The inspiration for this book originated in a series of lectures given, together with George A. Lane, S.J., to a number of religious communities in the midwestern United States. During preparation of the manuscript, Justin Kelly, S.J., helped considerably to shape and refine the ideas we were setting forth, particularly in chapters ten and twelve. Many others also contributed to our understanding, and, whenever the source is known, reference is made in the numerous footnotes.

We are happy that there has been a demand for a paperback edition of this book. Except for these concluding paragraphs of the Preface, no revisions have been made in the original text. To try to interpret and unify so many strands of socio-cultural history and theology was a very ambitious task. Fifteen years later we are tempted to nuance the way we treated some topics.[1] But we have resisted this temptation, convinced that the usefulness of our volume lies in the dramatization we gave to certain recurrent issues in the tradition—issues which have not disappeared, but are now even more pressing.

This book examines the Western tradition of Catholic Christian spirituality in the light of questions raised by contemporary religious experience in the United States. Modernity continues to pose very special challenges to this tradition by eroding the sense that its dominance is complete and its position is secure. The challenge of modernity lies precisely in its introduction of cumulative fragmentation at the levels of communal meaning and belonging. Basic Christian orientations are, consequently, under attack from all sides and people feel embattled. Piety may remain, but assurance does not. Even genuine piety cannot long endure in the face of increasing doubt, especially when alternatives to doubt are available in secular perspectives like positive science and revolutionary nationalism, or in faith substitutes like authoritarianism, fundamentalism, and moralism.

Yet beneath these modern manifestations of doubt moves the undertow of an ancient quest—for ultimate meaning and transcendence, for personal identity, for God. With this quest the never-quite-resolved issues persist: prayer and solitude, withdrawal and renunciation, engagement with the world, witness to faith, and service to one's fellow human beings. Social change demands familiar points of reference. Flexibility depends on fixity. People need markers: places, names, standards, sacred formulae. They need to know where they are coming from and where they are going. Without a firmer grasp of the past we are unprepared to face the present in a spirit of hope.

This book was first dedicated to Joseph F. Wulftange, S.J., who served us both as teacher and friend. We are pleased that we were able to offer him this tribute while he still lived. In the intervening years, the earliest and strongest encouragement for publishing a second edition came from Robert F. Harvanek, S.J.—a man whose thirst for the right questions, whose wisdom and magnanimity have been an inspiration to us and to many others. It is with respect, love, and gratitude that we dedicate this edition to him.

January 1, 1984   *Thomas M. Gannon, S.J.*
                                                              George W. Traub, S.J.

Chapter I

A SPIRITUALITY
FOR OUR TIME

To MANY A CATHOLIC standing in the midst of the wonders coming from Vatican II, it seemed as if the almost hopeless hopes of a century were being fulfilled before his very eyes. He was witnessing the sudden climax of an age that had begun with Newman, Scheeben, Lagrange—isolated figures raising their heads over the wall that surrounded post-Reformation Catholicism. It has not taken him long, however, to discover that the Council was much less a climax than a beginning. The energies it released and the hopes it created were so enormous as to leave in its wake inevitable tension, frustration, and disillusionment. It is indeed easy enough to pass off this malaise as a simple failure to hold fast to the tried-and-true formulas, structures, and habits of tradition; or, on the other hand, to blame it on the obstructionism of an ecclesiastical bureaucracy fundamentally out of sympathy with the spirit of the Council. But may it not be more accurate for today's Catholic to see the cause of this tension right within himself?

He tries to assimilate the recent advances in Scripture study, to participate in the new liturgy; perhaps he even ventures into the "new theology." But at the level of his own lived experience, he still feels uncomfortable. It is one thing to read about hierarchical authority as service; it is another to experience formal and impersonal treatment at the hands of an autocratic Curia. It is one thing to read the *Constitution on the Liturgy*, often another to attend Sunday Mass in the average parish. It is one thing to read the holy rule of one's congregation, another to experience what is all too often the anguish of living in a religious community bowed by the weight of anachronistic routine. Here the Christian is involved in no all-out war between the spirit and the flesh; would that the problem were as simple as that or as easy to articulate. Nor, hopefully, is anyone asking for a magic wand to make the tensions disappear. But in all honesty and without any idyllic expectations, present experience often bears little resemblance to the experience of Christian life recorded in the New Testament. What contemporary man is looking for might be called "spirituality," that is to say, the "lived unity of human existence in faith."[1] And this lived unity he does not find.

Over the past decade or more, a clear attempt has been made to satisfy this need for "spirituality"—especially as it exists within the lives of religious—by applying the insights of psychology to the dynamics of religious life. The names Van Kaam, Evoy and Christoph, Kennedy, and others come to mind.[2] Actually, a look through the many books and journals devoted to spirituality during this period reveals something of a preoccupation with the psychological. Seldom has any process of mass education taken place so quickly and effectively. In fact, one can hardly discuss the religious life today without speaking of "personhood," "personality development," or "fulfillment."

Few will deny that these terms are relevant for an integrated spiritual life. The human person is a marvelously complex phenomenon possessing basic requirements for growth on both the physical and psychological levels. Each of us has human affections and emotions, a need to love and be loved, a human need for friendship. We have human sensitivities: we need to be praised and encouraged, we are desperate for understanding and acceptance. Furthermore, each person is an individual: he thinks his own thoughts, makes his own choices, and demands respect for his own individuality. Perhaps the basic source of human unhappiness which religious psychology has attempted to correct is "the heresy of inhumanity"—the tendency to strive for the divine without striving for the truly human.[3] To ignore the needs and rights of humanity invites self-destruction. Holiness finds fertile soil in human wholeness; it finds growth in human integrity. Human nature makes inexorable demands and personality has its own dynamics. The failure to recognize these facts has tended to undermine genuine spirituality and has provided the religious psychologist with much grist for his mill.

The tangible results of introducing a psychological perspective into spirituality have been impressive. A deeper understanding of the human person has ushered in a more humane (and hopefully more Christian) approach to the religious life—something sorely needed also as a counter to the often mechanical piety of the nineteenth and earlier twentieth centuries. The change has perhaps been most evident among American women's congregations of relatively recent founding. A number of these have been able to effect *aggiornamento* with such dispatch as to leave behind not only the older and foreign groups of women but most male congregations and large segments of the diocesan clergy. Obviously, an increased knowledge of psychology has not been the only factor operative here; but the mere existence of movements like Sister Formation calls for courageous thinking about the place of "tradition" in the older and "better established" institutes.

Nevertheless, the very success of the psychological approach may have clouded over some fundamental limitations. First of all, much religious-psychological writing has been addressed rather exclusively to those in religious life, precisely where the need for "psychological liberation" is most sharply felt. This is an initial limitation of some significance. Religious form only a small, though not unimportant, part of the Church; the laity too are hungry more than ever for that "lived unity of human existence in faith," and for them "psychological liberation" does not seem to be the answer.

Even among religious, however, the original impact of psychological literature appears to be waning since the Council. At one time this writing, following Parkinson's Law, was able to create a seemingly unlimited need for more of itself. But today, the average religious becomes quickly sated with talk of fulfillment. He has been inoculated with just enough to be immune to all but the most potent doses. Perhaps he is coming to recognize the irony that the overly introspective tendencies which he so loudly deplores have themselves been increased by a fascination for psychology. Perhaps, too, as he finds greater "fulfillment" he has less need to read about it.

Finally, and this is crucial, psychology has made a limited contribution simply because it is psychology and not theology. As a liberating agent, as a propaedeutic to theology in an age when theological thought lay dormant, psychology has had an important contribution to make; there is no reason to suppose that it cannot continue to do so. But now that the Council has generated new interest in the possibilities of theological reflection, it is doubtful that psychology alone can ultimately satisfy the American in search of a spirituality.

What, then, of spiritual theology and "spiritual reading"? The picture is somewhat dismal. There are, of course, the standard sources of systematic spirituality like Tanquerey and de Guibert.[4] Despite the fact that their works went through many printings a generation or two ago and represent considerable scholarship, few find them satisfactory today—an indication of how much our theological discrimination has changed in a short time. Tanquerey's taxonomic treatment, for instance, seems now to communicate little of the enthusiasm for Christian living found, say, in the Acts of the Apostles; nor does it address itself to the spiritual life as man lives it today. In a typical section he asks what motives make the duty of perfection easier. He answers, first of all, concern for the welfare of one's own soul; if we strive for perfection, he observes, "we likewise increase daily *habitual grace* and acquire a title to a higher degree of glory in heaven. We have seen that every supernatural act done for God by a soul in the state of grace results in an increase of merit. Whoever is unmindful of perfection and is more or less remiss in the performance of his duty, acquires but little merit. . . . On the contrary, he who tends to perfection and strives to make progress, secures merit in large measure; he augments daily his store of grace and glory; each of his efforts is rewarded by additional grace here on earth and by happiness in heaven: 'An eternal weight of glory.' "[5] De Guibert's approach is less commercial than this. Still, the work remains a printed set of classroom notes cast in dry, scholastic form and written before it was possible to integrate spiritual theology with the findings of twentieth-century scholarship in Scripture, liturgy, systematic theology, and behavioral science.

Moving beyond de Guibert, one comes upon Louis Bouyer's *Introduction to Spirituality*.[6] Bouyer merits recognition for introducing some contemporary liturgical theology into his systematic spirituality, as well as for removing from it the myriad classifications and subdivisions of the virtues, vices, stages of prayer and the spiritual life, all of which so enmesh his predecessors. Inveighing against special pleading for a certain school of spirituality, Bouyer insists that there is but one spirituality in the Church—a true statement, given the necessary qualification. The problem is that, as a matter of fact, different schools of spirituality have been characteristic of the Church through the ages, even in her authoritative self-expression, the New Testament. A finer awareness of this diversity might have enabled Bouyer to temper the claim of universality for his own interpretation and to present a more sensitive reading of the distinctive facets of Christian spirituality.[7]

Such systematic spirituality as expounded by Tanquerey, de Guibert, and even Bouyer has for the most part been the diet of religious and priests. What sort of writing does one find broad enough to appeal to the laity as well? Early in this century, English-language works of spirituality took a theological turn in Columba Marmion and Anscar Vonier.[8] But this trend was short-lived. Moralizing rather than theologizing seemed to be the intent of Alban Goodier's very popular personal retelling of the gospel story,[9] while Edward Leen and Eugene Boylan showed their readers new difficulties in mental prayer.[10] Closer to the

present, Ronald Knox demonstrated the way that is open for
spiritual writing when little new theological insight is available:
a perfection of literary style which, unfortunately, did not draw
on his own deep religious experience.[11] A special feel for the
concrete and experiential may account for the greater popularity
of another stylist, Gerald Vann.[12]

On the American scene, the prayer-and-life manuals of Francis
LeBuffe and Martin Scott, with their "substitute spirituality" of
God and Myself individualism, far outlived the uneducated im-
migrant Catholic for whom they were originally written.[13] In the
forties and fifties, Fulton Sheen and his philosophical appeal to
common sense drew a large audience of Catholics and non-Catho-
lics alike, first on weekly radio and later on TV, as well as
through books like *Peace of Soul* and the five volumes of *Life Is
Worth Living*.[14] Mention must finally be made of the enigma of
Thomas Merton. That a contemplative monk, writing within the
context of his own special vocation, should be the single most
popular spiritual writer of a generation calls for more explanation than his being a genuine poet. At any rate, Merton is probably most convincing when writing about himself while refraining
from the implication that his is the special path for every dedicated soul.[15]

It seems unnecessary to make further assessment of spiritual
reading during the first half of our century. Here, as in the
religious psychology which brought some liberation, there has
been a fundamental absence of creative theology. A spirituality
for our time must above all be theological. Although Robert
Gleason has been credited with reintroducing theology into English spiritual writing,[16] the Council has made it painfully clear
that the English-speaking Catholic is almost totally dependent on
the European theologians. As more and more of this writing is
translated from German, Dutch, and French, one sees what an
enormous task of assimilation awaits us. The work of an entire
prolific generation is being dumped into our laps within a few
short years. And even while one struggles to digest it, there lurks
at the back of his mind a question about the viability of a theology born of a philosophy like existentialist phenomenology and a

culture like that of war-ravaged Europe—both so different from our own.[17]

Christian theological thought always has developed in service to the Church, and often as a result of a series of challenges to the "official" tradition. To accept the gospel of Christ is to create a new life; and in accepting the demands of this new life, it is most difficult to formulate the totality of revelation into a set of doctrinal beliefs or a manner of life that can be practiced. At the same time, the nature of the Christian message forbids one to take theology as a purely academic discipline pursued in isolation. The theology of the patristic age was a theology worked out chiefly by bishops grappling with the problems of their pastoral ministry. The theology of the early Middle Ages was the labor of monks trying to preserve and transmit the Christian heritage in the midst of barbarism. Scholastic theology arose as Christian thinkers entered the turbulent intellectual life of the newly founded universities. The theology of the seminary manuals was the result of the Church's attempt to meet the attacks of the Reformation. Surely we need a theology to serve the needs of the contemporary Catholic caught between the religious patterns bequeathed to him by tradition and the recent findings in Scripture study, liturgy, systematic theology, and behavioral science, as well as the tensions of his own times.

In any period of rapid change, however, the task before spiritual theology is even more precarious. How can we balance the changing with the changeless? How be faithful to the experience and learning of the present without destroying the viable traditions of the past? We pride ourselves on having laid to rest the old scholastic manuals of dogma and spirituality, but with what do we replace them? We may dip into the writings of Teilhard and perhaps Durrwell or Häring, listen to a series of lectures by Bernard Cooke, or catch up on the latest family scandal in the *National Catholic Reporter*. All this is well enough; but one runs the risk of myopia. In order to comprehend what is going on today and see precisely where we stand, do we not need perspective? Today must be seen in the light of the tradition of Christian yesterday.

Both some who favor and some who oppose the renewal of the Church assume that the Church is saying and doing all sorts of new things. Yet this "bringing up to date" has been principally a turning back—not to the partial tradition of the immediate past, but to the whole tradition of the Church—with a view to evaluating the entire course of development in the light of its origins. To cite but one example from the Council itself, the Fathers have charted the guidelines for tomorrow's liturgy with their eyes on the early Christian liturgies and the various forms they have assumed in the course of history. In all this, the Church has come to recognize and operate on a central methodological principle that has been emerging from the time of Hegel's *Phenomenology of Spirit* to that of Teilhard's *Phenomenon of Man:* one comes to an adequate understanding of a given situation only by retracing the steps that have led up to it. Any single stage in the evolutionary process is meaningless apart from what has preceded it and prepared its way. "Everything is the sum of the past," says Teilhard; "nothing is comprehensible except through its history."[18] We must, then, turn back and study the great currents —the writers, ideals, institutions—in the history of spirituality in order to discover what significant elements of the Christian tradition we have lost and to what extent we have accepted *as viable* elements which, in reality, are little more than cultural distortions of genuine spirituality. It is this fundamental conviction that grounds the whole of the present inquiry.

In order to provide a framework for analysis, it is important at this point to delineate the broad features of spirituality in general and to distinguish different ways in which the term spirituality can be used. Like theology as a whole, spirituality is integrally human, yet completely sacred—as vast and diversified as the reality of man's encounter with God. Unfortunately, the separation of theology from spirituality does not make the task of definition any easier. On the contrary, this dichotomy more often results in sterile theology, spirituality nourished by large doses of will power and sentimentality, or a combination of the two. Like the ill-fated Modernists at the turn of the century, we too face the challenge of rethinking the Christian message in a way that takes account both of historical development and personal experience.[19] This quest lies at the center of spirituality and must ground any attempt to define our terms in a more precise fashion.

Christian spirituality may be loosely defined as the way to holiness; in more theological terms, it is the way to man's full possession by the Father through Christ in the Spirit. In this broad understanding of the term there can be only *one* spirituality, since the one way to holiness must always be the Person of Christ. All spiritual life consists in a partial reenactment in our own lives of what happened once and for all in Jesus of Nazareth as the Incarnate Word.[20] All authentically Christian piety is, consequently, an *imitatio Christi*—not a mechanical, servile, mawkish imitation, but one which is spontaneous and free, proportioned to one's unique personality and life situation.

But when the brilliance of Christ's redeeming activity is refracted and applied in various historical contexts, the general means of union with God become specific and concrete in the lives of individual men and women. It is through their example that something of the power of Christ is mediated to us and we are shown the way to new and creative realizations of Christian sanctity. From particular visions of God, certain styles of approach result, and these are also referred to as spirituality. But no style of spirituality manifests completely the meaning of grace, redemption, or salvation. As John Courtney Murray has pointed out, God would have each man wholly to be his witness, but not necessarily a witness to the whole of Him. Only the Church, as the community of all the faithful, in her many-splendored variety, is a witness to the whole counsel of God.[21]

This distinction between man's union with God and more individual styles of approach has important implications. At any given time and place in history society challenges men to respond to God. These challenges have brought forth responses from extraordinary people. So penetrating was their vision of the relevance of Christ to their society that they were followed by large numbers of men and women who wished to share this vision. In this way schools of spirituality emerged, such as the Benedictine,

Dominican, Franciscan, and Jesuit—each of which sprang from definite needs of the Church at a given historical moment. But within each school it is further necessary to distinguish between a vision and a technique. The vision, or the new inspiration which a group produces and the religious universe in which its activity is situated, constitutes a permanent mental framework, a perspective in reference to which the service of God and one's own search for God take on new value and direction. The technique, or the way in which one's vision and the needs of a given age intersect, is intrinsically fluid and changes as society itself changes. If it appears important for us to make these distinctions, it is because the need to develop the theological foundations of spirituality is being felt today in a particularly acute way. If, to borrow an expression from Karl Marx, we need to reject a theory which has never been expressed in practical, day-to-day affairs, we find equally distasteful a spirituality made up of practical directions but whose doctrinal justification or theological perspective is not apparent. In the final analysis, therefore, spirituality consists in the style of a person's response to the grace of Christ before the challenge of everyday life in a given historical and cultural environment.

Now the relationship between vision and technique, or between spirituality and its social context, is never unilateral, but dialectic. Spirituality is a social product. It is also a crucial factor in the changing life styles of Christianity. Once the vision of these extraordinary servants of God is embodied in techniques and raised to the level of a relatively autonomous system of meaning, a spirituality has the capacity to act back upon the group that produced it in such a way that the original vision can be partially or even totally obscured. For example, a group of Benedictine monks may break away from the conventional life of their monastery and settle in the forest of Citeaux because they have special problems as Benedictines in a situation where the original Rule of St. Benedict has become submerged under customs and where there is a complete absence of any machinery or external authority to maintain or re-create a standard of observance.[22] But once the reforming group has made a fresh and thorough start, not only may they look upon religious life from an angle that is no longer simply Benedictine, but their activities and over-all style of life change as a result of their newly acquired spiritual perspective.

Furthermore, the growing complexity and sophistication of one's spiritual world-view (in this instance, the Cistercian) makes it increasingly inaccessible to outsiders, and the enhanced autonomy of the perspective itself makes for special problems of legitimation for outsiders and insiders alike.[23] Alternative views of the Christian life have to be kept out. It sometimes happens that those who share the "true" spiritual vision form esoteric enclaves, "hermetically sealed" to all but those who have been properly initiated into their vision and techniques. If the new spirit catches on, it also constitutes the criterion against which other styles of spirituality are measured. Consequently, when a spirituality has been so legitimized, it tends to impose itself on the rest of the Church. As with the Alexandrian tradition of eastern monasticism, its definitions of God and the world are posited as *the* objective reality. Anyone wishing to be authentically spiritual thus discovers not only an objective organization like monasticism, but also an objective spiritual world to which his experiences must conform if they are to be "really spiritual." Of course, those who mediate this world-view modify reality in the course of transmitting their vision of it. They select aspects of it according to their own location in society and their own individual idiosyncrasies. The possibility of union with God is thus "filtered" to successive generations through this double selectivity. It is only when a perspective proves inadequate to religious experience and the challenges of concrete living (e.g., the Cistercian vs. the Benedictine) that alternate approaches emerge and are then granted legitimacy.

It is never a simple matter to explain how spiritualities become detached from their existential origins and from the contemporary challenges in which they operate. The extent of such disengagement depends upon a considerable number of historical factors—the urgency of the social and cultural interests involved, the degree of theological refinement of the spirituality in question (e.g., the Alexandrian vs. the Coptic monastic tradition), and the social relevance or irrelevance of this theology. These factors will become clearer as we proceed. For our present purposes, it is more important to grasp, in principle, the dialectic between the social situation and the spirituality that is its product, and to keep this in mind when we analyze different spiritual perspectives in the following chapters. For in disposing ourselves for union with God, no one of us starts from scratch. Previous currents in Christian spirituality never wholly run out in the Church. At the very least they turn underground. Either manifest or latent, they remain to influence our own approach to God even when the time of their relevance is past. Our chief task, then, is to bring these themes into sharper focus so that we might become sensitive to our own heritage and free to serve God in the present with critical understanding and love.

But what about this heritage? How is one to discern the faithfulness of any given element of tradition to the original revelation of God's Word? How evaluate the Alexandrian notion of prayer, for example, the numerous benedictions and consecrations that characterize the piety of the later Middle Ages, or the recurring idea that contemplation is the most sublime activity of the Christian life? If all spiritual life consists in a partial re-enactment of what happened once and for all in Jesus of Nazareth, then the New Testament stands as the chief criterion of any spirituality. Yet, as we have said, God's truth in human words is intended for vital encounter with man. Revelation does not possess a mere timeless intrinsic validity; it has earthly existence only by being actually believed in fact. In this way the pure truth of the gospel must bear the stamp of the age in which it is heard. Consequently, it is wholly understandable that early Christian theologians might conceive of prayer as an attempt to detach the mind from its bodily prison and unite the individual soul to the supreme immutable God. "When . . . your intelligence goes out of the body," says Evagrius, "and rejects all thoughts that come from sense and memory and bodily humors and is filled with awe and joy, then it is allowable to think that you are close to the confines of prayer."[24]

Unfortunately, an explanation like Evagrius' destroys the terms of the problem. Man is a unity of spirit and body. He achieves union with God not by abstracting from the dimensions of space and time, not by striving for insensitivity to his physical and psychological condition, but by opening himself to God in the totality of his being *as man,* not as disembodied spirit. The problem with Evagrius' notion of prayer is not merely that the best philosophical instrument within reach—the Neo-Platonic theory of the soul's imprisonment in the body and the consequent disdain for material creation—broke in his hands. It delivered only an abstractionist theory of prayer. This is neither an understanding of the Christian doctrine of man nor of the Incarnate God who became man in order that we might become gods. To attempt to understand man's response to God in this way is not to understand it at all. Evagrius' genial speculations (and, as we shall see, the entire Alexandrian tradition) had an enormous influence on subsequent theological thought and the history of spirituality. The fact is that this concept of prayer insufficiently, and in the long view, inaccurately, expressed the original revelation of Christ. Its endurance certainly does not make it more timeless or more universally valid; it does mean that this understanding bears the style of mind of an earlier age, a habit of thought which for a long time was wrongly regarded as possessing a validity identical with the eternal validity of the gospel. Such hardening of form is nothing else but a dangerous symptom of an indifference to truth; and for those who continue to accept this form uncritically, it is a symptom of their lack of strength to effectively assimilate the gospel.[25]

Actually, the Church can do very little against the danger of spiritual "heresy" unless, like Pelagianism or Jansenism, it arrives at more obvious and extreme conclusions. The Church is even more helpless against heresy that only makes certain correct assertions and is silent on others that do not suit it. But even though the Church has come out strongly against Pelagianism and Jansenism, few of us would be so naive as to think that these tendencies have by that fact been effectively flushed out of our system. Man's mental world today is undoubtedly determined in

large part by attitudes, doctrines, and tendencies which contradict or understate the teaching of the gospel. Part of the reason
for this may be that our former attitudes serve a function and
meet a need which newer approaches do not meet. But when this
is said, we are not implying that the main task of spirituality is to
get the Bible straight and then apply it, or to re-think the philosophical problems of God and man and then start talking in a
new language. In part, the solution does lie in measuring spiritual teaching by the New Testament and early life of the
Church, as well as by ascertaining to what extent these teachings
derive from a past, historically conditioned view of human life—
a view which may look Christian because of its long symbiosis
with true Christianity, but which, in reality, is strongly determined by latent heresies of earlier times. For religious, part of
the solution includes "the constant return to the sources of all
Christian life and to the original spirit of their institutes."[26]
Beyond this, we have the extraordinarily difficult task of creating
a contemporary Christian identity and purpose.

This is too large a topic to develop at length here, and quite
frankly, we are addressing ourselves to the prior question of
reconstructing the heritage of spirituality. Yet attempting to
initiate anyone into the spiritual life by means of a historical-
theological discussion is an uncertain undertaking, even when it
is needed. The only central point of the spiritual life is God;
and that center is everywhere. God's grace is greater than religious institutions or styles of spirituality; we can never elevate
any vision or technique into an absolute of the religious life.
Each individual man or woman, as Karl Rahner observes, is a
unique and unrepeatable term of God's creative love. Each must
find his path to God in a way proper to himself.[27] Yet the grace
of Christ never comes to us "like a bolt from the blue." It is
channeled to us through very concrete circumstances. The Word
became flesh to unite to himself a holy people. To experience
God is merely the beginning of the spiritual life. It is only within
the Christian community that one's "conversion" can be effectively maintained as plausible. Grace comes through the people
God has fashioned, and the experience of grace incorporates us

ever more deeply into that people. In other words, Saul may have become Paul in the aloneness of religious ecstasy, but he could *remain* Paul only in the context of the Christian community that recognized him as such and confirmed the "new being" in which he now located this identity.[28]

It is difficult to hold these two points of experience and tradition in balance. The question for the religious man today is not whether there are spiritualities in the Church, but whether there is a spirituality for our time—whether God is still revealing himself in our own experiences. A God who once spoke to Augustine, Francis, or Ignatius Loyola, but now speaks no more, is not only uninteresting but unintelligible. To put the matter crudely (paraphrasing the remark of Rousseau), if God wanted to talk to me then why did he go speak to Moses! But the question is neither irrelevant nor illegitimate. In the book of Jeremiah, the king Zedekiah asks the prophet: "Is there any word from the Lord?" Today the question would be more likely to read, "Is there any word from the Lord for us?"[29]

It is possible to dismiss this demand for a present revelatory spirituality as a lack of sophistication or as the unquenchable thirst for something new. Such a dismissal would only be justified if the question were not posed with ultimate seriousness. In the recurring dialogue with God as he comes to us both through the Christian past and our present experience, certainly we encounter His revelation and His grace continually. Life in the concrete "has an inward openness toward God through which grace is constantly being offered to us. Joy, seriousness, responsibility, daring, commitment to an unforeseeable future, love, birth, the burden of work and thousands of other aspects of life which everyone experiences have an undercurrent which comes from grace and leads to it."[30]

The problem here is twofold. In the ordinary routines of daily living we seldom meet God in his utter transcendence. The action of the Spirit is inextricably linked to natural and earthly values so that it is impossible, by mere introspection, to distinguish between that which is due to the limitless natural openness of man and that which is due to the gratuitously supernatural call of God. At the same time, any attempt to construct a spirituality for our time is a precarious enterprise when it constricts its glance to merely contemporary experience. Christian experience, while genuinely timeless and unique, is a fundamentally relational affair. It has no meaning if it is separated from the tradition out of which it springs. No one can acquire an authentically Christian identity which does not have a strongly biblical, historical, and ecclesial dimension.

Our sensitivity and appreciation for the history of spirituality can never shroud the value of freedom and spontaneity in seeking God. The ways in which God may call a man to serve him are countless; and the saints were often strikingly unsystematic people because they were aware of the overriding greatness of God. But unless we keep in mind the diversity of Christian spirituality, we shall be in danger of misunderstanding the import of our own contemporary problematic. In the dialectic between God's limitless grace and the humanly constructed styles of spirituality man himself is transformed. In this same dialectic man finds God and thereby finds himself.

Chapter II

IDEALS OF
THE DESERT

ANY CONSIDERATION OF THE ORIGINS of the spiritual life as a self-conscious pursuit must begin toward the end of the third century. Certainly the Christian life had been practiced with fervor by individuals and communities from the time of the Apostles; the New Testament gives ample witness to this fact. But spirituality—as the systematic concern over the ascent of the soul to God—did not appear for almost a century and a half. By then the Church was no longer capable of seeing itself as already possessed of the kingdom of God, seated at the heavenly banquet table. There arose, instead, an acute awareness of the Church as a Church of sinners, of people in search of purification, education, and sanctification. In becoming more self-concerned, the Church thus gave birth to specialized institutions and conceptual models which attempted to chart the path of this ascent to God.

It was at this time that monasticism emerged in the East as a distinct style of life, separated in theory and in practice from the life of the ordinary, everyday Christian. In order to understand the thrust of the eastern monastic movement, however, it must first be viewed within the context of the Gospels and developments of the early Christian community as depicted in the Acts

of the Apostles, for whatever else monasticism is or has become, it
consists, first of all, in a concrete and particularized expression of
the revelation of the New Testament. It is based on a distinctive
conception of that revelation, and on the way in which certain
men responded to the gratuitous action of God. After this it will
be necessary to consider in some detail the desert ideals of self-
surrender, protest, asceticism, solitude, and contemplation, as
well as the climate within which these ideals developed.

The casual, or even careful, present-day reader of the literature of the earliest monastic writers forms the strong impression
that, for these men, the whole spiritual teaching of Christ is
epitomized in Luke's formulation of Christ's invitation, "If any
one wishes to come after me, let him deny himself, take up his
cross, and follow me" (9:23). Here emerge the two fundamental
dispositions which many have felt lie at the root of the Christian
life: renunciation of oneself and the determination to follow and
imitate Christ. The hermits and early eastern monks expressed
their conviction to come apart from the world and find God in
the solitude of extended prayer and rigorous penance with an
unbounded enthusiasm that made them appear foolish even to
many of their Christian contemporaries. Men like Anthony,
Athanasius, Pachomius, and Basil felt they had made the greatest
discovery; they had found their earthly paradise. The letters of
Jerome give us many illustrations of this view. "O desert," he
cries, "enamelled with the flowers of Christ. O solitude where
those stones are born of which in the Apocalypse is built the city
of the Great King! . . . How long [he asks a friend] will you
remain in the shadow of roofs, in the smoky dungeon of the
cities? Believe me, I see here more of the light."[1]

The motive for such enthusiasm is not difficult to uncover. In
every man, except possibly the most depraved, there lies a yearning for self-surrender which rises at times to a passion. This kind
of instinct is not easy to explain, nor can it be laughed away or
simply ignored. It has led some men, almost in spite of themselves, in a moment of heroic decision, to give their lives for
others. And there are few people who do not some time come
upon the vision of a nobler life, a more perfect existence.

Freudian analysts might explain this drive as an escape from a restrictive and repressive superego; existential psychiatrists might call it the search for meaning, the desire for transcendence. Whatever name we finally settle on is, in the long run, of minimal importance. The desire for self-surrender is part of the ground of human personality; and it is to this longing that Christ appealed throughout his life, death, and resurrection. Those who plan to renounce only the things forbidden under sin are working to save their souls, which everyone must do; but those who desire perfection must do more. To the man who with a commitment of his whole person accepts Christ as Lord, self-surrender is not a counsel. It is an imperative call of the Master. As Christ advised the wealthy young man: "There is still one thing you lack. Sell all that you own and distribute the money to the poor, and you will have treasure in heaven; then come, follow me" (Luke 18:22). Although the form this surrender is to take in the history of Christianity will vary with the changing years, its starting point has always been an acceptance of and commitment to the Risen Christ.

Reinforcing this desire for surrender was the Christian notion that man is engaged in a struggle which will last as long as his life on earth. As St. Paul put it, "In my inmost self, I dearly love God's law, but I can see that my body follows a different law that battles against the law which my reason dictates. This is what makes me a prisoner of that law of sin which lives inside my body. What a wretched man I am! Who will rescue me from this body doomed to death? Thanks be to God through Jesus Christ our Lord! In short, it is I who with my reason serve the Law of God, and no less I who serve in my unspiritual self the law of sin" (Rom. 7:21-25). In addition to fighting their own internal moral disharmony, Christians felt the need to guard against the suggestions of the World and do battle against the machinations and plots of the evil spirits of whose existence man had been told by God Himself. Thus, man's innate yearning for self-surrender, coupled with the Christian's vision of spiritual combat, form a necessary part of our understanding of the eastern monastic movement.

Besides this, however, there were the social and cultural pressures of a fading Roman Empire. It is a truism that human thought is in certain ways sociologically conditioned. In the fourth century, as Owen Chadwick has observed, "the social outlook drew from the Gospel that element which seemed so accurately to fit its spiritual needs—the demand to reject the world."[2] It is important in sketching the background of eastern monasticism to probe some of the factors which made this spiritual movement a clamor of *protest*. It was not without reason that the whole Christian Church during these early years was in some sense fleeing the world.

The rise of monasticism roughly coincides with the accommodation of the Church to the world around it. In some ways such adjustment was inevitable. Every newly founded religious group has to face the problem of how it will handle its relationship to the established order. A. D. Knock, in his well known study of conversion in classical antiquity, has pointed out that new religious groups are often at odds with the established society, its norms, and institutions.[3] These groups offer a new community and a new pattern of life to their members. They represent a break with the past. There is ample evidence in the New Testament of this kind of radical reaction. "If anyone comes to me without hating his father, mother, wife, children, brothers, sisters, yes and his own life too, he cannot be my disciple" (Luke 14:26). Paul too speaks of the solidarity of the Christian community which obliterates the distinctions of the past and of the outside world: "All baptized in Christ, you have all clothed yourselves in Christ, and there are no more distinctions between Jew and Greek, slave and free, male and female, but all of you are one in Christ Jesus" (Gal. 3:28). In the long run, the Church did not follow this active revolutionary path. Abandoning its earlier apocalyptic conception of the quick return of Jesus, the Church settled down to an acceptance of the "world" as a definite part of the economy with which it had to come to terms. While clinging to its essentially other-worldly orientation and rejecting in spirit the pursuit of purely secular values, Christianity left the established forms of social domination by the aristocracy and the gaping distance between social classes relatively undisturbed; it thus avoided prolonged and active opposition to the established society. It is interesting, for example, that while unbending in its opposition to certain customs and prescriptions of Roman law and often persecuted as a result (at times bitterly), the Church in its early history never denied the legitimacy before God of the established governmental structures. This ambivalence in the Christian attitude would continue in various forms despite changing historical conditions down the centuries. The new group asserts its own superiority over established authorities, but in a way that neither challenges nor threatens their effective operation or legitimacy. While becoming a community unto itself, the Church at the same time recognized and came to terms with the legitimate political structure. Actually it baptized that authority and joined hands with it.

But such accommodation inevitably demanded more of the new religion than it bargained for. Unfortunately, whatever the ultimate issue of Constantine's adoption of Christianity as the official religion of the Roman world, its first effects were to lower the ideal of Christianity itself. In the striking comment of Harnack, it seemed as if the net result of Constantine's action was to leave the world "in possession of all except its gods."[4] The stalwart Christians whom Diocletian had murdered were replaced by a multitude of time-servers and half-converted pagans. The conviction of the imminent reign of Jesus gave way to an uninspired contentment with things as they were. Occupied incessantly with questions of divine relations and processions, the Church tended to lose sight of the message of Christ, his lordship of history, and his work of salvation.

We must beware, however, of attributing these changes wholly to Constantine. The startling canons of the Council of Elvira (c. 300 A.D.) show that rottenness had already eaten into the Church itself. In the phrase of the eminent Church historian Herbert Workman, originally the Church "had descended out of heaven as a bride adorned for her husband; now the bridal dress was torn, the orange flower had faded. She was rich and increased in goods, and knew not that she was poor and naked."[5] Heresy mounted; Arians monopolized the sees of the Church, and for a time even the Chair of Peter was suspect. The followers of Damasus, in their struggle with the anti-pope Ursinus in 366, won for him the papacy, but at the cost of one hundred and thirty-seven lives. Once the Christians had laid down their lives for their faith; now they slaughtered each other to secure the prizes of the Church. "The doctrines of the Fathers," writes Basil, "are despised, the speculations of innovators hold sway in the Church. Men are rather contrivers of cunning systems than theologians. The wisdom of this world has the place of honor, having dispossessed the boasting of the Cross. The shepherds are driven out; in their place grievous wolves are brought in which harry the flock. Houses of prayer have none to assemble in them; the deserts are full of mourners."[6]

Such was the climate in which monasticism took root and began to grow. Christians of an earlier age could look upon their heroic martyrs as the supreme models of Christian witness; for them martyrdom represented the pinnacle of Christian renunciation. But since the great peace which actually preceded Constantine's conversion and especially after the conjunction of Church and State, the possibility of martyrdom had been eliminated. In the new conditions of accommodation and increasing worldliness, the holy men of the time were driven to construct a new form in which the old ideal of religion as the great renunciation might once again find expression. This new ideal was no longer to be found in the Church; nor, with the exception of Apollinaris, did men seek for it in the apocalyptic visions of earlier days. Rather, as Workman has observed, the new ideal lay above the Church, and, in a sense, even *outside* it. "The saint preached once more the need of the narrow way and the strait gate, but the broad road with which he compared it was not only in the world. The hermit fled not so much from the world as from the world in the Church, from court bishops who fought for richer sees, from people who bore the name of Christ but who were still pagans at heart, from men who as soon as they were made clerics, 'enlarged the fringes of their garments, rode on foaming steeds,' and dwelt in houses of many rooms, with sculptured doors and painted wardrobes. It was the snake in the grass that the monk dreaded; the open foe he could meet and crush."[7]

Within this context, the New Testament attitude of *indifference to* the world became transformed into a *suspicion of* the world—expressed in distrust and disparagement of the flesh and in anxiety over, and even fear of, sex. As part of this reaction, some people voluntarily embraced lives of celibacy, at times accompanied by excessive self-inflicted punishments. Others went into the desert to live a hermit's life and do battle with the devil unencumbered by the distractions of the city.[8] The movement toward monasticism was not merely an exodus of despair from the evils of the age, but even "a veritable stampede from the Catholic Church, as though that great creation of Christian energy were no better than the evil world from which escape was sought."[9] Thus, despite a few notable exceptions, monasticism as a whole emerged as separate from the Catholic Church, with an ideal, a style of life, and a pattern of institutions of its own that claimed to be indepedendent of—and even superior to—the institutions, life, and ideal of the Church itself. The flight to the desert represented both a protest and an affirmation—a protest against a decadent and overly institutionalized ecclesiastical body and a restatement of the gospel teaching to fit the changed conditions of the times.

Over the centuries, with the adoption of the Rule of St. Basil by segments of eastern monasticism, the movement was partially returned to the mainstream of the Church, placing its fervor and energy at the disposal of the Church's ideals and aims. Because of these later developments, it is easy to underestimate how completely the earlier ideal of monasticism lay outside, and at times even opposed to, that of the Church. Understandably, the first reaction of the Church was to suspect the extremes of abstinence and self-denial, for many felt that the flight to the desert represented a protest movement that by-passed the Church's established means of salvation in the sacraments. Until the end of the fifth century, the monk was generally regarded as a layman, whose tonsure was neither an equivalent for orders nor an exemption from the pains and penalties of lay life. Anthony, easily

the most renowned of the early hermits, was not merely a layman. He neither went to church nor received the sacraments for
years; yet he continued in the closest union with God.[10] In
Nitria, some fifty miles southeast of Alexandria in the Nile Delta,
eight priests sufficed for the spiritual administration of five thousand monks. In the process of time the monk was often compelled, because of the need of providing for the ritual of the
monastery, to join the priesthood; but the special circumstances
which brought this about never succeeded in making the priesthood anything more than an accidental addition to the monk's
religious profession. It is most significant, then, that monasticism in its origin was the protest of the lay spirit against any
conception of religion which excluded the laity from the highest
Christian obligations or the highest perfection. The plea of
Montanus and his followers for the emancipation of the Holy
Spirit from the rigid fetters of an increasing sacramentalism and
a mediating priesthood had been set aside and condemned. Yet,
as Workman comments, against all growing sacerdotalism "the
monk by his very existence was a silent, unconscious, but nonetheless potent protest."[11]

That the early monks were laymen, and rather anticlerical
laymen, is not the only consequence that can be traced from the
fact that monasticism lay tangential to the Catholic Church.
"The dominating principle that pervaded Egyptian monasticism
in all its manifestations," writes Dom Cuthbert Butler, "was a
spirit of strongly marked individualism."[12] The very extravagances and eccentricities which can so easily be held up for
amusement or ridicule are merely illustrations of this pronounced individualism manifesting itself in a rivalry of asceticism. Whether in the East or West, the monk was the voice in the
wilderness crying the forgotten truth of the worth of one individual soul against the growing collectivism of the Church. He
recoiled from the growing conception of the kingdom of God as
an organized society. He responded instead to Christ's words:
"The kingdom of God is within you." In contrast to Cyprian's
notion of a great imperial institution as the channel of grace,
with its apostolically descended bishops, presbyters, and deacons,

its elaborate system of sacraments, and its idea of solidarity in a common organization, the earliest monks proposed the individual life of the soul, face to face with God, in direct, not intermediate, communion with the divine, outside all institutions, often cut off by the physical fact of their renunciation from all sacraments, generally independent of bishops and priests, and their solidarity with fellow solitaries limited to spiritual communion.[13]

To flee from the problems of the Church and the decay of the world rather than to stand one's ground and labor for renewal and reform, to abandon a sinking ship rather than to help guide it into port might appear to be a less noble, perhaps even cowardly, reaction. But in partial justification it must be admitted that reform seemed virtually impossible. What remedy could heal the lowered ideals, the routinization of religion, and the apparently weakened manhood within the Church? Who could repair an empire slowly sinking into ruin, as much from weaknesses within—bad finance, a poverty-ridden middle class, an army of hireling barbarians—as by attacks from without? Internally, the Roman world, writes Harnack, "had arrived, by all the routes of its complicated development, at the bitterest criticism of and disgust at its own existence."[14] Nor can we overlook the notion—so prevalent at the time of monasticism's inception and fostered by Diocletian's reorganization of the old Augustan Principate into a new absolutist empire—that the individual existed simply for the sake of the State, that outside of his political utility, man had no ground for being. In the East and West alike, pagans and Christians agreed that Rome's rule was, of its very nature, eternal. But that rule worked with such mechanical precision and domination that the individual ceased to have any place. Monasticism, of course, refused to accept this idea, and in its own way, unconsciously prepared for the modern concept that the State exists for individuals and possesses neither sanctions nor powers except those which the citizenry may confer.

Louis Bouyer has written: "What certainly makes it difficult for many Christians today, even very fervent Christians, to appreciate monasticism is that it is without any question a flight from the world."[15] Looking back, we may see that for the Christian intent on perfection there were other alternatives which quite possibly would have been more challenging than flight to the desert. In the fourth century, Christianity was still a religion for townspeople, and following the lead of St. Paul, the Church sought its converts and built its churches in the towns. Yet the hermit and the monk sought more. As Jerome wrote in a letter to his friend Paulinus, "If you wish to take duty as a presbyter, then live in the cities and walled towns. . . . But what has the monk to do with cities, which are the homes, not of solitaries, but of crowds? . . . We have our masters in Elijah and Elisha, and our leaders in the sons of the prophets, who lived in fields and solitary places, and made themselves tents by the waters of Jordan. After the freedom of their lonely life they found confinement in a city as bad as imprisonment."[16] Moreover, from the current Neo-Platonic philosophy these early monks accepted wholeheartedly the idea that the highest good attainable by man was knowledge of one's own self, a knowledge to be gained only by concentrated self-discipline. The monks thus fled to the desert that they might more fully pursue this self-discipline and self-knowledge in the "universities of its solitude."

It is important to dwell briefly on these ideals of solitude and self-discipline. It does not seem entirely fair to say that the monk's yearning for isolation was merely a desire for return to a more unencumbered life—the free life of the fields over against the artificial life of the cities. No doubt there are many places in the writings of the desert fathers that give this impression. And if, in the beginning, the Christian who fled from his City of Destruction was more conscious of that from which he fled than of the new life which he found, it was not long before the lure of solitude for its own sake captivated his mind and heart. As Thomas Merton explains it, Christianity is essentially a religion of the Word of God. It is easy to forget that this Word first of all emerges from silence. Underlying the search for interior solitude is the basic principle that silence is the actualization of a faith in the single Word of God. Here man takes responsibility for fostering his own inner life and his ability to hear that Word when it is spoken. The solitary faces the full mystery of this inner life, in the presence of the invisible God. And he takes upon himself the lonely, barely communicable, task of working his way through the darkness of this life until he discovers the Mystery which envelops it.[17] Even among those hermits who organized themselves into loosely knit communities, the desire for complete solitude was evident. As we find in an anonymous historian of the period: "The Abbot Marcus said to the Abott Arsenius, 'Wherefore do you flee from us?' And the old man, Arsenius, replied, 'God knows that I love you; but I cannot be with God and with men. A thousand and a thousand thousand of the angelic powers have one will; men have many. Wherefore I cannot send God from me and come and be with men.' "[18]

For these men, then, the true solitary was not one who simply withdrew from society. Mere withdrawal leads to regression, to a sick solitude, without meaning and without profit. Merton has written that the solitary "is not called to leave society but to transcend it; not to withdraw from the fellowship with other men, but to renounce the appearance, the myth of union in diversion in order to attain to union on a higher and more spiritual level—the mystical level of the Body of Christ."[19] He is one who is aware of a basic aloneness within himself which, in reality, unites him to all other men. It is not merely something which affects him as an isolated individual. Hence, his isolation is the foundation of a deep and gentle sympathy with other men; even more, it is the doorway by which he enters into the mystery of God and brings others into that mystery by the power of his love and his humility.

The apparent emptiness of the true solitary was thus marked by a great simplicity and a deep concern for banishing anything which might dim his inner union with God. Within this perspective the often fierce self-discipline and penance of the early monks assumed some meaning. To do penance was to impose on the body abstinence from food or drink, to contradict certain needs one has for enjoyment or comfort, or to demand prolonged and painful efforts from our bodies. Its function was to prevent slipping into the pleasures of the senses, to release man from the forces that drag him down and which would otherwise succeed in enchaining his spirit. Thus understood, penance and self-discipline were a certain physical and psychological training which, with God's grace, will condition man for deeper union with God. This divine union, then, was the goal, penitential practices only the means.

How complete was the influence of the ideal of self-discipline on eastern monasticism is evidenced by the tales that have come down to us, though it is well to remember that the very existence of these tales is proof that the deeds they chronicle were extraordinary, and not normal. Unfortunately, the wholly praiseworthy Christian notion of penance and renunciation was often deeply colored by the prevalent gnostic idea of the essential dualism of God and the world, the absolute unconnectedness and opposition between what is spiritual and what is material. As a result, many of the practices of eastern asceticism were followed more out of contempt for the body in an effort to destroy or strangle the lower forces of flesh and blood than from a desire to re-establish the harmony that was compromised by sin. In concrete terms, this gnostic passion for self-discipline was most aptly expressed in the axiom: "My body kills me, I kill it."[20]

A typical example of the extremes of Gnostic-Christian asceticism was Symeon the Stylite, whom the historian Evagrius calls "that angel upon earth, that citizen in the flesh of the Heavenly Jerusalem."[21] For thirty-seven years this singular individual practiced one of the crudest penances the world has ever known; he "existed" on the top of a column—which the devotion of his disciples or his own desire to escape the attention of admirers raised from six feet to sixty in height, and which seemed to an eye-witness but five feet in breadth. Even before he mounted the pillar to which he was chained, the extent of his asceticism was such that his faithful follower Antonius wrote of him, "When he walks vermin drops from his body." Symeon began his monastic life as an enclosed anchorite by dwelling for forty days in a cave with his right leg fastened to a stone by an iron chain, "even though," we are assured, "the chain did not hinder the flight of his soul." And when admirers removed the bit of leather which protected his skin from the iron, in it they counted twenty fat bugs which Symeon had refused to disturb. At another time, through a whole summer, he dug a trench and daily buried himself in it up to his head. His fame as a saint was unequalled throughout the East. Arabs, Persians, Armenians, and even strangers from Spain and Britain journeyed to gaze on this prodigy of austerity.

Although Symeon was regarded by many of the northern Egyptian monks as a radical innovator, he was far from being alone in his wild asceticism. Jerome speaks with admiration of a hermit who lived in an old cistern on only five figs a day. Others, as Cassian relates, buried themselves in the darkest caves or banished themselves "in islands near the Nile habitable by none but monks, since the saltiness of the soil made it unfit for cultivation," and where every drop of water had to be carried over three miles "with sandy mountains in between."²² These and almost innumerable other tales witness to the fascination of an impossible, even anti-human, ideal. These rigorous practices were regarded, in Theodoret's phrase, as *"pietatis palaestrae,"* wrestling rings in which the monks won the title "athletes of God."²³

The success attained by this exaggerated asceticism cannot be explained merely by Christ's warning: "Anyone who does not carry his cross and come after me cannot be my disciple" (Luke 14:27). In many ways it demonstrates the continued and potent infiltration of Christianity not only by Gnosticism, but from the end of the first century by Encratism as well. The Encratites (the continent, or the abstainers) asserted that abstinence from marriage, from meat, and particularly from wine were indispensable conditions for salvation. Although later condemned by the Church, the austerities of sects like the Encratites aroused the admiration of the people and threatened to mislead them. Understandably, many orthodox Christians felt they could not allow themselves to be outdistanced in asceticism by heretics. If the true Christian were less austere, they reasoned, would not Christianity itself be discredited?

If, in the end, the modern reader turns away from these extremes of austerity and condemns the thinking that produced them, he must not lose sight of the basic ideals which eastern monasticism pursued. As we have seen, monasticism in its origin was the effort of the nobler spirits in a dissolute age to recover more completely the lost ideals of renunciation, self-surrender, protest, and individualism. Such goals were pursued with avid enthusiasm in solitude and rigorous self-discipline. "We are of God," the desert fathers seemed to say, "and the whole world lies in wickedness." One of the oldest and briefest summaries of this rule of life is an old man's description of what a monk should be: "So far as I can, alone to the alone (*solus ad solum*)." Said the Abbot Allois, "Unless a man shall say in his heart, I alone and God are in this world, he should not find peace."[24]

So far in our consideration of the rise of monasticism we have dwelt both on the environment and on the content of the idea. More has yet to be said about the intellectual climate which surrounded the movement and how it figured so strongly in the writings of these men on prayer. But before turning to these all-important topics, it would be well to focus on the development of eastern monasticism as a social and religious institution, for the ideals enunciated so far never existed in a vague and indeterminate state; they were sharply defined and made concrete in every detail by the communities of solitaries which developed in northern Egypt, but especially in the deserts of the south under the leadership of Pachomius.

We have already noted the enthusiasm with which Christianity in the East adopted the monastic life as the highest ideal and expression of renunciation and self-surrender. We must now briefly consider the organizational growth of this style of life within the Church, for the history of monasticism is not the study of a fixed idea with a changeless content. Actually, monasticism demonstrates its vigor and life by its adaptation to different local needs throughout the centuries.

Monasticism, as we know, began with individuals. Turning their backs on society, men went out to deserted places to live as hermits, "eremites," or "anchorites." For all practical purposes, the first historical figure in the development of monasticism is Anthony, an Egyptian Christian whose biography, after the manner of the times, is attributed to Athanasius. It is difficult to overestimate the extraordinary influence which this biography exerted on the religious life of the entire fourth- and fifth-century Church. No doubt Athanasius' *Life of Anthony* is largely a result of editorializing upon a few "historical" facts. But it is precisely the theme of the book which accounts for its subsequent popularity and attraction. By the grace of God and by the help of his hermit life, a simple, unlettered Copt triumphs over every form of temptation. The story seems to have hit Christianity at precisely the right psychological moment.

Anthony was born about the year 251 in the village of Coma in Middle Egypt not far from the Thebaid. After the death of his parents, when he was twenty, he was left in possession of a large farm and considerable wealth. Upon entering church one morning, as Athanasius tells us, he listened intently as the Gospel of the day was being read—"If you would be perfect, go sell what you have and give it to the poor." As Francis of Assisi did at a later date, Anthony took the words as addressed to himself. He disposed of the land and wealth he had inherited and went to live in a neighboring hut near a venerable old man who was pursuing an ascetic life. Later he moved to a desolate ruin in the Thebaid from which he visited other hermits and attracted a number of disciples. By the time of Anthony, then, the first or eremitical stage of monasticism was well under way.

But almost as soon as it was born, monasticism passed through its first transition. The hermit's complete isolation gave way to a loose association of solitaries in what was, at least partially, a community life. This phase of monastic development probably began under Anthony himself. Certainly about the year 325 there was such a community in the desert of Nitria under one of Anthony's followers, a certain Ammon. Here the community of 600 rapidly grew to over 5,000 men.[25] In this semi-eremitical stage each monk had his own hut, but these were gathered in a "colony." The monks were thus able to meet together for worship once or twice a week, but apart from such gatherings each one was free to organize his own life. In the larger colonies there was a natural tendency to centralize both worship and work under an appointed leader. It was these loose monastic federations which paved the way for the third and final stage in the evolution of eastern Christian monasticism—the growth of a fully communal or "cenobitic" life.

The man rightly credited with this fuller development is Pachomius, a former army officer turned Christian who seems to have lived for some years under the direction of a well-known hermit, Serapion. Whatever may have been his debt to Serapion, Pachomius developed the notion, already articulated by the author of the *Acts of the Apostles,* that to save souls you must bring them together. It is this simple insight which entitles him to a prominent place among religious leaders.

That the common life was, in its origins, an attempt to create an ideal Christian community on the pattern of the primitive Church recurs frequently and explicitly in the teachings of Pachomius' followers. "It is by a favor of God," writes Theodore, "that the holy community appeared on earth . . . by which he made the Apostolic life known to men desirous of modeling themselves after the Apostles."[26] Such an idea is found decades later even among the anchorites of the north. While John Cassian, who clearly regarded the eremitical life as superior to the cenobitic, lived with the monks of northern Egypt—themselves anchorites—he learned their conviction that the cenobitic way of life was of the apostles' own foundation!

There is little question that Pachomius' military experience figured significantly in his organization of the monastic life. Poverty and chastity had already been practiced by the desert hermits and had become stable elements in the monastic idea; to this structure Pachomius added, as a third element, an obedience colored by the simple but strict discipline he had learned in the imperial army. The monks lived in houses, each with its own appointed leader and all following the rules of the group. While the life of the monastery itself was communal, each monk had his own cell. To the regular times of prayer, hours of study and manual labor were added. The sale of their reed baskets and other products in Alexandria made the monks self-supporting. Dress, food, fasting, even conversation were under the rules of

the monastery, and soon candidates had to undergo several years
of probation before they were admitted to the group. Thus, in
embryo, the permanent pattern of communal monastic life as we
know it in both East and West was taking definite shape in the
experience of the Church.

Especially in its Antonian form, monastic life spread rapidly
throughout Palestine and Syria. After the middle of the fourth
century it flourished in Cappadocia (what is today south-central
Turkey) in a form that in many ways resembled the Pachomian
pattern, although there is no clear evidence of any direct dependence on Egypt.

One of the problems which, we have seen, plagued monasticism from its earliest years was the rivalry in austerity which led
so many of the ascetics of the desert to the wildest forms of
penance. Self-torture has no merit in itself; and competition in
self-denial makes asceticism an end rather than a means to union
with God. Moreover, the heart of the Christian gospel is the
message of love toward God and therefore toward man, and love
is one virtue that is not easily practiced in solitude. It was left to
the next historical figure in the development of monasticism,
Basil of Caesarea (c. 330-379), to see what was lacking in so much
of the asceticism of his day and to give the Church of the East a
more balanced and healthy rule for monastic living. It is also to
Basil's credit that he situated his monasticism in the mainstream
of the Greek Church, thus making it a style of life and a pursuit
of ideals, not alongside of or set in opposition to the Church, but
integral to the institutional pattern of Christianity.

Basil was a man of considerable natural talent, and few bishops of the eastern Church have left behind them a greater reputation for saintliness and indefatigable energy. As a young man
he had been attracted to the ascetic life, and a visit to the monastery of Pachomius in Egypt confirmed his desire to embrace it.
His own experience as a hermit as well as his visits to other
monastic communities in Palestine, Syria, and Mesopotamia
taught him what was needed in such a life. His personal holiness
attracted others to him; and though he was soon to give up the
monk's life in order to serve the Church as bishop of Caesarea

and defender of the faith, he never lost his love for the monastic life. The Rule he drew up sets out, in the form of questions and answers, the details of the dedicated community life.

Clearly, Basil preferred neither complete solitude nor the isolation of the monasteries. Ascetics should live together, practicing Christian love in community, but monasteries should be established near cities rather than in the deserts. Asceticism was thus a means to an end: the service of God in prayer, in learning, in labor, in the service of others. The life of the community was to be one of ordered simplicity, not of competition in austerities; and there were to be set hours for prayer, for meals, and for work. Poverty, chastity, and strict obedience stood as the principles of community life. Each monastery was to be supported by the fruits of its manual labor and its agriculture, and each was to have its own superior and assisting officers. One of these was responsible for distributing charity to the neighboring poor; another instructed boys in the school attached to the monastery. By introducing agriculture, learning, and the service of others, Basil thus saved eastern monasticism from complete self-absorption as well as from the extremes of asceticism. Through structures he established, Cappadocian monasticism was to have a particularly powerful and lasting influence on the entire history of monasticism as a religious and social institution.

We have dwelt in some detail on the organization of monasticism because of its importance in the history of spirituality. Unfortunately, not a few writers have failed to consider this aspect. They have given the impression that eastern monasticism was wholly made up of fanatics with merely a sprinkling of more ordered communities. But extremists are rarely representative of an entire movement. In every age there is the tendency to judge a project by its most prominent exponents, forgetting that the tales of special devotion or fanaticism which have survived have done so precisely because they were exceptional. Certainly eastern monasticism contained within it not a few fanatics and madmen, and in the East, the madman has often been regarded as but one step removed from the saint. But monasticism contained a much larger number of well-regulated, even if sometimes indiscreet, adherents. Even though the figure of Basil does not captivate the popular imagination as does Symeon the Stylite, his importance is vastly greater. Of the two lines along which monasticism developed—the eremitic and cenobitic—the cenobitic became predominant. In the same way, the figure of Anthony is ultimately of lesser influence than that of Pachomius. As Workman has pointed out, "If instead of devoting his pen to the praise of the hermit life, Athanasius had written an account of the community life inaugurated by Pachomius and established by him under a Rule, the two centuries that were to elapse before its principles were developed by Benedict might have been considerably shortened."[27]

Up to this point we have treated monasticism both as a set of ideals and an evolving institutional style of life. Before leaving these monks of the East, however, it is important to retrace some of the steps we have followed. Here we must concentrate on several other powerful factors, mainly philosophical, which left an indelible stamp on the character of monasticism as well as on later thinking about the nature of union with God and the pursuit of the spiritual life. As indicated in the previous chapter, concrete religious experience and practice almost certainly dies with the people who live it. Only what they write or what others write about them is assured of propagation beyond the narrowest boundaries of space and time. Thus, it is necessary to detail how certain apparent accidents of history enabled the peculiar spirituality of a tiny minority of eastern monks to dominate almost the entire history of spiritual writing. In the course of this survey, we shall return to third-century Alexandria and its pagan intellectual climate. Next, we move through the attempts of Clement and Origen to Christianize that climate only to find their Christian philosophical synthesis appearing in a de-Christianized form in the spiritual writings of the influential desert monk, Evagrius of Pontus. A brief account of the spread of Evagrianism to the West by John Cassian and of its continued hold on the East as exemplified in the Pseudo-Dionysius will bring this chapter to a close.

Although historians often refer to the last quarter of the fourth

century as the golden age of Egyptian monasticism, the period is
also marked by the struggle which issued in the decline of monasticism in that part of the world. Until the middle of the century
the vast majority of monks were not only native Egyptians, but
Copts also, like Anthony and Pachomius. They knew little if any
Greek, the universal language of the learned Mediterranean
world. By 350, however, Athanasius' *Life of Anthony* and stories
of other heroic Egyptian monks turned the eyes of the Christian
world toward the land of the Nile. Many men and women came
as pilgrims from East and West to tour the deserts and sometimes
they settled down to live among these athletes of God. From
Rome came Jerome with his entourage of matrons and widows,
Rufinus, and the famous widow Melania; from Basil's community in Caesarea came the priest-monk Palladius; from Roman
Scythia by way of Bethlehem came Germanus and John Cassian;
and most important, from Ibora in Pontus via Constantinople
and Caesarea came the man who was to become the intellectual
leader of Egyptian monasticism at its height, the deacon Evagrius.[28]

Although these foreigners always remained a small minority in
the Nile Delta, they assumed a position of dominance and authority by reason of their superior education. Because they spoke
Greek and many were conversant with the intellectual currents
of the time, they attracted followers. It was only a matter of time
before rivalry, even hostility, sprang up between these new-
comers and the native Copts.

For the Copts, the flight to the desert had the character of a
national movement, a revival of Coptic culture. These men—
simple, unlettered, untouched by the philosophic currents in
Alexandria—spoke only Coptic and were proud of it. The evidence also indicates that some of them possessed rather grossly
materialist notions of God and his action in the world. When
they were taught that the "hand of God" aids men, for example,
they expected to see a real hand emerging from the clouds. When
told to seek the "vision of God," they looked for a material vision
not unlike that of the god Asclepius sought by their pagan ancestors. "Spirit" they conceived as a substance of light capable of

making its physical presence felt, and prayer was a means for obtaining such favors as instantaneous transportation from place to place.[29] Although aberrations of religious imagination and practice such as these were hardly universal among the Copts, they did give some foundation to the Greeks' damning appellation of "anthropomorphite." The Copts returned the insult by calling the Greeks "Origenist," a term that implied contamination of the gospel with the pagan philosophy of Alexandria. This philosophy and some of the attempts to baptize it must occupy us at some length.

As the intellectual and cultural center of the Mediterranean world in the third and fourth centuries, Alexandria had become a melting pot for all the philosophical ideas of the time—the Hellenic Judaism of Philo,[30] Stoicism, Manichaeism, and especially Gnosticism and Neo-Platonism. An educated man of the time encountered these crosscurrents in a sort of natural synthesis which helped to explain his own nature and the universe he inhabited. This Alexandrian world-view was basically dualistic. The philosophers taught that the universe consisted of two distinct and antagonistic orders, the spiritual and the material. The spiritual order emanated from a simple and immutable supreme principle—often referred to as the "One" or "Mind"—whose absolute goodness and perfection consisted precisely in its immutability. Opposed diametrically to this spiritual order, and the result either of some principle of evil or of a catastrophic mistake on the part of lesser spiritual beings, was the material order.

Between these two forces stood man, himself an enormous misfortune. Originally an emanation from the Absolute and hence by nature a pure spirit, man had been mysteriously cast down into the material world and there imprisoned in a body. In fact, the soul's chief task in this world was to escape from the confinement of its body, break its link with the evil world of matter, and thus make its way back to the purely spiritual order, where it would eventually reunite with the One where it had originated.

Such an escape, according to this philosophy, involved a long and arduous battle. The soul had to fight the body, overcome it, and reach a state of insensitivity (*apatheia*) where it would be oblivious to all things of sense and body. Over and above the various ascetical practices needed to reduce the body to passionlessness, there remained the further task of bringing the mind into a harmony with the world of spirit, anticipating its eventual reunion with the One. The latter process—called *gnosis* or contemplation—involved reflection of the soul on itself as well as on ever higher, simpler, more abstract realities. Such high destiny, of course, was open only to an initiated elite.[31]

It should not be difficult to imagine the challenge these philosophical currents presented to the Christian community in Alexandria. Under the patronage of the late second- and third-century patriarchs, a catechetical school for the defense and explanation of the gospel grew up. In Clement (150-217), this school found a renowned master, although Stoicism and Platonism tended to exist side by side and apparently unreconciled with his Christianity.[32]

It was otherwise with his successor, Origen (c. 185-253), who developed the most successful synthesis of pagan Hellenism and Christianity in the third century. This man led a most austere, yet scholarly and apostolic life. In both his teaching and his life, he fused philosophy, poetry, and Scripture into a passionate union that marked the beginning at once of dogmatic, ascetical, and mystical theology. Although most of the elements previously attributed to Alexandrian philosophy are present in Origen's thought—the prior existence of pure spirits, their fall through sin, and their consequent subjection to matter—he radically alters that philosophy by making Christ its focal point. Christ it is who leads all men back to God and so to their initial state as pure spirits. Even more, Origen does not locate perfection in knowledge as did Clement, but in love manifested by works of charity. As we might expect, great emphasis is placed on renunciation and contemplation as the means for conquering man's evil inclinations and achieving that perfect love of Christ which reaches its fulfillment in martyrdom.[33] In this view, Christ is ever the center, the goal, the motivating force, the one reality of the world. However, Origen's Christ is more cosmic and divine than human, and it is consequently difficult to find in his theology a meaningful place for time, history, or the human body.[34]

A century after Origen (350), we find a view of man's condition which had become typical of learned Alexandrian Christianity. Athanasius' exegesis of the early chapters of Genesis offers a good example of this. What the Bible presents as man's free converse with God in the garden, Athanasius allegorizes into a state of habitual contemplation. Since the knower is like the thing he knows, this habitual contemplation of God is an absolute necessity for man if he is to maintain the likeness to God graciously bestowed on him and preserve himself from falling into the creature's state of change and decay. Alas, however, instead of keeping their gaze habitually fixed on God in contemplation, our first parents allowed themselves to be distracted by the material world around them, particularly by their own bodies—and so they fell. In brief, Adam's fall, according to the Alexandrian exegesis, was a distraction in prayer.[35]

Neither Origen himself nor Athanasius can rightly be considered guilty of teaching what the Coptic monks stigmatized as "Origenism." Although elements of Origen's doctrine undoubtedly had some influence on the fourth-century flight into the desert,[36] Origen would indeed have been dismayed to see how truncated his spirituality appeared in the teaching of the learned Greek desert fathers like Evagrius of Pontus.

Of the life of Evagrius (346-399), we know relatively little. A native of Ibora on the Black Sea, he probably spent his early manhood at Caesarea, where Basil ordained him reader and where he apparently gained fame as a rising theologian and preacher. After Basil's death in 379, Evagrius moved to Constantinople to seek the company of the famed Gregory of Nazianzus, as Jerome and others had done. Gregory ordained him deacon and regarded him so highly that when he abandoned the city during the Council there (381), he left Evagrius as support for his successor. Shortly, however, a potential love affair led Evagrius to seek the seclusion of Rufinus and Melania's monastery on Olivet. There a six-month illness—partly psychological—was finally ended with his decision to become a monk. He left Palestine for northern Egypt, spent two years on the Mount of Nitria, and then settled at the neighboring Cells. Here, except for periodic trips to Alexandria for conversation with the philosophers, he spent the remaining fifteen years of his life. He soon became the most influential teacher of the Origenist school, living a life of the greatest austerity, instructing those who came to him for advice, and turning out extensive writings, principally in gnomic form, for the monks to memorize.[37] Most of his works were lost until their rediscovery during the last sixty years.

On the evidence of these recent findings, there is no longer any doubt that Evagrius was the "chief founder of the spirituality both of East and West."[38] He was the great systematizer. Before him, the practice of the spiritual life had never been wrought into a logically complete system. Evagrius welded his ascetical and mystical teaching so tightly to his metaphysics, anthropology, and cosmology that subsequent writers experienced considerable difficulty in separating them.[39]

In skeleton, the Evagrian system bears a remarkable resemblance to the intellectual tradition of Alexandria and Origen. But where Origen is warm and full of the fire of enthusiasm, Evagrius seems distant, cold, rigid. Origen exhibits an apostolic interest in others; Evagrius preaches total isolation from the material universe and therefore from other men. While Origen's universe finds its center and fulfillment in Christ, Evagrius is consumed with the importance of the individual soul, so his system seems complete without Christ. His periodic mention of Christ and of the Trinity might mislead us into thinking that these are essential to his system. But as a leading student of Evagrianism has observed, "Evagrius never integrated the theology of the Trinity into his mysticism. Although we may often find the phrase 'contemplation of the trinity' in his *Centuries*, neither the Father as Father, nor the Son as Son, nor, above all, the Holy Spirit play any significant part in the ascent of the intellect. 'Holy Trinity' is only a Christian way of speaking of the Divinity, the 'Monad.' Evagrian mysticism remains more philosophical than properly theological."[40] In brief, Evagrius gives us Origen de-Christianized. In fact, he managed to lose nearly everything that Alexandrian Christianity had achieved through long generations.[41]

According to Evagrius, the spiritual life is divided into two phases, the "active" life and the "contemplative" life—a distinction he borrowed from Aristotle through Origen. But where Origen saw the two lives as complementary, Evagrius treated them as mutually exclusive stages on the way to God.[42]

A person begins, says Evagrius, by pursuing the "active" life. This is not to be confused with the current usage in which the term implies direct apostolic work for and in the midst of others. To Evagrius, activity signifies the acquisition of virtue through the analysis and avoidance of vice. His preoccupation with evil is patent. Only if a person comes to understand the many varieties of evil and enticement can he rid himself of sin. In his preoccupation with evil, Evagrius produced a catalogue and description of eight fundamental evil "thoughts": gluttony, lust, avarice, melancholy, anger, boredom with the life of asceticism, vainglory, and pride. And he devotes the major portion of his writings for beginners to direct and indirect means of eliminating them. As the term "thoughts" suggests, it is not only by physical austerities like fasting, deprivation of sleep, and exposure to extreme heat and cold, but also by coming to understand the nature of evil thoughts that the soul rids itself of them. The "active" life is oriented toward a single negative goal—acquiring the virtue of insensitivity, a state in which the mind has become inpervious to the senses, the body, and all things material, and can therefore pray without distractions.

If and when such insensitivity has been acquired, the soul is ready to begin the "contemplative" life. In this state, grosser forms of self-discipline are unnecessary, but there still remains a further and more spiritual asceticism. For although the avoidance of vice and practice of virtue "has purified the sensible part of the soul, the energies of the commandments will not be sufficient to heal the powers of the soul perfectly unless contemplations in turn take possession of the mind."[43] Insensitivity leads to charity—that "higher state of the mind in which it is impossible to love anything in the world more than the contemplation of God."[44] Now the mind begins to strip itself of all images, thoughts, concepts, leaving behind the contemplation of God in creatures so as to arrive at that final and highest insight into the absolutely simple and immutable Godhead. The more the mind empties itself, banishing all multiplicity and complexity, the more it approaches that Absolute One. The supreme goal of the contemplative life is a state of *anaesthesia* in which the mind, though seemingly unconscious, is actually aware of its approaching union with the Absolute, and so enjoys an angelic condition in the anticipation of its reabsorption into the Godhead.

Perhaps the easiest way to penetrate this complex world of Evagrian contemplation is to listen to the words of the author himself.[45] Prayer, first of all, is defined as "a habitual commerce of the intelligence with God." It is "an attitude free from all feeling" in which the "intelligence goes out of the body." Yet "even if the intelligence raises itself above the contemplation of bodily nature, it has not yet perfect contemplation of God because it can still mingle with the intelligibles and share in their multiplicity." Therefore prayer involves the "suppression of thought"; the intellect must achieve "perfect emptiness." The process is so sublime that prayer rightly deserves to be called an "angelic practice." Clearly it is so great a thing that everything else is to be sacrificed for it. As Evagrius rewrites the gospel: "Go sell all that you have and then take up the Cross; deny yourself so that you can pray without distraction."[46]

In summary, then, Evagrian doctrine divides the spiritual life into two rigidly distinct phases. The soul first seeks to achieve a state of insensitivity to the body and senses; then it proceeds to empty itself of all ideas in the hope of reaching the state of pure prayer or contemplation. Not for the love and service of Christ is everything to be forfeited, but for intellectual inactivity. If you would be perfect, acquire pure prayer. Can we call this doctrine anything less than "the cult of contemplation"?[47]

With Evagrius' death in 399, we come to the end of an epoch in the history of monasticism. Shortly thereafter, Theophilus, the Patriarch of Alexandria, took the step which inaugurated the downfall of Origenism in Egypt. At one time associated with Nitria, perhaps as a monk, Theophilus was a close friend of the prominent Origenists. From their number he had appointed his suffragan bishops, although some of them recoiled in horror at the thought of leaving the desert and a few even mutilated themselves to prevent the possibility of their having to accede. Theophilus was so ambitious for more ecclesiastical power that the existence of desert settlements beyond his control disturbed him. Consequently, he planned to use his Origenist friends to increase his hold over the other monks. In his Paschal letter for 399, he delivered an extended condemnation of anthropomorphism as heretical and in its place promulgated a "spiritual" theology of the Godhead. As copies of the letter circulated to the various monastic communities, they encountered violent opposition. The Egyptian ascetical leaders grew so bitter at Theophilus' anathemas that the vast majority favored condemning him as a heretic.

Tempers on both sides rose to the boiling point. A mob of Coptic monks made their way to Alexandria stirring up riots as they went, with the hope of murdering the Patriarch. Ready for any challenge, Theophilus went out to meet them and cried from a distance, "When I see you, I see the face of God." "If you really believe that," the leaders of the mob shouted back, "condemn the works of Origen." And on the spot, Theophilus agreed to do so. Instead of employing the Origenists against the mass of Copts, he quickly decided to use the Copts to crush his former friends.

At once he sent letters ordering the expulsion of all Origenist monks from Egypt. While many were thus forced out of the country, those at Nitria were less willing to go. It is difficult to disengage the tragedy that ensued from the propaganda of both sides. Theophilus accused the Origenists of arming slaves and with them securing the church at Nitria both against the remaining monks who wanted to attend divine worship and against a visitation by him and his bishops, to say nothing of an attempt on his own life. Palladius, who presented the Origenist propaganda complete with a host of inaccuracies and contradictions, alleged that the Patriarch, accompanied not by his suffragans but by an army of drunken soldiers, burned the cells of the Origenist leaders, their copies of the Scripture, the consecrated species, and even a boy.

We know that at least there was violence and brawling at Nitria in 399, and late in that year the Origenist leaders led some three hundred of their monks into exile in Palestine. By the year 400 or 401, fifty of them had arrived in Constantinople seeking the protection of John Chrysostom. Theophilus, in the meantime, held a synod at Alexandria in order to have Origenism officially condemned and, with a view to preventing the exiles from finding a home elsewhere, encouraged similar condemnations in the Church at large.[48]

As an ironic sequel to the whole controversy, the generally orthodox works of Origen were often looked upon as suspect and went into eclipse, while the works of Evagrius were circulated throughout the East (either in the original Greek or in Syriac and Armenian translations), but under orthodox by-lines like "Nilus of Ancyra" and "Basil the Great."[49] The basic Evagrian doctrines were personally carried to the West by John Cassian (c. 360-c. 435).

Cassian was an associate of Evagrius in northern Egypt for more than a decade; leaving Constantinople as a politico-religious refugee after the downfall of Chrysostom in 405, he made his way first to Rome and then to southern France. There he dreamed of perpetuating the spirituality which he felt had been so disastrously wiped out in Egypt by the explusion of the Origenists. He set up two communities, one for men and one for women, after the style of Nitria. But it was principally in Cassian's writings—the *Institutes* and especially the *Conferences*—that Evagrius' angelic ideal of contemplation was introduced to the West and lived on there, even if in tempered form.[50]

Back in the East, spirituality for a millennium could be characterized without exaggeration as a series of footnotes to Evagrius. One of his more creative successors, however, does merit at least brief consideration. The man called himself Dionysius. According to his own testimony, he was a contemporary and intimate of the apostles, a witness to the eclipse at the time of the crucifixion, one who was present with Peter and James when our Lady died, and a correspondent with St. John while he was exiled on Patmos. He is also the Dionysius mentioned in Acts as one of St. Paul's hearers on the Areopagus and so Eusebius mentions him as the first bishop of Athens. According to a tradition less easy to verify (but unquestioned through the Middle Ages and beyond), he subsequently journeyed to Paris, was made its first bishop and, at the age of one hundred and ten, died a martyr. Actually, the man was none of these things: hence his more accurate title *Pseudo*-Dionysius. The best evidence points to his having been a Syrian monk of the early sixth century.

This renowned writer achieved a refinement of the techniques of contemplation, advocating a method of psychological negation whereby the intelligence would slowly arrive at a state of unknowing and ultimately union with God. Although such a process sounds like a repetition of Evagrianism, Pseudo-Dionysius made his *gnosis* sound immensely more enticing, as this excerpt from his *Mystical Theology* illustrates:

O Trinity
      beyond essence and
      beyond divinity and
      beyond goodness
    guide of Christians in divine wisdom,
direct us towards mysticism's heights
      beyond unknowing
      beyond light
      beyond limit,
    there where the
      unmixed and
      unfettered and
      unchangeable
    mysteries of theology
        in the dazzling dark of the welcoming silence
lie hidden, in the intensity of their darkness
    all brilliance outshining,
      our intellects, blinded—overwhelming,
        with the intangible and
        with the invisible and
        with the illimitable.
Such is my prayer.
And you, beloved Timothy,[51]
    in the earnest exercise of mystical contemplation abandon
      all sensation and

                    all intellection and
                    all objects
                         or sensed
                         or seen and
                    all being and
                    all nonbeing and
                    in unknowing, as much as may be, be
                         one with the beyond being and knowing.
            By the ceaseless and limitless going out of yourself and
                         out of all things else
            you will be led in utter pureness,
                    rejecting all and
                    released from all,
                    aloft to the flashing forth,
                         beyond all being,
            of the divine dark.[52]

Is it difficult to imagine how people might be seduced by the sheer flamboyance of this incantation into thinking they would become mystics provided they followed the method and persevered?

Because of Dionysius' supposed authority as an intimate of the apostles and as the bishop-martyr at Paris, his works enjoyed enormous popularity in medieval Europe. He is cited by Aquinas more often than anyone except Augustine. But the most significant Dionysian influence is discernible in the writings of the great "negative" mystics like Meister Eckhart in the fourteenth century and John of the Cross in the sixteenth.[53]

We have seen how the intellectualist spirituality of a few desert fathers developed despite vigorous opposition and came to dominate the tradition of early Christian spiritual writing. According to these Origenist monks, everything must be sacrificed for pure prayer, a state so high that to reach it is to become perfect. Through such contemplation man becomes like the angels; he achieves heaven on earth. Of course, underlying this notion of prayer and spirituality are a number of intriguing assumptions. "What angels do, men ought to do." Or again, "What men will do in heaven, they ought to do now on earth."

And beneath this second assumption lurks the further notion that life after death is a totally immaterial, intellectual activity. Finally, "What men did before the fall—namely, habitual contemplation undistracted by the body—they should attempt to do now in order to regain the lost idyllic state."

The discerning reader will notice that these and other aspects of Origenist spirituality contain both more and less than the original revelation of God in Jesus Christ. Evagrian prayer is certainly more indebted to the intellectual climate of fourth-century Alexandria than to Scripture. But is not a certain amount of cultural influence upon Christianity to be expected— even welcomed? While prayer itself is an essential of the Christian life, the precise form it assumes in any given age should be suited to the mentality of that age. Consequently, we should be less concerned about the presence of Alexandrianism in the prayer-style of a few learned desert monks, than about its possible presence in the styles of eleventh-century France, fourteenth-century Germany, sixteenth-century Spain, or even twentieth-century America. Could it be that something in our own notion of prayer needs to be de-Alexandrianized?

The history of eastern monasticism poses for the contemporary Christian questions as complex as they are important, and we must be careful in our evaluation of them. The Christian certainly has more than a private concern about his salvation. Generally speaking, he simply may not settle down in some quiet corner and seek his salvation there, quite unconcerned about the passage of history. At the same time, it may be impossible in a particular age to achieve anything lofty or great, and a man may recognize this and thus know himself to be released from his duty toward the world. In other words, there are entirely legitimate withdrawals from public life, from politics, from the market places of an impoverished age. Indeed, in certain periods this may be the only possible way of existing for a wise, honest, and courageous person. Even he is not capable of everything, nor is he bound to consider himself capable of it.

Yet all this does not mean that the Christian may *in principle* withdraw from history. He has a duty toward this world, for he can only find the eternal in the temporal. Yet again this does not mean that the temporal and eternal are simply the same. To this extent the Christian has the right and duty to make the world and its history something relative, and in a true sense, to devaluate and disarm it and uncover its value. Part of Christ's message concerning the world and its incalculable possibilities is that a man profits nothing if he gains the whole of it but loses his soul. *This* kind of flight, which sees the significance of world events as something inherently relative, is part of what it means to be a Christian. Such an attitude cannot be equated with cowardice or cynicism, although there are too many instances where it has been used to defend a wholly negative stance.[54]

For the hermits and monks of the East this faith was expressed in enthusiastic renunciation and a solitary search for God. They began with the belief that the world and all it contained lay under the power of the Evil One; their response was flight both from the world and their fellow men. In a sense, then, monasticism was the triumph of the individual. But by withdrawing to the unencumbered isolation of the desert to fight the evil in themselves, quite possibly they exposed themselves to greater conflict than they would have encountered in the world—a self without an objective life. Moreover, salvation must be a matter of the whole man, not of a soul artificially divorced from mind and body. As the eventual excesses of the movement demonstrated, man is not built of water-tight compartments with bulkheads and automatic doors to cut off one part from another. The mistake of many eastern monks was, as Workman has well indicated, that they tended to think of self-conquest as the mastery of only two passions—the pride of life and the lust of the flesh.[55] This exaggeration threw life out of perspective, and the result was disastrous. The monks grew indifferent to sins of the spirit, while morbid introspection and concentration on sins of the flesh often produced diseases of the soul as deadly as the sins themselves. One wonders if those attacked by the lust of the flesh would have suffered so severely if they had given themselves less time to think about their temptations.

Nor did the special type of environmental determinism espoused by eastern monasticism prove itself adequate. The monk, like the Catholic agrarians of early twentieth-century America, exaggerated the spiritual value of environment. He denied that the highest life was possible except in certain favored conditions. He surrounded his soul with walls to keep out all evil. Life, he thought, should be a ceaseless round of praise and thanksgiving. Everything was done to make the path to perfection the natural road of the soul, and contemplation the consuming task of life. Yet, in too many cases, this spiritual environment proved useless. The power of environment to change a soul, after all, to produce the true spirit of self-surrender, is limited. But the power of a soul on fire with love to change an environment is as limitless as the strength of God.[56]

Nevertheless, when all qualifications have been made for aberrations and extravagances, monasticism did preserve for us two great truths: without discipline there can be no holiness, and discipline which costs nothing—which is not renunciation in some form or other—is valueless. If a man would master himself and open himself to the gracious action of God, he must pay the price. The monks preached, even if in somewhat strident tones, that there is a higher, more inspired gospel than that of comfort, that a spiritual vocation is neither cheaply accessible nor based on sporadic, impulsive renunciation. Pursuit of the spiritual life must rest on settled conviction and be tested by trial over a period of time.

In the end, we cannot overlook the fact that, perhaps in spite of itself, monasticism provided a safety valve for those in the Church who sought a more intense Christianity. It underscored the need for protest, prayer, solitude, and renunciation. If these monks today appear to be narrow-minded, egotistically anxious about their own salvation, desperate to salvage their souls from the chaos of the times, we cannot fail to admire the magnificent strength of their faith over the world. In its own way, this lesson is an important one, even though monasticism failed to understand that the true Christian can take history seriously because he knows it to be already overcome by the victory of Christ. History thus grows in value, since in it the limitless and lasting salvation of God takes place.

Monasticism as the single great expression of the Christian life has long since passed away. The world moves on for good or ill, and the message of Christ must take on new forms and be translated into new patterns of thought. Yet we must be careful not to confuse the essential message of eastern monasticism with the strange and bizarre manifestations through which it has sometimes expressed itself. Today we tend to look down upon these coarse forms of self-sacrifice, self-surrender; leisure and contemplation are vanishing arts. And who is to say that our own view is more adequate? Nevertheless, as Christ searches our souls for the marks of his cross and the furrows of his passion, for the signs of our own personal union with him and commitment to his standards, there must be some trace of solitude, renunciation, and the refusal to capitulate to the world. And it is this challenge which represents the continuing importance of the hermits and monks of the desert.

Chapter III

THE EVOLUTION OF WESTERN MONASTICISM

IN THE EARLY FIFTH CENTURY when John Cassian brought his mitigated Origenism to the West and tried to implant it in southern Gaul, monasticism had already established itself as an accepted feature of Christian life. As in the East, it began unobtrusively with the dedication of virgins and ascetics who continued to live at home in the cities. Although the Near East possessed hundreds of monastic establishments and tens of thousands of monks by the last quarter of the fourth century, monasticism in the West had only a small following; the educated and travelled Augustine was still unaware of its existence at the time of his conversion in 386.[1]

Beneath the surface, however, seeds were beginning to germinate. The recent translation into Latin of Athanasius' *Life of Anthony* began to have a gradual but deep influence and helped to create a climate favorable to the solitary, ascetic way of life. Eusebius, bishop of Vercelli in north Italy, gathered members of his clergy in community in order to have them lead a monastic life. Jerome (340-420) never ceased bombarding the often degenerate Roman circles with ascetical propaganda. And with more finesse but no less persuasiveness, Ambrose (340-397) used his cathedral pulpit in Milan to eulogize the state of virginity, holding up the Blessed Virgin as a model so perfect that her life should be the norm for all. Inspired by this eloquence, young men and women began to renounce the world and to lead lives of prayer and asceticism in their own homes, much to the chagrin of their families. These efforts of Eusebius, Jerome, and Ambrose were part of a larger drive that persisted through the fourth century and, despite fierce opposition, succeeded in tying the ascetic and monastic ideals—especially celibacy—to the life of the clergy. While it had always been relatively common for bishops and priests not to marry *after* receiving orders, celibacy now became a prerequisite to ordination for bishops in the East and for bishops, priests, deacons, and subdeacons in the West.[2]

The final momentum for this movement arose not only from a conviction of the intrinsic superiority of virginity to marriage but, as so often has happened in the history of the Church, from the need to respond to the heretics of the time, who seemed intent on removing the cross and all asceticism from Christianity. The layman Helvidius began by questioning whether Mary had remained a virgin throughout her life. The ex-monk Jovinian proceeded to deny the superiority of fasting to indulgence and of the single state to the married life. The direction he was headed can be seen from his claim that baptism conferred a kind of impeccability guaranteeing salvation; what need, then, for the Christian to have any discipline in his life? Finally, the priest Vigilantius belittled as pagan various popular practices of piety like the veneration of the martyrs and of their relics and burial places, and he exhibited a strong dislike for withdrawl into the desert ("desertion" rather than combat), virginity, and other practices of monasticism. At a time when the tide was moving toward obligatory celibacy for the clergy, he taught that all priests should be required to marry if they had not already done so.[3]

These anti-ascetical figures were hardly more extreme in their positions than the propagandists of asceticism who opposed them. We have already referred to the invasion of the Christian mind by Gnosticism and Manichaeism and the resultant aversion for anything having to do with the body. This attitude betrayed itself especially in an extreme reserve toward, if not disgust for, sexual matters. The histories of the time delight in recounting their apologias for celibacy—stories of wives who run away from their husbands to practice virginity, or of couples who decide on the night of their wedding to observe perpetual continence.[4] A contempt for the marriage act and the "impure" desires accompanying it (often associated with an Augustine said to be unable to dissociate sex from his own earlier debaucheries) can too easily be detected in the general spirit of the times. Already available were all the ingredients that would go to make up what C. S. Lewis has called the "sexology" of the medieval Church.[5]

Augustine himself (354-430) is too towering a genius and saint to be passed over with nothing more than an unkind reference to his teaching on sexual morality. The man must simply be recognized as the most influential teacher the Christian West has ever possessed. His language and thought, as well as the personal experience which formed them, have become the very fabric of Western man's mind, the first clear example of his self-conscious, introspective nature. Yet for all his existential individualism, Augustine is the theologian of the City, of society, and of the Church as "the whole Christ," of "grace" and man's helplessness without the free gifts of God, of the primacy of charity—all dimensions which are blurred or nearly absent from many of his predecessors and contemporaries.

The lifelong struggle to throw off the Manichaeism of his youth, which we have alluded to above, represents only one facet of Augustine's intellectual evolution. He also faced the task of baptizing his Neo-Platonism. For some time after his conversion, his quest for Wisdom still operated within the Neo-Platonic categories so familiar to us. He sees the ascent to truth as taking place in seven steps, each of which follows the preceding with the inexorable necessity of Plotinus' movement toward the One.[6] How far this is from his later conception that God graciously reveals himself to man where and when he (God) wills!

After his conversion to Christianity, Augustine was drawn irresistibly to the ascetic life. He relinquished his chair of rhetoric

and went into seclusion outside Milan with his mother and a few
friends. Returning to his native Africa after his mother's death,
he converted his father's house at Tagaste into a monastery. He
sold everything he possessed, gave the money to the poor, and
then settled down with his friends to a life of prayer, fasting, and
study of the Scriptures. Nor did he reject his monastic life when
he became bishop of Hippo in 396. By that time he had founded
a number of monasteries from which houses spread all over
North Africa; now he gathered his own clergy around him into a
community. His monastic priests were strictly forbidden to possess anything as their own; they ate together in temperance and
charity; and to avoid all suspicion, no woman was ever to dwell
in their house. Their fervor and regularity was so celebrated that
many of them were eventually elected to fill neighboring sees.

Important as his monastic foundations were, Augustine's writings on monasticism were even more significant. A treatise *On the
Work of Monks* he directed against those all-too-numerous religious who, under pretext of needing time for continual prayer
and meditation, refused to work while they spent their time wandering, gossiping, and living off the alms of the people. In 423 he
wrote a letter to pacify a rebellious community of nuns in Hippo.
In order to re-establish peace and religious discipline he laid
down a number of prescriptions. The sisters, for example, were
all to live under the same roof and, whether rich or poor before
their entrance, were to share everything in common, receiving
from the superior only what they needed. At the prescribed
hours, they were to appear in the chapel for the common singing
and recitation of psalms and prayers. Not only were they to
follow all the external directives for this common worship but
they ought to perform it from the heart. They were to mortify the
flesh by fasting as far as their health permitted, and their dress
was to be simple, modest, and designed to avoid attracting attention. Finally, all were to obey their superior as if she were their
mother; and she in turn was to give her commands in all charity,
so as to be loved rather than feared. Originally intended merely
to resolve difficulties in an early fifth-century nunnery, this letter
became a key document in the history of spirituality. On it was

built the famous Rule of the eleventh-century Canons of St. Augustine and the thirteenth-century Order of Preachers.[7]

Interestingly enough, neither the home-convents of Italy, the secular-priest monasteries of bishops like Eusebius and Augustine, the strictly monastic houses of men and women in North Africa, nor the elusive army of hermits, cave-dwellers and vagabonds were most representative of fourth- and fifth-century religious life in the West. This distinction must be reserved for the half-eremitic, half-cenobitic settlements that sprang up under the charismatic influence of Martin of Tours (317-397). Conscripted by his soldier-father to thwart his plans for an eremitical life, Martin spent his years of military service in caring for the poor and unfortunate. After being released from service, he became a disciple of Hilary, bishop of Poitiers in central Gaul. Five miles away at Liguge, Martin founded the first monastery in Gaul, about the year 360. Here each of his monks had his own hut or cell where he worked, ate, and slept, and from which he came out only for religious exercises in a common oratory. Although Martin headed the monastery, he did so more by example than by precept since there was no formal rule. After ten years of happy seclusion, he was called to become bishop of Tours. Although he undertook this pastoral office with great zeal, the hermit soul in him had not died. He used his travels as a means of propagating monasticism, and he himself continued to live a life of poverty and renunciation. Whenever he could spare the time, he retired for prayer to his monastery at Marmoutier.[8]

In southern Gaul, where Martin's influence did not penetrate, two other important monasteries were founded around the turn of the fourth century. Honoratus (d. 429) gave up wealth and family to retire to the island of Lerins off the Riviera coast where followers soon joined with him to form a quasi-eremitic community that was to become a major center of learning. A few years after the foundation of Lerins, John Cassian arrived in Marseilles to found his monasteries and to transcribe the wisdom of the desert for the semi-solitary monks of Gaul whose style of life so closely resembled that of the north Egyptian ascetics he had known. On the whole, however, Gallic monasticism resisted codification; it did not fashion a rule, but spread through personal contact. Never highly organized, it could disappear as quickly as it had arisen. Within little more than two centuries, in fact, it would be totally absorbed by a new style of structured religious life brought from Italy. But before its demise it was to cross the Channel to Britain, Wales, and Ireland and take such root that monasticism and Christianity there would at times become apparently identical.

In 429 and again in 447, a disciple of Martin named Germanus travelled the "unexplored sea" to southern Britain and there by his miracles suppressed "damnable unbelief" among the invading Saxons and Picts. British Christianity, he found, was virtually indistinguishable from the fierce monasticism introduced from southern Gaul some time earlier; and he took pains to present the natives with more recent Gallic monastic practice.[9] Important as this work of Germanus was, it is overshadowed by that of a man who lived under him in the monastery of Auxerre for more than a decade—the great Patrick. This monk, heathen-born in Britain around 389 and named Sucat, was kidnapped from his father's farm at age sixteen and taken with thousands of other Britons to Ireland. There, according to the man himself, "the Lord opened my eyes regarding my unbelief." After five years in slavery, he escaped on a ship carrying Irish wolf dogs to Gaul. Although it is difficult to follow his wanderings, we do know that he spent more than twenty years as a monk there, living for a time at Lerins and also at Auxerre. Consequently, when in 432 Pope Celestine sent him to Ireland, the Christianity he brought was rather exclusively monastic. Some years later, after a visit to Rome, Patrick made an attempt to centralize ecclesiastical authority around Armagh, but the interminable feuding and mutual hostility of the clans made exercise of central authority difficult. After his death in 461, such organization became practically impossible.

For centuries thereafter, Irish Christianity was that of the "saints"; it was organized totally around Irish monasticism. And the latter was often difficult to distinguish from the life of the clans in which blood relationship was the sole determinant of membership. "No real Irish tribe," it has been said, had legal existence "without the two branches, the tribe of the 'saint' and the tribe of the land."[10] Frequently the two branches were under one chieftain, the "abb" or abbot, who himself admitted no earthly superior. His office was strictly hereditary, and detailed rules were drawn up to retain the control of a monastery in the founder's family.

Whole sections of a tribe or clan—even the entire clan—were thus brought to live a sort of monastic life. At Bangor we are told that the monastery had two thousand members, and there were three thousand at Clonard and at Clonfert—figures probably taken from the size of the clans themselves. To keep order under such circumstances, the members were put under a strict daily regime. They had six to eight periods of communal prayer, complete with great numbers of psalms, genuflections, and prostrations. Though a considerable amount of manual labor was demanded, their work was not always exclusively physical, and many monasteries became centers of genuine culture and learning during the golden age of 550-650.

Despite this scholarly refinement, Celtic monasticism seemed to have taken for granted a rough system of enforcing moral and religious observance. Exhaustive catalogues of sins were drawn up and condign punishments specified. Failure to make the sign of the cross over one's spoon at table, for instance, merited six strokes with the "lash"; failure to kneel for a blessing when leaving the monastery merited twelve strokes; and speaking alone to a woman without someone else present merited two hundred. Major crimes like murder, fornication, or even detraction against the abbot might call for as much as twelve years on bread and water.[11]

A final important feature of Celtic monasticism is the restless wandering of so many of its monks. Their prototype is undoubtedly Brendan of Clonfert (d. 577), celebrated in song and romance, who crossed the sea "through a thick fog" in order to find an earthly abode "beyond which shone an eternal clearness."[12] These itinerant enthusiasts from the great settlements of Ireland and Wales spread their brand of monasticism, culture, and learn-

ing across most of western Europe—all the way from Scotland
and its Western Isles and even Iceland to the plains of Italy, and
from Brittany to the sources of the Rhine and the Danube. The
greatest of them were Columba (c. 521-597) and Columban (c.
543-615). Columba, a scion of Irish kings, founded the monastery
on the island of Iona from which all of northern Britain was
evangelized through the establishment of daughter houses. Columban carried on the same activity in Gaul, setting up one
monastery after another as the populace flocked to him, and
writing the harsh rule on which much of our knowledge of Celtic
monasticism is based.

Perhaps these monks had inherited the wanderlust of
their ancestors. Perhaps also the boredom of a settled life led
them to seek adventure away from home. But for the best of
them, the motivation was more consciously religious. As the
monks of the East before them, they sought a "desert" of solitude
and renunciation. They were, first of all, giving up their home
and the tightly knit clan structure of Celtic society. They would
go on a journey, symbolizing their pilgrim state in this world—
making their way without fixed abode toward their heavenly
home. Finally, when they did settle down, it would be in exile, in
a foreign land with foreign people and foreign tongue. Columba,
it is said, sailed away for Iona "desiring to go into exile for the
sake of Christ."[13] Thus, constantly reminded that man is a
stranger in this world, the monks would fix their hearts on God
alone and await the day of their final journey to him.

While it is true that these "exiled" monks carried on some
preaching, more often they simply drew the people around them
in a new monastic community. Actually, they were only missionaries in spite of themselves. In the final analysis, then, the pere-
grinations of Celtic monasticism should be viewed, not as manifestations of missionary zeal, but as acts of asceticism. For all its
apparent charismatic success, Celtic monasticism outside Ireland,
Scotland, and Wales always remained a transplant. It failed to
sink any real roots in foreign cultures. It had few organizational
or administrative resources. Although some of these Celtic foundations were to survive for centuries, virtually all of them, like

the Gallic foundations of Martin, sooner or later adopted the practice and law of that Italian saint and legislative genius named Benedict.

Benedict (c. 480-c. 547), the "Father of Europe," was born, lived, and died in a central Italy loud with the death rattle of the Roman Empire. Rome had been sacked by Alaric and the Huns in 410 and again in 455 by the Vandals. Many of the provinces were under the control of barbarian tribes. In 476, the barbarian leader Odoacer deposed Romulus, the boy emperor, and sent the royal insignia back to Zeno in Constantinople. The early 490's witnessed the devastating way in which the Gothic king, Theodoric, with Zeno's support, eventually defeated Odoacer, treacherously killed him, and thus became ruler of the West. Despite the way he came to power, Theodoric—who like so many of the invaders had accepted Arianism rather than orthodox Christianity—ruled with a strong and relatively just hand, maintaining a semblance of order and peace for more than thirty years (493-526). Beginning with 527, however, another period of total chaos ensued. Justinian, the new emperor of the East, was bent on reestablishing control over the West. The cost of this ambition was a bloody war of twenty years against the Goths. For the second time in less than a century, practically the whole of Italy was laid waste.

The conditions of the age may explain why we know so little of Benedict. It seems that he came from a prosperous family in the Umbrian town of Nursia. As an adolescent he was sent to Rome by his parents to pursue further studies. There he encountered all the crumbling grandeur and learning, the sophistication and the vice of that great city. Although Christianity seemed to be thriving if one judged only by the outward appearance of attendance at Mass, Benedict found a people still half pagan. After some years, despairing of ever leading a truly Christian life in Rome, Benedict retired some forty miles outside the city to a deserted region called Subiaco. There, in imitation of the Egyptian solitaries he had read about, he led the life of a hermit.

He practiced such austerity that he might have died of starva-

tion had not a neighboring monk periodically supplied him with
a loaf of bread. In order to overcome a violent temptation
against chastity, we are told, he threw himself naked into a thorn
bush and rolled around in it. His fame as a holy ascetic spread.
The monks at nearby Vicovaro importuned him endlessly to become their abbot. He finally relented, only to find them a rebellious lot unwilling to accept a needed reforming hand. They
even tried to poison him, whereupon he beat a retreat to Subiaco
and to the relative quiet of the solitary life. Soon disciples again
gathered around him; he set up twelve little monasteries, each
with a prior and twelve monks, and a thirteenth in which he
himself could instruct the novices. This time the hatred of a
dissolute parish priest of the area made Benedict decide to leave.
With a few faithful companions, he journeyed down the old
Latin Way and stopped at the impoverished town of Cassinum,
eighty miles south of Rome. Overlooking the town, on the impos-
ing hill we now know as Monte Cassino, Benedict leveled a
pagan temple and built what was to become the most famous
monastery in Christian history. The year was 528.

In the two decades remaining to him, Benedict developed a
new style of Christian life and bequeathed it to the ages by
writing his *Rule for Monks*. If we are disappointed at knowing so
little about this great man, we may take comfort in these words
of Pope Gregory the Great, his first biographer (594): "I would
like . . . to tell you much more about this venerable abbot; but I
am purposely passing over some of his deeds so as to move on to
the lives of others. Yet I would not have you ignorant of this, that
Benedict was eminent, not only for the many miracles that made
him famous, but also for his teaching. In fact, he wrote a Rule
for monks that is remarkable for its discretion and clarity of style.
Anyone who wishes to know Benedict's character and life more
precisely may find a complete account of his principles and practice in the ordinances of that Rule; for the Saint cannot have
taught otherwise than as he lived."[14]

Life at Monte Cassino little resembled that which Benedict
had first adopted after leaving Rome. From his own experience
and from what he saw of monasticism around him, he was con-

vinced that the only life suited to the average monk was an ordered life in community "under a rule and an abbot." All the varieties of free-lance monks—stylites and carpetbaggers—he considered perverters of the monastic ideal. Despite all their austerities, they lacked true order and discipline in their lives; they were "liars before God," "given up to their own wills," not God's. "Of the wretched observance of all these folk," Benedict wrote in the first chapter of his Rule, "it is better to be silent than to speak. Therefore . . . let us proceed with God's help to provide for the strong race of the Cenobites."[15]

For the eastern ideals of solitude, individualism, competitive austerity, and angelic contemplation, Benedict substituted community, humble obedience, moderation, and vocal prayer. He was not a philosopher, but a legislator. Gone was the hyperbolic language and the angelic ideal of the desert idylls; in their place we find "this little Rule for beginners" (ch. lxxiii). Experience had taught Benedict that monks were neither angels nor supermen. Therefore, with a balanced appreciation of good will, human weakness, and God's grace, he drew up a way of life that could be realized by all. His monks were to have sufficient food, clothing, and sleep. As he made clear in the prologue to his Rule, he was establishing "a school of the Lord's service in . . . which we hope to ordain nothing . . . harsh or burdensome."

Evidence of this realistic humanism is to be found not only in the individual prescriptions of the Rule, but in the tone of the entire work and in its peculiar literary genre—not exhortation and sermon, but legal code. Although western monasticism had been in existence for several centuries, the history of monasticism as an institution with constitutionally established structures of government can only begin here.

In Benedict's conception, the abbot is the central pillar of life for the community. Although subject himself to the law of God, the example of Christ, and the religious Rule, he is the final interpreter of that Rule for his monks. To him they owe complete obedience, for they have freely chosen him to be the representative of Christ in their midst. He appoints all the lesser officials of the monastery to serve as long as it suits his pleasure; his office alone is for life. On serious matters of common concern, he must hold a council of the whole community and on matters of lesser concern, a council of elders; but in neither case is he obliged to follow the advice given. Because he has such extensive powers, the abbot is warned against harshness and favoritism and is reminded of the accounting he must eventually give of his stewardship.

In establishing these features of monastic government, Benedict was legislating for a single monastery. In fact, to insure against the kind of restlessness current in the monasticism of the period, he required his monks to take a vow of stability binding them to lifelong residence in the house of their profession. He removed the need to leave by insisting the monastery be "so arranged that all necessary things, such as water, mill, garden, and various crafts may be within the enclosure, so that the monks may not be compelled to wander outside it, for that is not at all expedient for their souls" (ch. lxvi). Hence, as David Knowles has observed, "The Rule . . . deals only with a single self-contained, self-supporting, and self-sufficient family. There is no suggestion of any supervision by an external authority, save that of the bishop in the case of a notoriously culpable abbot, no hint of any association for discipline or legislation, no instructions even to govern the making of new foundations."[16]

With his attention thus centered on the individual monastery, Benedict was able to prescribe in greater detail than any of his predecessors the daily routine his monks were to follow. Among the community's activities, "nothing [was to] be put before the Work of God" (ch. xliii), the simple and dignified reading and chanting of the divine office in choir at fixed times throughout the day and night—about four hours in all. Benedict devoted no fewer than twelve of his seventy-three chapters to this liturgical practice and he legislated its rubrics with meticulous care. Despite these prescriptions for liturgical service, Benedict paid no direct attention to the Eucharist, which seems not to have been a part of the daily observance in his monastery. From several oblique references, we know that it was customary to have Mass on Sundays and major feast days.[17] For this purpose a priest was brought in or, if a priest-monk were living in the community, he officiated. Here, as in the East, Benedict's community was made up of laymen rather than clerics; and he clearly feared that the presence of a large number of priests in his house would weaken the spirit of monastic observance.[18]

A second substantial of Benedict's daily order was the quiet, meditative reading of Scripture and the Fathers which he called *lectio divina*. With some four hours a day to devote to this private reading, it is clear the average monk could absorb an enormous amount of sacred learning in his lifetime. Yet this exercise was to be as much an affair of the heart as of the head; not erudition, but affection and spiritual development was its goal. *Lectio divina* thus provided a fine complement to the communal prayer of the divine office. This Benedictine prayer clearly differed from the eastern cult of contemplation. Such "contemplation," which, we have seen, constituted the summit of perfection for Evagrian spirituality, Benedict never mentions. He probably does not mean to exclude the possibility of a monk reaching the so-called higher forms of prayer, but from his Rule, one can only conclude that the highest form of prayer is the corporate worship of the liturgy. Even private prayer should grow out of the Church's book, the Bible—not from an emptying of the mind.

Unlike Cassian, with whose work he was familiar, Benedict did not think that "even momentary departure from contemplation is fornication."[19] In addition to the times for liturgy and for prayerful reading, he set aside a total of some six hours a day to be spent in work with the hands—some kind of farm or domestic work or craft.[20] Here again is evident his sense of reality, moderation and discretion, of what is possible and good for a man. Formal prayer during much of the day—no matter what kind— was simply out of the question. Man had to earn his bread; he also needed a change from sedentary mental activity in some form of physical exercise. The result, as Workman has justly pointed out, was nothing short of a revolution in man's attitude toward work.[21]

Such, then, were the principal daily activities of Benedict and his monks—a rhythmic balance of liturgical worship, private

prayerful reading, and manual labor. This kind of life "under a
rule" constituted his approach to spirituality:

> The monastery . . . is to be a self-sustaining unit, independent both
> economically and constitutionally. The abbot rules a community
> which is supported by the sufficient produce of its own fields and
> gardens, and has within its own enclosure facilities to make and
> repair clothing and other articles of common use. The monastery is to
> provide for those who wish to live its Rule a delicately ordered way of
> life drawn from the Gospel, by means of which its members can serve
> God and sanctify their souls apart from the world. The life is to be a
> family life and the father is the abbot. The daily order is carefully
> regulated and characterized by an "unvarying routine" and a strict
> regularity. On the average day it provides four hours for liturgical
> prayer in the oratory, about four hours for thoughtful spiritual read-
> ing and prayer, and about six to be spent in some kind of manual or
> domestic work or the exercise of a simple craft. It is a life to be spent
> in silence and withdrawal from the world. For its spiritual develop-
> ment the monk has the teaching and counsels of the abbot and more
> experienced monks, the monastic literature, and the prayers of psalter
> and liturgy. The Rule contains, in principle at least, the answer to
> most of the practical problems which might arise in such a life.[22]

In assessing any great document of history, it is important to
ask not only what it says but also what it does not say. Benedict's
Rule makes no mention whatever of the apostolate. Its spiritual
ideal is personal sanctification—the seeking after God through
perfect living of the Christian life in a community separated from
the outside world. In this, it already made a significant departure
from the ideal of solitude so prevalent in the East, for the Bene
dictine monk was at least taken out of himself by having to live
together with others under a common rule and superior. But we
must not attribute to this original Benedictine ideal elements
which were only later to emerge. Montalembert demonstrated an
awareness of this danger when he wrote in his classic *Monks of
the West:* "Historians have vied with one another in praising
Benedict's genius and clear-sightedness; they have supposed
that he intended to regenerate Europe, to stop the dissolution of
society, to prepare the reconstruction of political order, to re-

establish public education, and to preserve literature and the arts. . . . I firmly believe that he never dreamt of regenerating anything but his own soul."[23]

Still the fact remains that Benedict, despite an almost constant dependence on other sources,[24] fashioned in his Rule an entirely new, dynamic, and independent organism. He himself must have recognized its chances for widespread adoption. Because his approach supplanted the uncertain and vague exhortation of previous rules with the "reign of law," it possessed an inherent superiority. Benedict was consciously attempting to correct rigid and extravagant asceticism on the one hand, and reactionary laxity on the other—two extremes not entirely unlike each other. Such self-restraint must not be confused with the self-conquest of earlier monasticism; it was rather a *giving of self* than a conquering of self. "As we progress in our monastic life and in faith," Benedict wrote in his prologue, "our hearts shall be enlarged, and we shall run with unspeakable sweetness of love in the way of God's commandments." With the Rule of Benedict we can thus discern new beginnings of evangelical extroversion—as opposed to Origenist introversion—in the history of organized spirituality, though Benedict would undoubtedly not have thought of it this way. Beyond his conscious goals of stability, order, and moderation, Benedict's Rule possessed a dynamism capable of development in directions he never dreamed.

Within a half century of Benedict's death, two figures appeared on the Italian scene and introduced important new elements into the stream of western monasticism—Cassiodorus and Pope Gregory I. A one-time associate of Theodoric, Cassiodorus (c. 477-570) gave up his distinguished political career and retired to his estates in southern Italy. Establishing a monastery there, he first instilled in his monks a great love for scholarship and learning, then set them to transcribing and translating manuscripts. Through this personal example and the dissemination of his writings, he had a profound influence on the western monastic ideal.[25] Perhaps more than anyone else he was responsible for turning the earlier shop and field work of monks into the work of the scriptorium.

Pope Gregory (c. 540-604) was also involved in politics in his younger days. After his father's death, Gregory used his inheritance to set up a series of monasteries in Rome and later became a monk himself. Subsequently, he served as papal nuncio in Constantinople, as abbot of St. Andrew's, one of his own monasteries, and in 590 was elected pope. Evidently Gregory had long been concerned with conditions in Britain, where repeated waves of barbarian invaders drove the Christian inhabitants to the north and west, and brought their paganism to most of the island. He himself had planned to become a missionary to this territory. But when this become impossible, he turned to the monks of his old monastery for help. Under the pope's commission, the abbot Augustine set out with several companions. First discouraged by rumors of terrible savagery in England, the group begged to be released from their mission. But Gregory would not give up his plans. He increased their number and sent them out again. Early in 597, therefore, Augustine and a group of forty monks landed on English shores to begin their work of preaching and conversion. Gregory continued to strengthen the mission by sending more missionaries as well as frequent letters of direction and encouragement.

It is not to our purpose to narrate the story of England's rapid conversion through the acceptance of Christianity by one tribal king after another, the confrontation between Celtic and Roman Christianity with the eventual triumph of the Roman style of ecclesiastical organization and monasticism, or the immense missionary enterprise undertaken a century later by innumerable English monks and nuns—the most famous of whom was Winfrid (675-753), renamed Boniface by Pope Gregory II.[26] Within little more than three hundred years virtually the whole of barbarian Europe—from England to the Slavic lands and as far north as Scandinavia—was brought into the Christian fold. It is important, however, to direct our attention to several over-all characteristics of this conversion from barbarism to Christianity First of all, the rapidity with which it was effected was due to the approach of the missionaries. They often addressed themselves to the kings and tribal leaders; when these accepted Christianity all their people were baptized with them. It is questionable, therefore, how many among the baptized masses were convinced and committed individuals. Even more questionable was the practice of Frankish princes who in their expansionist drive to conquer Saxony and central Europe used the prospect of political advancement and material gain to lead pagan nobles to the baptismal font.[27] Secondly, this vast missionary endeavor was often carried on with direction and support from Rome. In sending Augustine and his companions to England, the pope himself inaugurated the initial phase of this activity, and Boniface made no fewer than three visits to Rome in the midst of his herculean labors in Germany. Having the seal on one's missionary enterprise of a papacy growing mighty with religious and political power must have been a distinct advantage in approaching the local barbarian potentates. The episcopal and diocesan structures established at an early date in the mission territories provide further evidence of Rome's influence.[28]

Finally and most significantly, the missionaries themselves were all monks. What led these men, devoted to a life cut off from the world, to leave their cloisters and travel to a foreign land? Does the frequency of missionary trips among the monks of the seventh to ninth centuries indicate a fundamental change in the monastic ideal? According to Leclercq, this phenomenon represents not apostolic interest, but a personal and rare extension of the monastic vocation of renunciation. Just as a few cenobites were, after some years, called to the heroic life of complete solitude, so others were called to leave their monastery and go into exile after the manner of Abraham, sojourners in a foreign land.[29] Of course, there is still no reason to believe that the "exile" motive was the only one; it is just as reasonable to suppose that a gradual but real transition of ideals was taking place among many monks.[30] Their prototype would be Pope Gregory himself. His family background, his cosmopolitan education, his previous involvement in political life, left him with no desire for permanent dissociation from people and affairs. Here then, was a new breed of monk—peculiarly western, less willing than his eastern counterpart always and everywhere to consign the world to the condemning judgment of God.

One must be extremely cautious, however, in identifying this transition as a change in the *Benedictine* ideal. That any of these missionaries were actually Benedictines must be proved rather than assumed. "The traditional picture of Benedictine monachism spreading over the map of Europe like oil from Monte Cassino has been obliterated by modern research."[31] It is unlikely that, as a group, this community survived the sack of its monastery by the Lombards in 581. Neither Gregory nor his disciple Augustine followed Benedict's Rule as a code. Far from being a second founder of Benedictinism, Gregory actually held views on prayer and apostolic labor that were irreconcilable with Benedict's.[32] Life under the Rule again makes a significant appearance in England and France a century later, but its use spread only gradually. Although toward the end of his reign, Charlemagne decreed that all monks in his domain should observe the Benedictine Rule, he died shortly thereafter, and it was left to his son Louis the Pious to execute his father's plans. Louis' initiative, however, would never have succeeded without the zeal and inspiration of the reforming abbot Benedict of Aniane (751-821), "the second founder of Benedictinism." Like many before and after him, Benedict of Aniane had been a courtier and a soldier; the sudden death of his brother and his own narrow escape led him to enter a monastery.

Monasteries were then in a deplorable state. Many of them had grown so wealthy that they were transferred, willingly or forcibly, to the control of outsiders—laymen or prelates. Many of the monks were without order or discipline in their lives, despite what was sometimes oppressive treatment at the hands of a despotic abbot. Although Benedict's monastery was probably much better than average, he left it to withdraw to Aniane where he managed to lead the life of a hermit for a few years. Inevitably, men came to join him. After several expansions, his hermit's cell grew to a monastery peopled with a thousand monks. By this time he had concluded that the salvation of monasticism would come only with literal observance of the original Benedictine Rule. Benedict met with such success that when Louis became emperor he called him to the capital, Aachen, and gave him authority over all the monasteries of the realm. Uniformity was what Benedict preached and uniformity is what he accomplished. Henceforth every monk of the realm was to follow the same daily schedule, wear the same dress, eat the same type and amount of food, and pursue the same course of studies. Thus, the Benedictine Rule, long held in esteem, now became law throughout the Empire. But such standardizations also carried with them customs purely Frankish and out of harmony with the original ideal of Cassino. In keeping with feudal social order, for example, the monks turned their lands over to serfs so that they would be able to devote more time to the celebration of the liturgy. The new legislation also gave the force of law to the great ornamentation and duplication that characterized the Carolingian liturgical revival. The monks were expected to attend two Masses each day; and the office of the dead and that of all saints, along with numerous extra psalms and ceremonial visits to special altars, were added to the daily liturgy as it was once practiced at Monte Cassino.

Despite Benedict of Aniane's insistence on rigid uniformity, his reform did not survive long after his death in 821. He provided no administrative structures for regular meetings of a general chapter, and the Empire itself broke apart from internal dissension and from the attacks of invading Danes and Huns. Monasteries that were not burned or destroyed were appropriated by some grasping lord, for, whatever the state of their religious observance, the monasteries had grown wealthy. Many of them were burgeoning little cities, complete with church and revenue, shops, and large holdings of farmland with serfs to work it—too ripe a plum for an avaricious lord not to pluck.

There was, after all, nothing temperate about the age. The years 900 to 1050 must go down as the most corrupt period in the history of the Church. Men bought and murdered their way to the papacy, maintained their position with terror, and then handed it on like a fief to an illegitimate son. Bishops and priests fought over each other's concubines. A Roman observer of 1040 claimed that "it would be very difficult to find a single priest who was literate, innocent of simony, or without a concubine." The

priests of Milan fought over "who should have the most sumptu-
ous dresses, the most abundant tables, and the most beautiful
mistresses." And monks were little better. In 936, for instance,
two monks murdered the abbot of Farfa and seized control of his
monastery. For years they fought one another for supreme control, all the while squandering the monastery revenues on their
followers and soldiers. One of them fathered seven daughters and
three sons, bringing them up in ostentatious splendor. Not to be
outdone, the other monks had their own mistresses whom they
dressed in remade altar vestments and decorated with the jewelry
made from sacred vessels. While it would be patent exaggeration
to say that these instances were typical, the fact that they occurred at all is an indication of the moral climate of the times.[33]

In the year 909, Count William of Aquitaine founded a new
monastery at Cluny in Burgundy. In order to guarantee that it
would not fall prey to some grasping hand, he wrote in a solemn
charter: "Through God and all His saints, and by the awful day
of judgment, I warn and admonish that no one of the secular
princes, no count, no bishop, not even the pontiff of the . . .
Roman See, shall invade the property of these servants of God, or
alienate it, or diminish it, or exchange it, or give it as a benefice
to any one, or set up any prelate over them against their will."[34]
Owing nothing to any secular lord or bishop, the monks of Cluny
thus followed the Rule of Benedict with absolute strictness,
elected their own abbot with complete freedom from outside
interference, and rested under the protection of the Holy See.
Although for the next century and a half this last proviso would
confer only the negative benefit of freedom from local and regional meddling, it eventually led to great advantages both for
Cluny and for the papacy. In the meantime, Cluny was blessed
not only by the guarantees of its charter, but by the administrative ability, wisdom, and holiness of four long-lived abbotts—
Maieul, Odilo, Hugh, and Peter the Venerable. Under them it
enjoyed two full centuries of leadership in the reform of western
monasticism and ultimately that of the whole Church.

As the fame of Cluny spread, one monastery after another
sought its help for reform; occasionally, the help was given without the asking. Such monasteries were brought, first of all, to

accept strictly regular observance according to the Cluniac interpretation of the Rule. In short, this meant spending the better part of each day in the oratory. Going a step further than Benedict of Aniane, the Cluniacs had followed with absolute literalness Benedict's original admonition to put nothing before the Work of God. They practically eliminated manual labor and *lectio divina* in favor of long and elaborately performed liturgical ceremonies. Thus engaged, they would be less apt to become involved in worldly occupations, much less in the vice of the world around them.

The more significant aspect of the Cluniac reforms, however, was its governmental structure. Cluny had gained independence by removing itself from outside local control and submitting to the immediate protection of Rome; other monasteries could achieve similar freedom by submitting to the protection of Cluny. More than a thousand monasteries all over Europe thus came to be affiliated with Cluny at the height of its power. In theory, every monk in a Cluniac monastery belonged to the community at Cluny and became a subject of its abbot, to whom alone he made his profession. The relationship of monasteries, therefore, was not one of the horizontal equality, but of vertical dependence analogous to the feudal bond of contemporary European society. As David Knowles has pointed out:

Cluny thus made use of the two most powerful ideas in early medieval society, that of the religious obedience of a monk to his abbot, and that of the fidelity and mutual obligations of vassal and lord. The pivot of the whole system was the abbot of Cluny, who was at once in his spiritual capacity the father and sovereign of all Cluniac monks and in his forensic capacity, as *persona* or lord of the church of Cluny, the overlord to whom all the churches linked to her owed fealty. Cluny had stumbled into empire and there was no element of reason or statecraft in her system. Each of the two elements . . . was in a sense artificial and false, for obedience to a titular abbot whom one never saw was an unreality, and so was the fictional feudal relationship of one monastery to another, or rather of a part of one great family to another more honorable part. Nevertheless, it worked for a time because it exactly met the capacities and estimates of value of its age.[35]

For a short time in the eleventh century Cluny could be called the spiritual capital of Europe. It was the most magnificent establishment of the period. It drew its men from the best Europe could offer. The papacy strengthened it with full powers of exemption and Cluny, in turn, strengthened the papacy in its struggle with the decadence of the times. More than one of the great reforming popes came from a Cluniac house; and the greatest of them all, Gregory VII, though not himself a Cluniac monk, could never have mounted his massive assault on a faltering Europe without the support of Cluny. In some respects, the result of this great reform movement was, writes Workman, "the most wonderful fact in the history of the Church. For a while the world lay at the feet of the monastic ideal; no longer an ideal outside the Church, but dominating the Church itself. For the tenth and eleventh centuries the hope of Christendom lay in the monastery. The monk and not the secular represented all that was vital and progressive. The ultimate failure of this movement to bring the Church within the monastic mould was inevitable, but should not blind us to the measure of its then success."[36]

Cluny went into rapid decline during the twelfth century. It was drained by the very wealth of its empire. Further, there was no constitutional framework to insure the running of its enormous mechanism once it was no longer blessed with abbots of the stature of Odilo and Hugh. Some of them were not merely weak, but downright evil. Abbot Pontius, finally deposed by the pope after thirteen years of misrule, did not scruple to make war on the monastery itself and to melt down the gold and silver vessels to pay his henchmen. Times too were changing; the agricultural feudalism upon which western monasticism had been based was giving way to the commercialism of growing cities. Since the eleventh century new movements had already emerged to enrich the religious life of Europe. Inaugurated in an age of social change and upheaval, these would undoubtedly assume a variety of forms—first, a return to the past, later a departure into the future.

Benedict of Aniane and the leaders of Cluny clearly thought of their reforms as a return to the golden age of Monte Cassino. But other reformers looked much farther back for their ideal—to the desert origins of eastern monasticism. At Camaldoli in Tuscany, Romuald of Ravenna (c. 950-1027) founded the first western institute of hermits living under a rule. Consciously modeling themselves on their eastern forbears, the Camaldolese monks called their settlement a "desert." Each monk had his own cell from which he emerged only at certain times for common prayer, meals, or chapter meeting. In 1084, Bruno of Rheims and a few companions began a similar hermit colony in the cold and desolate mountain territory of Grande Chartreuse. By constantly refusing to lower their standards, lessen the austerities of their rule, or make any adjustment to changing times, these Carthusians have remained to this day a spiritual elite, "never reformed because never deformed."

John Gualbert of Florence (990-1073) was the first eleventh-century founder to institute a reform by return to the original Benedictine ideal. He and his congregation of Vallombrosa interpreted the Rule in a strict sense, "thus probably exceeding the severity intended by its author."[37] In one respect, however, Gualbert showed himself an important innovator. Benedict's "family" at Monte Cassino had lived in complete equality; literate and illiterate, patrician and ex-slave—all lived and worked and prayed together without distinction or discrimination. This arrangement functioned well for a small community of the early sixth century, but it gradually gave way as monastic work demanded literacy and monks went on to holy orders. The menial farm work in which they had employed themselves was now transferred to hired laborers. For several centuries thereafter, the primitive, austere community could be distinguished from the more opulent one by the fact that its own monks did the farm labor. Finally, a new class—called oblates, lay monks, bearded monks, or *conversi*—sprang up all over Europe. In some instances they may have been privileged servants; in others, dedicated oblates or illiterate, unordained monks. It seems that Gualbert was the first monastic leader to integrate these *conversi* with his monks and make them recognized members of the community. They administered and carried out all the farm work, thus freeing the monks from the burden and temptations of temporal affairs.

Except for its integration of the *conversi*, Vallombrosa must go down in history as unimportant when compared with another Benedictine reform a generation or two later. When some monks in the community of Molesme, disgruntled with the growing wealth and laxity of their monastery, persuaded their abbot to lead them into the deep, dank forest of Citeaux, they could not have known that they were founding the first international order in the Church. All they desired was a life of honest, hard, religious simplicity. They located their abbey in the remote forest, hoping to cut off all sources of property, wealth, and power. Their buildings—even the chapel—were plain and austere, totally lacking in Cluniac splendor and ornamentation. They also removed the many repetitions and embellishments which previous "reforms" had added to the divine office. Hence, they would be able to spend the time Benedict had prescribed both for *lectio divina* and for manual labor. Furthermore, they refused to accept members under sixteen years of age, thus doing away with the system of infant oblation in practice since before Benedict's time. Consequently, they readily abandoned the monastery school which heretofore had educated young oblates as well as boys from the surrounding towns and countryside. In fact, the whole intellectual enterprise—teaching, study, copying, translating, writing—was considered foreign to the simple pursuit of spiritual progress.

With extra liturgical and private prayer on Sundays and some forty feast days each year, the monks of Citeaux worked only four days a week, and the greater part of the abbey's menial tasks was quickly assumed by an eager band of *conversi*. These simple, illiterate men were forbidden to have books or to learn anything beyond a few short prayers. They were given more ample meals and sleep, and were expected to attend Mass on Sundays and feast days, receiving Holy Communion seven times a year. With *conversi* to bear the burden of hewing a living from the isolated forest, Citeaux hoped to avoid the temptation of accepting serfs or the income from estates, churches, and other ecclesiastical benefices repeatedly urged upon the medieval monastery. Actually, so many men flocked to Cistercian houses seeking the lay brother's life that the *conversi* became an economic factor of major importance, vastly extending the boundaries of cultivated land throughout Europe.[38]

The first great task of the new community at Citeaux came in 1113 with the decision of Abbot Stephen Harding to establish a second foundation. How were Citeaux and her future daughter houses to keep the fires of reform from being extinguished? How accomplish this without departing, like Cluny, from the original Benedictine view of the abbot as the father of a single monastery? The answer, developed gradually on the basis of experience, has come down to us in a final, codified form in the famous *Charter of Love*. As the title suggests, the bond between mother and daughter houses was not to be one of feudal subservience—lord and vassal—but of love between equals. The abbot of the founding abbey exercised his spiritual responsibility toward the daughter houses by annually visiting them to insure exact observance of a common rule. Each house had its own abbot, and when all of them gathered each year in general chapter for counsel and legislation, the abbot of the mother foundation stood among them as a peer subject to judgment as much as any of them. As history would prove, this system of central government with relative local autonomy worked as effectively even when the Cistercian order had grown to a federation of hundreds of abbeys.

For many years, it has been thought that Citeaux faced a much earlier crisis than the constitutional one just described. The story of an ever-dwindling group of men eking out an existence until the day when Bernard (1091-1153) with twenty-nine relatives arrived to save them can now be dismissed as more melodrama than history. What Bernard did bring to Citeaux—and to the whole Cistercian order—were the anti-intellectual and anti-aesthetic extremes which many have thought belonged to it from the beginning.[39] In fact, Bernard brought much more—a great enthusiasm for religious life, a magnetic ability to preach and lead men, and a power of passionate poetic expression in writing about the love of God. He was undoubtedly the most illustrious Cistercian of them all; yet it is difficult to think of him as typical. The Cistercian lived a life of stability and seclusion in the forest, free from the distraction of learning and wordly activity. Bernard, however, was an international figure. He wrote volumes, preached, travelled throughout Europe, and influenced the decisions of popes and kings. It was he who made Citeaux a truly international force. Although he belonged to an order that took its inspiration from the idea of return to the simple past, his way of life pointed toward a more complex future. He was the harbinger of styles of Christian life yet to come—the canons of the twelfth century and the friars of the thirteenth.

In looking back over the seven centuries of western monastic life just sketched, we may feel that the panorama is too diverse to exhibit any recurring patterns. The fundamental question, of course, is, What is a monk? Is he a stabile or itinerant religious? a cenobite or a hermit? Is he typified by Martin of Tours, Columban, or Benedict? by Benedict of Aniane, Odilo of Cluny, Stephen Harding, Bernard, or Bruno? Despite the complexity of the period, some tentative observations on the nature of monasticism and its evolution are warranted.

To begin, we ought to recognize that the very diversity of western monasticism is itself of significance. With some assurance we may call Benedict the central figure of the earlier Middle Ages and his Rule the central document. Yet even among the followers of Benedict's Rule, no marked uniformity of interpretation and observance is discernible. Despite its being a law code, the Rule is animated, not by legalism, but by freedom and a gentle suasiveness. Its ultimate appeal is to interior charity rather than to external organization. Consequently, the long life of Benedictinism, as Newman claimed, has been "rich rather than symmetrical, with many origins and centres and new beginnings, and the action of local influences. Instead of progressing on plan and system it has shot forth and run as if spontaneously, and has shaped itself according to events, from an irrepressible fulness of life within, and from the energetic self-action of its parts."[40] On the other hand, a number of contemporary interpreters look upon many phases of monastic history—from missionary enterprise to the intellectual life of teaching and scholarship—not as legitimate and spontaneous developments, but as probable deviations from the original ideal—the personal sanctification of the monk. "While it may be sanctifying to sacrifice oneself to the needs of others," warns Van Zeller, "it may not be *monastically* sanctifying."[41] If one accepts this view, then what characterizes the monk is that he has time for God; no other goal may be allowed to interfere with this pursuit.[42] Such an understanding probably motivated the great reformers like Benedict of Aniane and the Cluniac and Cistercian leaders to preach a return to the original Benedictine ideal. Yet, reviewing what these men actually accomplished, it would be difficult to say that they were more successful in achieving their stated goals than in regularizing customs of a more recent tradition—customs often enough at variance with Benedict's ideal.

Let us reenact the Benedictine story in brief. Benedict was well acquainted with the extremes of asceticism as well as the laxity to which the free-lance monk, hermit or vagabond, was prone. Accordingly, he designed a "school of the Lord's service"—a balanced life of prayer and work to be lived with others under a superior in the same place for life. While remaining faithful to the gospel, Benedict created an interpretation of it at once possible and attractive to the average dedicated Christian. However paradoxical it may sound, his way was too successful. Men flocked to the monasteries. Their stability and dedication to work gave them an advantage over a world in turmoil; they became wealthy; they grew lax. When a reformer arose and led a small group of followers into the far-distant forest to begin a new life of simplicity based on the true interpretation of the Rule, the same cycle repeated itself—order, stability, and work led to wealth, to corruption, and ultimately to another reform.[43] Occasionally, as with Bruno, the reform might establish a life of such simplicity, austerity, and renunciation that this cycle would never have occasion to begin. But in general, western monasticism has clearly been otherwise. It exhibits a pattern of more moderate renunciation, a preference for association with others—at least in common prayer and work in the religious community, if not with the world outside—rather than for eremitical isolation. The tendency to move outward toward others, although only implicit and often unacknowledged, is too pervasive a factor in the history of western monasticism not to be one of its distinguishing characteristics. While obviating the dangers inherent in the path of the desert solitary, it gave birth to its own problem: how far could the monk become involved in the world and still be a monk?

Some of this tension was alleviated at the beginning of the high Middle Ages. For with the demise of feudalism and the rise of the city as a new center of cultural and economic stability, the full burden of the world was lifted from the shoulders of monasticism. Not only was the monk freed of many temporal obligations to the world, but with the rise of a new kind of monk-in-the-city—the friar—he was also spared many religious and apostolic occupations as well.

With this new freedom, monasticism has lived on as a numerically small but distinguished feature of the Church's life to our own day. Could it have been otherwise with a style of Christianity whose inner spirit was great enough to survive so wonderfully the dark centuries we have just chronicled? Here, in the familiar words of John Henry Newman, the story is summed up:

When the bodily frame receives an injury, or is seized with some sudden malady, nature may be expected to set right the evil, if left to itself, but she requires time; science comes in to shorten the process, and is violent that it may be certain. This may be taken to illustrate St. Benedict's mode of counteracting the miseries of life. He found the world, physical and social, in ruins, and his mission was to restore it in the way, not of science, but of nature, not as if setting about to do it, not professing to do it by any set time or by any rare specific or by any series of strokes, but so quietly, patiently, gradually, that often, till the work was done, it was not known to be doing. It was a restoration, rather than a visitation, correction, or conversion. The new world which he helped to create was a growth rather than a structure. Silent men were observed about the country, or discovered in the forest, digging, clearing, and building; and other silent men, not seen, were sitting in the cold cloister, tiring their eyes, and keeping their attention on the stretch, while they painfully deciphered and copied the manuscripts which they had saved. . . .

And then, when they had in the course of many years gained their peaceful victories, perhaps some new invader came, and with fire and sword undid their slow and persevering toil in an hour. . . . Down in the dust lay the labour and civilization of centuries—Churches, Colleges, Cloisters, Libraries—and nothing was left to them but to begin all over again; but this they did without grudging so promptly, cheerfully, and tranquilly, as if it were by some law of nature that the restoration came, and they were like the flowers and shrubs and fruit trees which they reared, and which, when ill-treated, do not take vengeance, or remember evil, but give forth fresh branches, leaves, or blossoms, perhaps in greater profusion, and with richer quality, for the very reason that the old were rudely broken off. If one holy place was desecrated, the monks pitched upon another, and by this time there were rich or powerful men who remembered and loved the past enough to wish to have it restored in the future. . . .

To the monk heaven was next door; he formed no plans, he had no cares; the ravens of his father Benedict were ever at his side. He "went forth" in his youth "to his work and to his labour" until the evening of life; if he lived a day longer, he did a day's work more; whether he lived many days or few, he laboured on to the end of them. He had no wish to see further in advance of his journey than where he was to make his next stage. He ploughed and sowed, he prayed, he meditated, he studied, he wrote, he taught, and then he died and went to heaven. He made his way into the labyrinthine forest, and he cleared just so much of space as his dwelling required, suffering the high solemn trees and deep pathless thicket to close him in. And when he began to build, his architecture was suggested by the scene—not the scientific and masterly conception of a great whole with many parts, as the Gothic style in a later age, but plain and inartificial, the adaptation of received fashions to his own purpose, and an addition of chapel to chapel and a wayward growth of cloister, according to the occasion, with half-concealed shrines and unexpected recesses, with paintings on the wall as by a second thought, with an absence of display and a wild, irregular beauty, like that of the woods by which he was at first surrounded. And when he would employ his mind, he turned to Scripture, the book of books, and there he found a special response to the peculiarities of his vocation; for there supernatural truths stand forth as the trees and flowers of Eden, in a divine disorder, as some awful intricate garden or paradise, which he enjoyed the more because he could not catalogue its wonders. Next he read the Holy Fathers, and there again he recognized a like ungrudging profusion and careless wealth of precept and of consolation. And when he began to compose, still he did so after that mode which nature and revelation had taught him, avoiding curious knowledge, content with incidental ignorance, passing from subject to subject with little regard to system, or care to penetrate beyond his own homestead of thought—and writing, not with the sharp logic of disputants, or the subtle analysis of philosophers, but with the one aim of reflecting in his pages, as in a faithful mirror, the words and works of the Almighty, as they confronted him, whether in Scripture and the Fathers, or in that "mighty maze" of deeds and events, which men call the world's history, but which to him was a Providential Dispensation.[44]

Chapter IV

THE CITY,
THE FRIARS,
AND THE PEOPLE

WITH THE OPENING YEARS of the thirteenth century, spirituality in the Church entered upon one if its greatest revolutions. When a religious group—or religious life in general—is unable to identify itself with the environment in which it operates, it is time for a searching reappraisal. And it was precisely this problem of relevancy to its own age that stimulated the kind of religious reaction in the twelfth and thirteenth centuries which we will refer to as the "mendicant transition." Certainly part of this upheaval concerned the religious imagination and practices of the medieval layman, an aspect which will call for careful consideration in the second part of the present chapter. But first, the ramifications of these alterations on religious life, strictly so-called, will occupy our attention.

Western Europe at the time was in the throes of one of the major changes of its history—the shift from an essentially rural, agrarian culture to an urban, commercial one. The basic framework of society, medieval feudalism, was breaking apart and being replaced by a new phenomenon—the medieval city. In the earlier agrarian society the life of the people had been structured around the individual feudal manor; the manor was the center of existence for the local community, producing within itself all that was necessary for life. Commerce was virtually nonexistent, and hard currency was used sparingly. Whatever cities did exist were merely centers of administration or armed fortresses where people could flee in times of emergency; their permanent populations were small—most often no more than three to four hundred.

But toward the end of the eleventh century, changes took place which affected every aspect of society. People began to cluster in the urban centers, while merchants and artisans emerged as the nucleus of a new and developing middle class. As feudalism proved an anachronism and an impracticality, commerce became the stable and fundamental support of a new social order. Hard currency was adopted as the medium of exchange. People lived in closer contact, and new human values were discovered. Romanticism captured the heart of southern Europe; love stories of the troubadours abounded. The great medieval universities began to develop during these years, so that by the end of the twelfth century there were institutions at Bologna, Paris, Oxford, and Salerno. The time was also one of religious revival, a period in which the new, free, middle-class man expressed his enthusiasm and exuberance for authentic Christianity and, as we shall see later, for almost every kind of religious extravagance. The great mendicant orders of Dominic and Francis sprang up to meet the challenge of the new bourgeoisie, the new city, the new commerce, and the new intellectual life of the university. And with their mobility and peculiar adaptability, the mendicants were finely equipped to face the contemporary situation.

But there were other factors which also figured in the religious climate of the times. Despite improvements over the eleventh and twelfth centuries, the Church was still in a gloomy state. It is sufficient to point to the growing attachment to luxurious living, which, since the Crusades, had spread even among the clergy and monks. "I met on the street," wrote Thomas of Chantimpre, the Dominican prior at Louvain, "an abbot with so many horses and so large a retinue that if I had not known him I would have taken him for a duke or a count. . . . Only the addition of a circlet on his brow would have been needed."[1] In the wake of such excesses, we find reactionary movements emerging such as the Humiliati ("Poor Catholics"), who emphasized work, poverty, and preaching. The collective, liturgical worship of the time proved insufficient to meet the need for a spirituality with an individualistic appeal, although the Church did respond with hymns such as the "Jesu Dulcis Memoria" and extra-liturgical devotions to the Blessed Virgin Mary, the saints, the humanity and especially the sufferings of Christ, and the adoration of the Eucharist. In the long run, the Church was helped, not so much by the genius or energy of her popes, great as many of these pontiffs undoubtedly were, nor by the self-sacrifice of some secular bishops and secular clergy, but by the labor of two men of penetrating vision. "Master Dominic and his Preaching Brothers," founded in 1216, revived the forgotten duty of preaching, while Francis and his "Little Brothers," beginning in 1209, showed an astonished Europe how to remove mountains by a faith wedded to love.

The essential thrust of these two men and their followers, however, cannot be defined simply as a group response to the changing structure of medieval society or to the laxity within the Church, for both groups were as much a response to the theological heresies of the time. Consequently, it is important to give some consideration to the religious errors from which the mendicants derived their challenge.

While it may not be quite fair to say that the general piety of the Middle Ages was out of joint, it was certainly crooked. Heretical sects sprang up from every corner of the medieval world. At the risk of oversimplifying the labyrinth of names under which these errors passed, the two most pungent streams of underground opposition to the Church were the Waldensians and the Catharists.[2] The first of these groups began at Lyons, although it found its most coherent expression in northern Italy, where the Waldensians survive even to this day. The movement takes its name from a Lyons merchant, Peter Waldo, who in the famine year of 1176 gave away his property and tried to live literally by what he considered the Gospel of Christ. His basic direction was toward the simple life. Dissatisfied with the worldliness of many of the hierarchy, he and his companions tended to disregard ecclesiastical authority and to exalt the position of the layman. In their own way, the Waldensians were an Evangelical sect, interested in neither criticizing the general structure of Christian medieval theology nor quarreling (at least in the beginning) with the sacramental doctrines of the day.

Originally quite orthodox, the Waldensians were forced into heresy by the failure of the official Church to meet their challenge.[3] Waldo and his followers ("The Poor Men of Lyons") were condemned in a decree of Lucius III in 1181, but they still hoped for papal recognition. Eventually, it was granted them on the condition that they preach only at the request of the local clergy. Thus, in the gradual separation of the Waldensians from the Church it seems clear that the main point at issue was whether lay preaching, organized around an independent center, could be tolerated within the framework of the institutional Church. Ironically, it was not thirty years later that Innocent III, with hesitations for which the Waldensian precedent was probably responsible, granted just such recognition to the burgeoning order of St. Francis. As Ronald Knox has commented, "If the Church welcomed the Poor Man of Assisi, while she rejected the Poor Men of Lyons, it must be supposed that the latter had given the world an early taste of their quality."[4]

The Catharists, on the other hand, were at least partially influenced by those Manichean doctrines which, while originating in the Near East, seem to be a recurrent tendency in human thought. The Catharists taught that matter, as such, is evil; that the world was created by a fallen spirit who acquired, in consequence, a status little less than divinity; that our Lord did not take on real human flesh by being born of Mary; that he carried through life a phantom matterless body and so did not die on the Cross; that procreation is evil (thus the perfect believer will neither use marriage nor eat any food of animal origin); that the idea of sacraments in which God's saving power came to man through material means could only be blasphemy; that the body will not rise again, and indeed that the soul's whole effort must be directed toward its own escape from the body. Doctrines such as these formed something like a coherent theology, but one which was certainly not Christian. Nor was it a casual heterodoxy like the Puritanism of the Waldensians, for it undermined the whole mystery of the Incarnation. To reassert that mystery against these emerging opponents, to insist on, even glory in, that wedding of things human with things divine which the Incarnation involves, the Church through Dominic's inspiration was to forge a new weapon whose primary significance has been obscured by our familiarity with it—the rosary of the Blessed Virgin.[5]

Both the Waldensian and Catharist movements were propagandist; where their preachers went, little communities of converts would form. Precariously affiliated with the parent body, these groups soon began to develop their own heterodoxies. Moreover, two propagandist sects of such growing strength must, from time to time, meet in a common mission field. What would be their attitude to one another? Would they fight or fuse? In all probability they fused; at least there is no record of their fighting. The place where such mingling most certainly occurred was the city of Albi in southern France, where their activities culminated in a massive popular movement called Albigensianism. As the Albigensian proponents grew in number, they also increased in local patronage. As a result, when the Lateran Council of 1159 took pains to condemn the heretics of Albi by name, local action was slow and fumbling. The Council of Lombez rounded up a group of Waldensians and tried to incriminate them as Catharists. Philip Augustus, although repeatedly urged to interfere, was nevertheless full of evasions. In 1209, Pope Innocent III was provoked by the murder of one of his own commissioners, and so launched the Albigensian Crusade. The Abbot of Citeaux with some of his brethren was sent to combat the heresy after the manner of St. Bernard, but this too failed. Many of the representatives of the Church became judges rather than missionaries, particularly the incendiary papal legates. Their lack of Christian tolerance plus their appearance in immoderate, worldly pomp stripped them of any moral advantage they might have possessed.

To relate the history of the wars which followed during the next twenty years and the subsequent measures by which the Albigensians were suppressed, or at least driven underground, is not to our purpose here. We are concerned with what the heretics believed and the threat which they posed, for it is against this background that the rise of Dominic and Francis takes on its proper dimension. In order to understand this atmosphere of apprehension, we have only to recall that the Albigensians boasted of an elaborate organization which they were prepared to set up against the Catholic Church. It is true that they claimed to have only sixteen dioceses in the world, but they did ordain their own bishops and deacons (apparently not priests) in defiance of the Catholic hierarchy. They denied the efficacy of the Christian sacraments and substituted their own rites. And the theology they preached was not, in any recognizable sense, Christian.

Against all this, as well as against the degeneracy within the Church, the friars were a protest. Without changing the basic monastic principles of poverty, chastity, and obedience, the mendicants sought to work out their ideals not by withdrawing from men, but by seeking them. In fact, their conception was so different from earlier views of the religious life that originally friars were forbidden to go within the walls of any monastery. Previously, the highest religious life had been identified with retreat from the world, with retiring like Bruno to some Grande Chartreuse, where in the rarer air, far from the world's noise and whirl, men could save their souls and rule into their characters fine lines of virtue and piety.

But the friars were entirely different. They were a group of social laborers and theological disputants. Charity still constituted the guiding principle of their spiritual life, but it was charity from a different viewpoint. The monk had said: "Live as if you were alone in this world with God." The friar replied: "Live as if you only existed for the sake of others." As Humbert of Romans writes in his commentary on Dominic's Rule: "Our order has been founded for preaching and for the salvation of our neighbors. Our studies should tend principally, ardently, above everything, to make us useful for souls."[6] As Francis records it, his most ecstatic joy was when he heard the voice of God "that it behooved him by preaching to convert many people. Thus says the Lord, 'Say to Brother Francis that God has not called him to this estate for himself alone, but to the end that he may gain fruit for souls, and that many through him may be saved.' "[7] But it is time that we look more closely at each of these two men and the styles of spirituality that they and their followers preached and practiced.

Francis was born in the little town of Assisi, about midway between Rome and Florence, as the twelfth century was running out (1182). Although his father, Pietro Bernardone, was a wealthy cloth merchant, the education Francis received had the usual limitations of the times. He wrote with difficulty and in later years signed all his letters with the simple sign of the cross. Because of his father's business journeys to the fairs of France, however, Francis did have the advantage of familiarity with the language and songs of the country to which, in fact, he owed his name. To his father, the youngster who had been born in his absence was not Giovanni, as he had been baptized, but his little "Frenchman."

There was little in Francis' early life to foreshadow his future. Conversion for him was a radical change—not the slow breaking of dawn, but the opening of blind eyes. After his dissipations brought him face to face with death at the age of twenty-one, and a second fever contracted on a military expedition to Apulia nearly took his life, Francis arose a new man. He spent his days in a cave from which he came home at night pale with his interior conflicts. But the love in him went beyond the confines of solitude and, ministering to the outcasts in the leper hospitals, he found in the least of these brethren Christ himself. He went about dressed in rags and would sell all he had to repair a ruined roadside chapel, or give his last coin to a beggar.

No doubt Francis' behavior was trying to his family and friends. Finally, his father cast him bound into his cellar and applied to the local magistrates to deal with him as a madman.

Fortunately the magistrates referred the case to the bishop. On the appointed day, in the presence of a great throng of curious townsmen, the bishop gave his decision. He advised Francis to give up all his property, which was precisely what the young man longed to do. So, then and there, he made a solemn renunciation of all his possessions and stripped himself even of his clothes. Henceforth he was free, free as the birds who seemed to him to live the perfect life—they build no barns and yet sing unceasingly.

We must leave the interested reader to search out for himself the record of how eleven men, drawn by the same desire for complete consecration, one by one joined themselves to Francis; how in the summer of 1210 Francis went with his companions to Rome that he might obtain from Innocent III the sanction of his simple Rule; and how from these beginnings the new order spread with marvelous speed to every land.[8] It is more important here to attempt to recapture Francis' vision. This is no simple task, partly because of the difficulty of understanding Franciscan spirituality without a detailed study of its history, partly because of the divergent views among contemporary commentators on Francis himself and his spiritual legacy.[9]

It would seem, nevertheless, that for Francis and for his followers the central core of man's approach to God was to be found in a kind of spiritual, Christocentric attitude. The term "spiritual" is chosen designedly, for Francis' Christ-centeredness was more than a theological cornerstone as it was with Bonaventure some years later; rather it constituted Francis' fundamental approach to the Christian life. For him, all men were children of the heavenly Father, and therefore his brothers in Christ. His chief concern was Christ, the Incarnate Word, and his mission of salvation. Moreover, as the German Franciscan Cajetan Esser has written: "Francis' eyes were ever fixed on the entire course of salvation history. He immersed himself in God's entire redemptive work, realized in and through Jesus Christ. He and his followers were interested not so much in delineating and copying our Lord's historical life, as in sharing the saving work revealed in his mission—in being its witness and living image."[10] Christ's

Incarnation was of such importance to Francis because it both demonstrated God's goodness and taught men how they must live. Thus, true Franciscan spirituality outlaws formalism and long discursive prayer; involved theories like the Evagrian or Dionysian stripping of the mind have no place. Francis simply takes his men to the foot of the Cross or to the altar so they may see the Victim of Love, or he leads them to nature to see traces of God's goodness and majesty—emphasizing always the joy and dignity of our grace as adopted sons of God.

But how did Francis interpret and apply this Christ-centered approach? The answer is deceptively simple: he did not interpret it at all. "Since the Lord revealed to him that he was to live according to the Gospel, he simply consulted the Gospel in every crisis and carried out blindly and with reverent trust whatever he found there."[11] Here we get the clue to the secret of Franciscan idealism—simple, childlike acceptance and fulfillment of the Gospel. Such simplicity, however, is but the manifestation of deep-seated convictions Francis held regarding our relationship to God. For Francis, the fundamental truth of the Gospel was that God's name is Father. One may safely call it the central truth, the unifying dogma of all Franciscan spirituality—God is our Father, and we are his children in Jesus Christ. Correlative with this notion of God's fatherhood, there was always present to Francis a sense of the divine childhood; and since all human beings must be our brothers in Christ under a single Father, they must be considered and treated as such. A common fatherhood and a brotherhood with Christ shared by all men—this was the scope of Francis' vision, and it was to find its common expression in love.

But what of the cult of poverty so vigorously practiced by the followers of Francis? Like any form of asceticism, poverty was intended to remove the obstacles that might prevent the full flowering of love. Unfortunately, there is a common misapprehension that poverty alone was what mattered most in Francis' life, and indeed in the whole Franciscan movement. Unquestionably, it did matter, but it was not the heart of Francis' vision. As much as anywhere, the distinction between means and end is important, as well as the distinction between spirit and its exterior manifestation. Poverty for Francis was simply a way of liberation and of freedom. It was only a means; the end was love. By poverty the holocaust was prepared; the flame of love ignited it.[12]

Interestingly enough, Francis' contemporary Thomas Aquinas takes a much different approach to poverty. For Thomas, the virtue and vow of poverty is an extension of the virtue and vow of obedience. Poverty consists essentially in dependence upon the will of another in the use of material goods.[13] For the Franciscan Bonaventure, on the other hand, the perfection of poverty is to be weighed solely by the degree of separation it brings from possessions. "That state is more sincere and more removed from the dangers of riches which has no property either proper or common, movable or immovable, in order that there may be no material for pride, nor occasion of lasciviousness, nor incentive of avarice."[14]

That Francis should attract some following is not surprising. But that a whole company of men, many of them laymen or at most in minor orders, should renounce all that the world held precious, wander barefoot over Europe preaching the gospel to the poor, and, what is more, live it out as men had never seen it lived before—this was indeed to bring back the living Jesus into the midst of his people and to restore his teaching in most vivid form. As Christopher Dawson has commented, "The movement which had the greatest influence on medieval religion and culture was not the speculative mysticism of the Dominicans, but the evangelical piety and the devotion to the Humanity of Jesus that found its supreme expression in the life of St. Francis."[15]

As might be expected from the saturation of Italy with underworld heresy, Francis' Little Brothers were at first exposed to considerable persecution. On their initial missionary journey "some [people] listened willingly, others scoffed, the greater part overwhelmed them with questions: 'Whence come you?' 'Of what order are you?' And, though sometimes it was a weariness to answer, they said simply, 'We are penitents, natives of the city of Assisi.' "[16] When local authorities threatened to hang some of them as vagabonds, they offered their own rope cinctures as halt-ers. But whether accepted or rejected, these mendicants every-where associated with the poor, helping the laborers to gather olives or strip the vines, singing all the while their hymns of joy or making merry like children at a feast.

History tells us that this early enthusiasm did not last. The primitive rigor of the Rule was beyond human strength, as Inno-cent III had foretold in his first interview with Francis. Though differences in the order did not come to a head until later, even in his own lifetime Francis had to mourn that the first simplicity had become perverted and that it seemed unlikely his vision would come to pass. The main part of his Rule begins with the sentence, "And this is my advice, my counsel, and my earnest plea to my friars in our Lord Jesus Christ that, when they travel about the world, they should not be quarrelsome or take part in disputes or criticize others; but they should be gentle, peaceful, and unassuming, courteous and humble, speaking respectfully to everyone, as is expected of them."[17] Here and in what follows, Francis had pictured his friars traveling in larger or smaller groups, as active apostolic men whose monastery was the whole world. Everywhere they went they used the greeting of peace, and they stayed wherever they could find lodging. Francis in-sisted that they provide for themselves by daily wage-labor, but the work should not lead either to the ownership or to the accu-mulation of property. Diversified in their activities, the group was to be formed in a loose organizational structure, with au-thority divided among the various individual Franciscan families rather than flowing from one single head. Thus, the bond which held Francis and his early followers together was not a detailed plan of activity smoothly carried out by everyone. The union of Francis and his brothers was rather the magnetic personality of Francis himself. Indeed, since they were true beggars and pil-grims in this world, the Brothers had little source of unity "on the road" but each other. It was Francis the man, then, not Francis the organizer, as well as the mutual love of one member for the other, that held his many children in over-all unity.

Clearly, Francis of Assisi was a charismatic leader, a personality set apart from ordinary men and endowed with exceptional natural and supernatural powers. Because they are out-of-the-ordinary, such leaders are sources of instability as well as innovation; because they elicit followers and evoke respect, they possess that kind of authority which is voluntarily accepted and followed. But charismatic phenomena are inherently temporary; they can prolong their existence only by becoming "routinized" —that is, by becoming transformed or incorporated into the institutionalized structures of an organization. It was precisely in this process of routinization that Francis' spiritual vision underwent modification. And when, a short time after their establishment, the Little Brothers were joined by hundreds, the majority of these new members, unlike the early disciples, had no chance of coming under the personal spell of the master.

As with any growing organization, leaders are selected on the basis of their ability to meet the needs of the group, not because of their private inspirations. Among the early Franciscans, leaders were usually legal-minded and unable to grasp something as original and intuitive as Francis' ideal. From the very beginning, the ministers and learned men of the order argued, criticized, and complained when Francis attempted to draft his original Rule; written on the spiritual, not on the legislative level, it was at once too demanding for the many and too imprecise for the canonist. The majority were unwilling to accept absolute poverty, yet they felt the need for definite rules of conduct as well as some kind of hierarchical structure. Thus, after two years of mental anguish and some sharp pressure from his closest companions, Francis produced a shorter and more commonplace edition of his rule. This was the *Regula Bullata,* approved by Honorius III in 1223; when it was promulgated the Friars Minor entered the ranks of the religious orders.

Francis' revised rule, even with all the formalism that had been added to it, was still something new. Even after all the canonists and conventional objectors had done their work, the greatest novelty of the *Regula Bullata* was its spirit of freedom. All previous religious founders had led men away from the world and set before them life inside a monastery as the norm.

Francis, though escaping in spirit from everything worldly as thoroughly as Benedict or Bernard, wished his friars to go about in the world working, reaching others, and helping them. Moreover, in order that the friar might fully imitate Christ, his passage through the world must be unhampered by any possession of property. Francis, after all, would never allow his men to own property either as persons or as a group. In his original conception they had neither land nor house nor chapel; they were to be always as were the apostles when sent to preach penance under Christ's command. They were to live on what was given them for the spiritual or material work they did; failing that they were to live on charity or to beg. To Francis, money—hard coin—was dirty and impure, and his friars were never to accept, keep, or even touch it. The insuperable difficulties in holding to this idea, when numbers became large and when sickness, study, and the training of novices became a major concern, is obvious to everyone. The attempts of Francis himself as well as later friars to resist relaxations both in the spirit of freedom and the practice of poverty, and the various shifts and changes on the part of well-meaning authorities, are a recurrent and distressing feature of subsequent Franciscan history.

John Parenti, the first elected general of the order, was sympathetic to Francis' original ideals but it was he who was more than a little responsible for the general decline of Franciscan simplicity and flexibility. He encouraged three developments which were maintained by succeeding generals: the advancement of learning, governmental changes which favored the more educated friars, and the acquisition of ecclesiastical privileges. Because of his own past legal training, he possessed both a strong respect for the letter of the law and the temperament of a strict disciplinarian. The generalate of Brother Elias, one of Francis' earliest companions, had more far-reaching negative results. His disedifying personal behavior and provocative methods of government stimulated many laws designed to prevent the recurrence of such abuses. Furthermore, his own championing of the lay brothers within the order had both unfortunate and unanticipated consequences—the gradual formation of a clerical order in which the lay brothers declined in number as well as importance.

Although it would be hard to imagine controversies more removed from the spirit of Francis, the pervading problem during these organizational years still remained the ideal of poverty. By the middle of the thirteenth century, within a few decades of Francis' death, there existed several developed interpretations of his notion of poverty. By the time of Bonaventure (1260), the extreme patterns—the Spiritual and the Relaxed—were clearly in evidence, and elements of both continued into the fourteenth century. Thanks to Bonaventure and others like him, the Brothers of the Community—the mainstream of the first order's spirituality—were able to persevere. Yet the question of poverty was certainly not settled. Francis himself had enjoined the strictest form of poverty for his followers—neither the friars themselves, nor the order as a whole, could own anything. Under his inspiration the new order officially renounced all property and placed it in the hands of the papacy. Though excellent in theory, such a program encountered considerable practical difficulty. By 1322 these problems had become so extensive that John XXII decided to renounce papal ownership of Franciscan property and return it to the first order. Although this move naturally weakened the original ideal of poverty, there is little wonder that the Pope acted as he did, in view of the record of the civil war that beset the order during these years.

With the restoration of property to the Franciscans in 1332, a new movement called Conventualism sprang up, although it was not until two centuries later that the group now known as the Friars Minor Conventual separated from the other first-order groups. As early as 1334, an anti-Conventual reform or Observant tendency began to emerge within the order. The Observants rapidly grew in strength so that by 1428 they were important enough to receive special consideration from Rome. In that year Pope Martin V revoked for them the decree of 1322, thus returning the ownership of their property to the Holy See. Though officially the Observants continued under the administrative control of the Conventualist group, the split between them gradually widened.

At first the new Observant reform might appear to be primarily a return to stricter material poverty, the result of relatively minor quarrels over fixed incomes and legacies. But in reality, poverty lay only on the surface. The root of the divergence was deeper, revolving around the twofold life of prayer and the apostolate. The key to much of the internal history of the Franciscans and to the series of struggles and reforms that marked their development would seem to be the "observance" or "non-observance" of the spirit of prayer and devotion; on this depended, in turn, the observance or neglect of the whole Rule of St. Francis.[18] In point of fact, the Observants differed from the current Conventual way of life in three specific points: the strictest observance of Franciscan poverty, a greater use of bodily mortifications, and especially a greater cultivation of the life of prayer and solitude—particularly the practice of contemplation. It was, therefore, not one or another point of rule that separated the two, but the whole style of their lives.

Finally, after three centuries of incompatibility, the split was formalized by Pope Leo X's division of the order into Conventuals and Observants in 1517. The final separation was but a single phase in a more extensive series of movements brewing beneath the surface, even within the Observant faction itself. In 1496 the Alcantarines had broken away from the First Order and, shortly after the major division of 1517, several other subgroups came into being, of which the Capuchins are perhaps the best known. Within a few years other Observant groups, such as the French and German Recollects, emerged to meet various specialized needs and give outlet to the ever varying efforts of the Observants to imitate more closely the holiness of Francis. It would also seem that these splinter groups moved sharply in the direction of the monks of the desert in their practices of solitude, contemplation, and renunciation. Even among the stronger current of Friars Minor, the early idealism of Francis soon faded away and friaries were converted into the very things that Francis feared most—a new crop of monastic houses.

In discussing Francis and his order, our task was made difficult by the need to pick our way through rival Franciscan versions of both the legends of Francis and the interpretation of Franciscan spirituality. With St. Dominic the job is simpler; we have merely to clear away the manifest accretions and legends of later generations.

Dominic de Guzman was born in 1170 at Calaruega in Old Castile. The land of his birth was, in fact, to influence his whole life. The fairest provinces of Spain were still under control of the Muslims, and so from his earliest days Dominic was brought up to think of heresy as the great foe that must be overcome at any cost. The son of a nobleman and the youngest of two brothers, he was educated first at home, then by a clerical relative of his mother, and finally in the schools of Palencia. After ten years of training there, Dominic entered the cathedral chapter of Osma about 1195.

Soon after Dominic had been appointed prior of this chapter, he accompanied his bishop, Diego, on a diplomatic mission to Denmark and on a pilgrimage to Rome. Late in 1204, at the bidding of Innocent III, the two men set off for the frontier borderlands of Languedoc, a country besieged by the heretical Catharists. There he spent the next ten years preaching, while the country was deluged with the blood of the Albigensian Crusade. During the same time, he founded a school for women of gentle birth, mostly converts from the Albigensians, at Prouille, under the shadow of the Pyrenees. The two missionaries next went to Montpellier where they urged an entirely new plan of campaign against the heretics. Instead of depending on the authority of the bishops and the military aid of the barons as the papal legates hitherto had done, the two Spaniards wanted to appeal directly to the heretics themselves, addressing their preaching to them and winning them by example. Dominic and Bishop Diego began the missionary work first of all by taking the injunction of evangelical poverty seriously and, above all, by treating the heretics in all seriousness as people sharing a common humanity with themselves.

The first real disputation with the Albigensians, in which the heretics did not stand like defendants before their judges but as discussants with equal rights, took place at Montreal in 1206. The two parties searched for the truth according to prearranged rules of debate, one of which was that the man who could not prove his position from Scripture was to be regarded as defeated. This disputation seems to have been the seed of the Dominican order.[19]

Although Dominic and Diego gathered only a small band of kindred souls, the movement encountered serious mistrust from the start. The papal legates considered their method of evangelization folly. To be sure, there were exceptions—like the Bishop of Toulouse—who felt otherwise, but opposition continued. A year after the Montreal disputation, Bishop Diego died, and Dominic became the sole dynamic spirit behind this movement as well as the leader of the community they had established in Toulouse. What is most intriguing, perhaps, is that Dominic's reform movement arose out of Waldensianism itself. To him it was clear that Waldensianism could be conquered only if its demands were acknowledged and carried out within the Catholic Church; and like the Waldensians, he returned to the example of the primitive Church—its style of preaching and its simplicity of life. Dominic's point of view was undoubtedly strengthened by what he had to witness at this time and to the end of his life—the unspeakable cruelty of the Albigensian Crusade. He was present, for instance, at Lavaur in 1211 when the heretics were stoned, tortured, burned, and crucified by the hundreds after the capture of the city. While this kind of frenzy raged, the Dominican Order was born.

Although the Lateran Council had just decided that no new orders were to be confirmed by the Church, Dominic finally succeeded in obtaining sanction for his group from Pope Honorius III in 1216. Distinguishing themselves in highly revolutionary fashion from the older orders, Dominicans had no permanent bond to a specific monastery (*stabilitas loci*); they lived not in isolation but in the midst of cities; they practiced poverty in the literal sense—the poverty of beggars, which had hitherto been forbidden to clerics; and they devoted themselves to the study of Scripture and the sciences. The rules of the order, in fact, even stipulated that members could be excused from canonical prayers for the sake of study—a dispensation unthinkable among Benedictines.

Dominic's community was also different from that of the Little

Brothers of Francis, even though both groups came into being in response to the same challenge. In the first place, Dominic's was an order of priests from the start. Secondly, it was of a rational and sober complexion, altogether unromantic in its origins. Thirdly, it did not in principle reject culture and the pursuit of science, as Francis and his early followers did, but expressly turned its attention to the first universities of the western world, from which students were pouring into the newly established order. Fourthly, Dominic's Rule—based on the most severe interpretation of St. Augustine's Rule with supplementary regulations from the code of the Canons of Prémontré, the usages of Cluny, and the idea of corporate poverty adopted from Francis—set down a precise and detailed organizational structure with authority flowing from a single source.

But the differences between the Dominican and Franciscan friars went deeper than the organizational level. It was the contemplative vocation, after all, that Dominic first chose for himself and to which he dedicated himself by vow. Even though he was eventually to alter his more conservative approach to monasticism, there can be no doubt that Dominic and his Preachers always remained closer to this tradition than did Francis. After Paul's Epistles, Dominic's favorite reading was the *Conferences* of Cassian—this "mirror for monks," as Benedict had called it. Dominic's own first religious foundation was a convent of contemplative nuns, and even when he came out of his cloister in response to the needs of his age, his example was that of a contemplative at large, his words those of a contemplative praying out loud. In his own order, his chief concern was to make his followers preachers by making them contemplatives first.

This did not mean, as is clear from Thomas Aquinas' explanation of the nature of teaching, that the contemplative merely handed over his conclusions to others to be received by them on faith or as matters of opinion, but that he assisted his listeners to form in themselves minds like his own.[20] Thus Dominican work for souls was far more than pastoral; it was educational in the highest sense. It aimed to educate consciences, to train men and women to reflect and act for themselves. It was

Dominic's essential vision to draw into his own group any with whom he came in contact, making contemplatives active in the spread of contemplation and independent of monastic enclosure. Such an ideal was not an attempt to undo the notion of religious life already established, but a desire to enlarge the cloister by making it as wide as the world. While the older orders had provided the safeguards of a cloister for those who had decided to become contemplatives, the Order of Preachers went into the world to propagate contemplation.[21]

Part of the idea which grounded Dominic's viewpoint undoubtedly derived from his earlier experience as a Canon Regular of St. Augustine. Canons arose in the Church toward the middle of the eleventh century as one result of the need for priests to serve the people while still living a common, monastic life, and also as a response to the attempts of the hierarchy to enforce clerical celibacy. The canons differed from monks by being also clerics, with singular powers of adapting themselves to work of any sort—whether pastoral, educational, or even philanthropic, that is, in the hospitals attached to their houses. They also differed from monks by reason of the greater simplicity and elasticity of their organization. But while such a distinction could be clear in theory, in practice it was not always easy to separate these groups either from the monastic orders of the time or from the diocesan clergy.[22] Originally, the canons had no rule to guide the details of their religious life; eventually, they adopted the Rule derived from letters of exhortation Augustine had written for some nuns and priests in his own diocese of Hippo. Because of its origins Augustine's Rule was not an elaborate code for religious life, but a casual summary confining itself to fundamental principles and edifying exhortations.

In the development of his own Constitutions, Dominic clearly went beyond the general directives of the Rule of Augustine, first by interpreting it in the strictest possible way and, secondly, by adding elements from the code of Prémontré and from the Benedictinism of Cluny.[23] Nevertheless, it is easier to understand the overall direction of the Order of Preachers if we view them within the context of the canons regular from which they derived. The first principle which ruled the Dominican order from its inception was its dedication to the apostolic work of preaching and the salvation of souls. Immediately following this was the directive that its members must be men of prayer and renunciation, graduating by intense and uninterrupted study to become authoritative teachers. Both as a clerical and as a monastic body, its underlying position was one of absolute and immediate subjection to the pope. Under his authority, it formed an independent and autonomous society. Its rulers were elected by democratic suffrage; its laws were formulated by representative assemblies and administered by officials who, while ultimately responsible to these assemblies, still enjoyed full jurisdiction over their immediate subjects during the term of their office.

The corporate aim of the order was and remains to communicate by preaching and teaching the fruits which proceed by prayer and study from the fulness of contemplation. The means by which this goal was pursued were the solemn vows of poverty, chastity, and obedience, as well as monastic observance with solemn choral recitation of the divine office. With the exception of the vows, these means might be modified to suit varying conditions, but they could never be entirely dispensed with or changed in substance. Such a set of ideals obviously attracted a different group of followers than those who flocked to the Brothers of Assisi. But like Francis, Dominic struck a spark that soon flared into a conflagration. By the time of his death in 1221, there were burgeoning groups of Dominicans in Spain, France, Italy, Germany, Hungary, England, Sweden, and Denmark—a total of more than thirty monasteries.

From this brief survey of the lives of two great spiritual leaders and the mendicant orders they established, we pause to consider these movements from the standpoint of our theme—the special part they played in the development of Christian spirituality. Despite their differing emphases, both of these orders were part of a larger movement to evangelical and voluntary poverty which found enthusiastic adherents over all Europe among religious, clergy, and laity alike.[24] From a sociological point of view, it was a kind of youth movement, but one which flourished only on the soil of cities. Neither Dominic nor Francis would have encountered it in a Benedictine monastic community. Furthermore, it was an anti-movement, directed against the solid secularity of a Christianity that was making itself at home in the economic, intellectual, and political world. Against this the corporate poverty of the Franciscans and the rigorous intellectualism of the Dominicans stood in eloquent protest.

At the same time, we cannot overlook the democratic significance of the mendicants. Hildebrand's attempt to impose monasticism on the Christian world at large, especially on the clergy, had an essentially aristocratic tone, despite the pontiff's own lower-class origins. He had used the chair of Peter as his instrument, working his reform, so to speak, from the highest downward. The friars now renewed the religious ideal in an effort to work from the lowest upward. Previously, monks had generally belonged to the upper classes; only for the aristocrat was the refuge of the cloister easily accessible.[25] The poor, except in the towns, were serfs tied down to the soil; the heavenly gardens were not open to them, except perhaps as lay brothers. But in the brotherhood of Francis, caste distinctions were unknown, and these men whom feudalism had despised took the world by storm. Throughout their history they have been leaders in popular movements, and their recruits, for the most part, have come from the middle classes. Ironically, in attempting to reform monasticism on such a democratic basis, Francis enrolled forces greater than either Hildebrand or Bernard had ever dreamed of.

While Dominic's emphasis laid less stress on democracy and more on apostolic preaching and learning, it was just as timely. Here was a group dominated by a passion for the enunciation of truth and a drive for the better understanding and use of the Scriptures. In this latter orientation, Dominic embodied the same radical tendency which had fired Peter Waldo and his followers —a fundamental return to the Bible and a renewed dedication to the ideal of poverty. As a result of both these mendicant movements, Europe was now filled with a host of earnest laymen bound together in social service and church work and with a force of learned clerics who began to occupy some of the most influential university chairs. From the outset, both groups of mendicants were ardent missionaries. Rather than flee the world, they made the whole world their parish.

As with most reform movements, however, the mendicant ideals did not remain untarnished, and while some loss of enthusiasm is virtually inevitable, the very success of the movement involved a contradiction between the ideal and the real all the more striking because of the hope which the mendicants raised for the spiritual renewal of both religious and laity alike. Although it is true that Dominic had broken away from the monastic tradition less than Francis, he nevertheless quashed at the outset the monastic conception that it was necessary for a monk to do much manual work each day. But Francis' impact was even more profound. While he allowed in his Rule for those who wish to "live religiously in a hermitage," the bulk of the Rule demanded—in principle—total involvement in apostolic and missionary activity, without the slightest trace of monastic connections. This was, in fact, the keynote of his order, and even the vestiges of monasticism contained in the canons regular and to some degree in the Constitutions of Dominic were absent from Francis' Rule.

Nevertheless, the subsequent history of the Brothers of Assisi— their times of decay and reform, the civil war over "evangelical poverty"—symbolized the kind of difficulties encountered by the other mendicant movements, even if in less dramatic form. Crises arose when the spirit of prayer and devotion, so easy to cultivate in the confines of a monastery, was threatened by the demands of study or the call of the poor. And problems developed when the friars went into the cities, built large houses, and apparently forgot "Lady Poverty" or the exigencies of contemplation. Part of the explanation for these difficulties must be found in a basic ambiguity underlying the whole mendicant tradition itself. In a word, there was no theology of apostolic involvement, no framework in which the prayer life of the friar could be integrated with his activity. And while the lived experience of the founder could continue to inspire the group for a while, it was the theological understanding of the mendicant reform—or the lack of it—which remained to form and underscore the crises of the mendicants themselves.

In the beginning, of course, the mendicants certainly did not pursue action for the sake of action; they put themselves at the service of others so that the world might more readily discover God. They became enthusiastic apostles in everything so that they might bear witness to the all-embracing love of Christ and make him recognized as the one and only Lord. As the lives of both Francis and Dominic testify, apostolic involvement must feed on a life of continuous and intensive prayer and asceticism. But once the first enthusiasm had gone, difficulties in continuing both action and prayer did not fail to arise. One must have recourse to prayer in order that God may give His strength and courage, in order that He may enable us to accept the numerous sacrifices involved in any serious enterprise. Certainly a person can deceive himself for a time; the numberless, harassing activities, accepted at the outset with a view to God's service, can lead to the abandonment of prayer. But sooner or later one has to come back to the reason for his action; then potential self-deception can lead to inward renewal.

The problem with the mendicants, as we will develop in greater detail in a subsequent chapter, was not that they did not pray or that they were not active, but that in attempting to break away from the monastic ideal they did not construct an adequate and satisfactory understanding of the genuine innovation which they themselves had wrought. In the end, a movement which was anti-monastic (in the case of the Franciscans) or at least a significant expansion of the monastic ideal (in the case of the Dominicans) actually ended by adding new members to the long family of monastic orders.

We must be careful not to paint the later degeneracy of the mendicants in overly dark colors. That they did not completely lose the self-abnegation of their early days, even after more than a century of slow decay, was abundantly demonstrated during the Black Death of 1349, when the friars stayed by the sick and were swept away in their thousands. Even if the dream of Francis and Dominic passed away or underwent drastic modification, as other dreams had passed away or had been altered by succeeding generations, the inspiration of the mendicant friar would still bear its hundredfold. Refusing to share the Benedictine outlook, the instincts of the local landowners, or the Carthusian's attraction for his cell, he journeyed everywhere, with no other ties than the interests of his order, his duty of obedience, and his insatiable desire for souls. Seekers after God would ever feel this gentle influence and follow in flight the white wings of Francis as he soared toward Infinite Love or the straight arrow of Dominic's preaching as he searched endlessly for Infinite Truth.

The intellectual dynamics of the early thirteenth century were, we have said, determined chiefly by two forces, both revolutionary and both of tremendous vitality: on the one hand, the radical evangelism of the voluntary poverty movement which rediscovered a central demand of the Bible and attempted to make it operative in the Christian life of laity, clergy, and religious alike; on the other hand, the no-less-fierce urge to reconstruct the foundations of society on non-feudal soil and to investigate, on the plane of natural philosophy, the reality that lay before men's eyes. Both forces contributed to the climate in which the mendicant orders flowered. It will be important now to consider briefly the effect this climate had on the piety and religious practice of the ordinary medieval laymen to whom the friars addressed themselves and whose religious imagination they helped to shape.

Up to this point there has been little to report concerning lay spirituality. Although monasticism began as a strictly lay movement, in the West it did not long remain such. Besides, when one speaks today of lay spirituality, he invariably thinks of a style of Christian life suitable for all the people, for the masses—and this, monasticism never has been and never will be. Whatever the actual practice of the Christian life by the ordinary layman during the period of the Fathers and the early Middle Ages, the monastic ideal alone was preached as the pattern for all to follow. The involvement of the mass of men with the things of this world was seen as a debilitating concession necessary until the world could be converted into a monastery.[26]

By the beginning of the thirteenth century, however, the hard realities of the world had proved stronger than the renunciation rhetoric of the Church's monastic ideal. The wealthy monastery, the soft, easy-living pastor, and the prince-bishop were everywhere in evidence. The common layman could hardly be expected to turn to monks and clergy for the direction of his more spiritual aspirations. If indeed he wished to raise his material standard of living, the path before him led away from the country estates of clergy and gentry and into the growing cities with their new opportunities for business and commerce. Insofar as he sought religious inspiration there, his imagination was captured by the newly rediscovered ideals of the voluntary poverty movement.

The monk had never considered preaching the Word more than an accidental occupation and the parish priest had long ago abdicated this as his principal office; preaching demanded more learning or more energy than he possessed. The few priests who tried to continue preaching often encountered deaf, if not hostile, audiences. As late as 1281 an English synod found it necessary to insist that parish priests preach the basic fundamentals of the faith to their people four times a year.[27] Such absence of effective preaching in an age virtually without books or formal education explains how a populace nominally Christian could have been so utterly ignorant of the doctrine and practice of Christianity. It also explains why the early mendicant friars, with their learning, zeal, and honest poverty, met with such an enthusiastic reception. The people were hungry, and they found the friars' sermons a living experience, overflowing with sacred eloquence, spontaneity, and genuine devotion.

Although the friars usually restricted their preaching to fundamentals—the creed, the commandments, the works of mercy, the virtues and vices, the sacraments—their apostolate of the Word was otherwise unlimited. They preached to common people and to priests, to prelates and kings, to nuns and monks; they spoke in the street, in the market place, in house or castle, in cemeteries, in chapel and church and cathedral across the whole of Europe. To the friars, therefore, goes much of the credit for laying the groundwork of a spirituality addressed to the entire populace.[28]

Just as the friars were appearing on the scene, Church leaders

began to express concern over the ignorance of doctrine and
apathy of religious practice among clergy and laity alike. The
Fourth Lateran Council (1215) decreed under pain of excom-
munication that everyone was to go to confession and receive
Holy Communion once a year.[29] Behind this decree lay the fact
that the majority of medieval Christians, unlike Christians of the
early centuries, were not receiving the Eucharist weekly, probably
not even yearly. In regard to Penance, however, the decree implied not merely a decline in the frequency of people's reception,
but an evolution in the Church's thinking on how often this
sacrament should be received. There were centuries when the
monk-bishops of Gaul taught that a person should *do* penance
frequently but go to confession only on his deathbed. For a long
time, in fact, Church discipline forbade the reception of sacramental reconciliation more than once—hence the warning of several councils against administration of penance to a young person in danger of death, since he might recover and some day find
himself in need of a forbidden second administration.[30]

The fathers of the Council had no illusions in enacting the
decree on annual reception of Penance and the Eucharist. They
realized that neither the clergy nor the laity were properly prepared to carry it out. The Church would have to begin an elaborate program of education. As diocese after diocese took up the
campaign, it gained momentum through the thirteenth century.
A flood of instruction and sermon manuals testified to the seriousness with which Church scholars undertook the task of bringing the technical learning of the moral and canonical theological
treatises to the parish clergy. Most of these manuals were in
Latin; but with the advent of the fourteenth century, they begin
to appear in the vernacular along with books of moral instruction and devotion for the growing number of literate lay people.

The focus of the largest body of instruction for the laity is
evident in some of the most popular titles: *Manuel de Pechiez,
Handlyng Synne, Cursor Mundi* with its "Boke of Penance,"
Somme des Vices et des Vertues, Pricke of Conscience. The
reader may be familiar with Chaucer's Parson's Tale—really not
a tale at all, but a treatise of some thousand lines on penance,

replete with the citation of innumerable authorities and divided into the three requisite elements of contrition, confession, and satisfaction. The treatment of confession comprises the largest part of the work and is occupied principally with the seven deadly sins, the relation between them, the circumstances that lead to them, their various species and subspecies, and the remedies to be applied for each.

For all their preoccupation with sin, repentance, and punishment, the popular manuals offered little nourishment to a people more interested in being moved by their religion than enlightened by it. If we turn to the devotional literature of the period we find this inspirational dimension considerably more manifest. Notice the feeling expressed in a verse prayer that must often have been on the lips of literate and illiterate alike:

> Jesu, for Thy Holy Name,
> And for Thy bytter Passioun,
> Save me frome synne and schame
> And endeles dampnacion.

> Five Pater Nosters, Five Ave Marias and a Credo.
> Five thowsand days of pardon.[31]

This is prayer, not mere doctrine. Further, while it expresses fear over sin and the prospect of hell's torments, it focuses most of all on the person and passion of Christ. This kind of tender devotion to Christ was the center of medieval man's piety. The apocryphal gospels and various legends provided his imagination with picturesque details for the life of Christ and of our Lady. He loved to dwell especially on the nativity and the passion, both of which possessed great emotional impact. Again and again these two events were depicted in works of art and, of course, in the Christmas crib and the stations of the cross. Devotion to the Five Wounds and to the Precious Blood also became popular. The artist, much influenced by the mystics to be studied in the next chapter, could not be too realistic in treating the details of Christ's suffering—the stripes from the scourging, the thorns, the nails and the gaping wounds in hands and feet and side, and blood everywhere—all designed to excite piety to its highest pitch.

Perhaps the most characteristic art subject of the later Middle Ages is the Image of Pity, a representation of Jesus, crucified or standing in front of his cross, with bleeding wounds and blood spattered over his whole body, and appealing for a response of pity and tears from the onlooker. One version (a sort of advertisement for the Gregorian Mass!) shows Jesus standing in the tomb, wounded, and not yet able to ascend to heaven. These images might also serve as a sacramental which offered salvation and mercy in the form of an indulgence to one who would stop and contemplate. A typical inscription reads: "To all them that devoutly say five pater nosters, five aves, and a credo afor such a figure are graunted 32,755 [?] years of pardon."[32] A good case can be made for viewing the monologues of the mystery plays as animated Images of Pity in which an all-bloody Christ appeals to the audience for pity and repentance and offers his mercy.[33] Thus the highly popular medieval drama also acted as an element in the formation of the people's religious consciousness.[34]

Among the forms of medieval devotion to Christ, we must include devotion to the Blessed Sacrament. Despite the semi-superstitious practices which, as we shall see, tended to surround it and despite the negative attitude we might assume on the basis of a renewed theology of the Eucharist, it would be wrong to suppose that this devotion was not generally a beneficial nourishment for popular piety. In essence medieval devotion to the Blessed Sacrament consisted of looking in adoration at God present in the host. As the great historian of the liturgy, Jungmann, puts it: "To see the celestial mystery—that is the climax of the Grail-legend in which the religious longing of the Middle Ages found its poetic expression." It was as if the words of Jesus had been rewritten: "He who *looks at* my flesh shall have everlasting life." Actually, more immediate and tangible benefits were thought to result—for example, that on the day one looked upon the host he could not lose his eyesight or meet a sudden death. As a consequence of such beliefs, people would run from church to church in order to see the elevated host as many times as possible. They even initi-

ated lawsuits to get a place with a favorable view of the altar. In
some places the majority of the congregation entered the church
only with the consecration warning bell, witnessed the elevation,
and then left as quickly as they had come. For those under ex-
communication or interdict, the most painful privation was often
an injunction against looking at the host; some sought to cir-
cumvent this by boring a hole in the church walls.

Naturally there arose a movement for repeated or longer
"showings" at Mass, and the Church had to take action against
the priests who acceded—at times under the influence of a
stipend—to popular wishes for repetition and extension of the
elevation. It was not long, however, before the longer showings
won out in the form we know as benediction or exposition of the
Blessed Sacrament. From the beginning of the fourteenth century, on the Feast of Corpus Christi the monstrance was carried
through the streets for all to see and was then left exposed on the
high altar during the Mass that followed and indeed through the
week—a great octave of privilege.[35]

Such an attitude toward the Eucharist did not emerge suddenly.
In addition to an overemphasis on the divinity of Christ result-
ing from the long battle against Arianism, perhaps the most
contributing factor was the inability of the people to understand
the language of the Mass, Latin. This was the beginning of a veil
of separation between the priest and people. From the high altar
facing the back wall of the apse, the priest performed his function—saying the mysterious words and bringing God down on
the altar; far away in the nave, the people performed their function—looking on in awe. The period also witnessed a prolifera-
tion of ceremonial actions—genuflection, signs of the cross, kiss-
ing the altar, and incensation—adding solemnity and mystery to
the otherwise unintelligible rite. By means of allegorical interpretation, the people were led to endow various insignificant
aspects of the ceremony with arbitrary meaning. The hiding of
the paten under the corporal, for example, signified our Lord's
hiding of his divinity in the passion; the priest's extending his
arms in prayer showed Jesus on the cross; lifting his voice at the
Nobis quoque represented Jesus' cry before he expired; the five

crosses at the doxology signified the five wounds. Often the different symbols overlapped or contradicted one another and at times a new allegorical insight played havoc with an existing system of symbols, thus demanding a complete "theological" reinterpretation. Throughout this transformation of the Eucharist into a holy play, the one thing necessary—besides a fertile imagination —was ignorance of what was actually being said and done by the priest![36]

This one-sided view of the Mass, as a miracle wrought by God for the people through the instrumentality of the priest, led to an erroneous doctrine of the effects of the Mass and hence to numerous abuses. During the time a person hears Mass, it was said, he does not grow older and the souls in purgatory do not suffer; or again, after hearing Mass, food tastes better, or one will not die a sudden death. Views such as these led to the initiation of the so-called votive Mass. New Mass formularies were composed to ward off various illnesses and to invoke the saints who protected against them. What was questionable here, as with the series or Gregorian Masses for the dead, was the assurance of unfailing results attached to the practice. In this context, the demand for Masses increased enormously. Many Masses came to be said simultaneously at different altars in the same church, and large numbers of priests derived their entire income from Mass stipends and endowments.[37]

Anyone who takes a comprehensive look at the later Middle Ages cannot help but be struck by the anomalous mixture of fear and tenderness in its piety. Over the high altar in church, medieval man looked with fear and trembling at Jesus the terrible judge casting sinners into the fiery, eternal torments of hell; and yet he could call upon him with these words:

> Swete Jhesu, king of blysse,
> myn herte love, min herte lisse [joy].[38]

Christ in the Eucharist was so divine that medieval man no longer dared touch the host, seldom dared partake of it; still he could stage a spectacle in which the same Christ was played by an ordinary human being. Medieval man shrank in terror at the prospect of plague, famine, and death and surrounded himself with armies of mediating angels and saints for fear of being unable to approach God directly; yet he could contemplate with joy an Image of Pity, speak of Christ's "blyssful Passion," and in tears say to him:

> Jhesu, late me fele whate joy it be
> to suffren wo for love of the.[39]

These observations on the contradictions of the age are not made to accuse late medieval man of logical inconsistency; certainly he must have been well aware of such contrasts. In fact, as the Dutch historian Huizinga has pointed out: "To the world when it was half a thousand years younger, the outline of all things seemed more clearly marked than to us. The contrast between suffering and joy, between adversity and happiness, appeared more striking." Life seemed to consist in extremes—fierce religious asceticism and unrestrained licentiousness, ferocious judicial punishments and great popular waves of pity and mercy, most horrible crimes and most extravagant acts of saintliness— and everywhere a sea of tears. So much for the stark contrasts in the life of the people.

Huizinga continues his picture, pointing to other aspects of the mentality of the age: "All experience had yet to the minds of men the directness and absoluteness of the pleasure and pain of child-life. Every event, every action, was still embodied in expressive and solemn forms, which raised them to the dignity of a ritual. For it was not merely the great facts of birth, marriage and death which, by the sacredness of the sacrament, were raised to the rank of mysteries; incidents of less importance, like a journey, a task, a visit, were equally attended by a thousand formalities: benedictions, ceremonies, formulae."[40] It only remains to fill out in more detail these characteristics of the popular religious imagination.

First, we can observe a pervasive attempt to raise the ordinary activities of daily life to the level of the sacred. "There is not an

object nor an action, however trivial, that is not constantly cor-
related with Christ and salvation." For example, the Dominican
mystic Henry Suso eats three quarters of an apple in honor of the
Trinity and the remaining quarter in commemoration of "the
love with which the heavenly Mother gave her tender child Jesus
an apple to eat"; and in consequence Suso eats the last quarter
with the paring, since little boys do not peel their apples; he does
not eat it after Christmas, for then the baby Jesus was too young
to eat apples. When drinking, Suso does so in five swallows because of the Lord's five wounds, and since blood and water
flowed from the side of Christ, he takes the last swallow twice.[41]

This mentality produced an endless growth of religious interpretations, votive Masses, offices, hymns, special benedictions,
images, relics, churches, saints, vigils, and holy days. Responsible
and perceptive writers of the period recognized in all this that
the Church was shouldering a burden of superfluous particulars
which it could not long support. Repeatedly they cry out: "The
Church is being overloaded." Yet what was or what could be
done about the situation? It is difficult not to see this prolifera-
tion as an indication of the failure of normal religious activity,
especially the liturgy, to provide genuine religious experience.
The world was clearly undergoing progressive secularization;
what was needed was a viable lay spirituality—one that would
help the people understand the intrinsic Christian value of their
activity. That no such spirituality was given them is evidenced
by their frantic and misguided attempt to protect themselves by
re-sacralizing the world.

The inevitable result of trying to superimpose a religious
meaning on earthly reality was that the truly sacred and holy
tended to sink to the level of the commonplace, the profane, and
even the vulgar, obscene, and blasphemous. The veneration of
saints' relics—in its origin and intent a salutary way of honor-
ing the martyrs' bodies which had played a part in their triumph
for Christ—thus tended to become mixed with crude, primitive
ideas and practices. When Thomas Aquinas died in their monastery on his way to the Council of Lyons, the monks of Fossanuova
so feared losing such a precious relic that they decapitated his

body, boiled, and preserved it. At a great feast, Charles VI of France gave his guests the ribs of his ancestor St. Louis as mementos of the occasion. Similarly, as the number of patron saints multiplied out of all control—one for each guild and occupation, one for each town, one for each activity—devotion to the saints became tinged with increasing superstition. Each malady and disease was associated with its particular saint, to whom one prayed for deliverance from it, e.g., St. Maur's evil (gout), St. Vitus' dance. Since the saint was thought to have power over the disease, it was only a short step to feeling that its contraction was also due to the saint.[42]

Finally, we may ask ourselves what constituted sanctity in the estimation of the later Middle Ages. An answer might be found in the life of Blessed Pierre de Luxembourg (1368-1387). This descendant of the royal house of Luxembourg and relative of the King of France and the Duke of Burgundy was clearly an example of William James' "under-witted saint," a mind so narrow it could live only in a carefully isolated sphere of devotion. Because of family connections, Pierre was made Bishop of Metz at fifteen and a cardinal soon after. At first his parents opposed his propensity for extreme asceticism, but soon they grew proud of their little "saint." In an attempt to appreciate the peculiar witness of his life, we must picture him amid the unbridled luxury and vice of the court—a sickly, undergrown boy, dressed in rags, horribly dirty, and covered with vermin. He is ever occupied with his sins and carries around with him a notebook in which he is continually recording them. In the middle of the night, he wakes his chaplain in order to go to confession and during the last year of his life must always have the priest by his side should he need to be shriven. After his death at age eighteen, an entire trunk full of the sin-slips was found! The cause for his beatification was introduced at once by two kings and the University of Paris. Only because of the current pope's negligence was the beatification delayed for a century and a half. Many miracles, of course, followed immediately upon Pierre's death.[43]

Although our picture of the Middle Ages will not be complete until we take a look at fourteenth-century mysticism in the next chapter, it is time to bring this chapter to a close. One stands in amazement at the prodigious energy and imagination of high medieval religion. The move to the cities and rapid economic change, as well as the challenge of heresy, brought forth the friars; the new secular learning was met by the universities, various treatises of theology and the great Thomas Aquinas. Architecture, music, and drama nourished popular piety.

Yet within a century the friars went the way of the monks before them and scholasticism became sterile; the unhappier tendencies in religious art, imagination, and practice grew like cancer. In the wake of catastrophes like the Black Death, the Hundred Years' War, and the Western Schism, it seems the Church had not the energy to effect reform. By the time it did muster its efforts, whole nations and peoples had withdrawn their allegiance and joined the Reformation. Moreover, the great Council of Trent, for all its concern with anathematizing abstract doctrinal error, did little to attack the source of the problem—the decadent religious imagination of the populace.[44] Nothing very effective, it seems, would be done about it for another four centuries.

Chapter V

THE MYSTICISM
OF THE LATE
MIDDLE AGES

No DISCUSSION OF MEDIEVAL PIETY would be complete without some attention to the great flowering of mysticism in the fourteenth century. It is a curious phenomenon in the history of spirituality that mysticism seems to flourish at a few specific times and places. In fact, there have been only three great periods of mysticism in the history of the Church: the third and fourth centuries in the East (Egypt, Palestine, and Asia Minor), the fourteenth century in northern Europe, and sixteenth-century Spain. While the historian can be satisfied with reporting the phenomenon of such schools of mysticism, their existence has always been something of a difficulty for the theologian, who finds himself asking: Can one man teach another how to become a mystic? Does God give his mystical graces to entire groups of people at a few given times and places and yet withhold them from virtually everyone in all other eras? In the last part of this chapter, we shall address ourselves to these and other questions which involve the nature of mysticism itself. For now it is enough to observe that unlike the majority of Christian epochs, these three periods were marked not merely by genuine mystics, as any age might well be, but by people (some of them genuine mystics) who talked, preached, and wrote about mysticism.

With this comment in mind we can say that fourteenth-century "mysticism" was restricted, with the one notable exception of Catherine of Siena, to northern Europe, more specifically to the Rhineland and England. In our following consideration we want first to look at some of the principal mystical writers during this period and then to illustrate several important characteristics and tendencies of the mysticism they described.

Certainly the first and most controversial of the Rhineland mystics was Meister Eckhart of Hochheim (1260- before 1329). This Dominican teacher, preacher, spiritual director, and master of theology combined the scholasticism of Albert the Great and Thomas Aquinas with the Neoplatonic mysticism of Pseudo-Dionysius. Although he spent much of his life in high administrative positions in his order, Eckhart still found time to compose lengthy Latin philosophical and theological treatises. But he was best known as a preacher of great poetic and rhetorical power, who could discover for himself and his hearers astounding "truths" by translating abstract Latin theological ideas into the language of the people. For some of these "truths" Eckhart was accused of heresy, and he spent the last years of his life defending himself—in the judgment of ecclesiastical courts, unsuccessfully.

Eckhart had two great disciples, John Tauler (1300-1361) and Henry Suso (1296-1366). Like him, they were Dominicans and preachers; but in view of his condemnation they were restrained in presenting his doctrines. Tauler was also less speculative, more homely, than his master; his emphasis on the will gave a more practical bent to the mysticism of the times. Suso was a poet, a *Minnesinger* of God; and although he retained the basic tenets of Dionysian mysticism, the way he wrote about following the suffering Christ may remind the reader of Francis of Assisi. Of these three mystical writers, Eckhart and Tauler seem to have learned their "mysticism" from those they directed, while Suso alone spoke of his own personal experience.[1]

A final important Rhineland mystic, John Van Ruysbroek

(1293-1381), spent the first twenty-five years of his priestly life serving a parish in Brussels. Then he retired to a forest with some relatives to form a contemplative community which eventually came under the Rule of St. Augustine, devoting itself to the "mixed life" of contemplation and activity. Since Gerard Groote visited this foundation and was much taken by the spirit of its founder, we may say that Ruysbroek had at least an indirect influence on the tradition which produced the *Imitation of Christ*.

It is a coincidence that fourteenth-century England also produced four great mystical writers. The most celebrated of these is the anonymous author of *The Cloud of Unknowing* and *The Epistle of Privy Counsel,* works written in the tradition of unadulterated Dionysian mysticism and expressly intended for those advanced in the spiritual life. A second writer, the hermit Richard Rolle of Hampole (c. 1300-1349), tried to express his intense feelings of love for Jesus in works like the *Fire of Love;*[2] while critical of the active life, of priests, and of monks, he admired the friars and especially the Franciscan Spirituals' ideal of complete poverty. The Augustinian canon Walter Hilton (d. 1396) was more moderate than Rolle or the author of *The Cloud* in praising the contemplative life over the active life; his *Scale of Perfection* teaches gradual progress through three degrees of contemplation to perfect mystical union with God. A fourth figure, Dame Julian of Norwich (1343- after 1416), although an anchoress at least during the later years of her life, was certainly no introvert. She stands out as a prophetic exception to the English Dionysian tradition. Her only work, *The Revelations of Divine Love,* because of its theological profundity and poetic beauty, is perhaps the finest single piece of devotional writing in the English language.

This account of some leading mystical writers provides only an initial picture of late medieval mysticism. We must also take note of the Benedictine visionaries of the thirteenth century, Gertrude and the two Mechtildes, and of the great visionary Church-reformers of the fourteenth, the Dominicans Bridget of Sweden and Catherine of Siena. As might be expected in a society where women far outnumbered men, the women religious and therefore women mystics also outnumbered the men. There was such a demand for the religious life among women that the orders could not set up houses fast enough to accommodate all who wished to enter. Hence groups of women were led to form their own pious societies in which they lived a common life, earned their living by working at crafts like spinning and weaving, and sought spiritual direction where they could find it. Eckhart, Tauler, Suso, and Hilton all spent much time directing communities of women in the ways of contemplation. Men too came under the influence of these and other teachers of mysticism, so that the atmosphere of northern Europe was pervaded by an enthusiasm for mysticism. Both sexes and all classes of society, including clergy and laity, were included among groups like the "Friends of God," a pious association, neither a religious order nor a sect, cultivating an intense interior life in the face of the widespread laxity and moral decadence of the age.

As the spirit of mysticism took hold and spread, various currents of questionable orthodoxy, perhaps latent in the teaching of more learned men like Eckhart, began to appear in balder form among the people. The Beghards (also called the Brethren of the Free Spirit) and their female counterparts, the Beguines, it was charged, thought themselves capable of such perfect union with the Godhead that they became impeccable and had no need for the mediation of the Church, the sacraments, and the humanity of Christ.[3] Although many of these people led lives of honest asceticism and were orthodox at least in intent, their doctrines could easily be used as justification for erroneous beliefs and practices. Similar dangerous tendencies grew out of fantastic prophecies like that of Joachim of Flora and his apocalyptic interpreter, Gerard of Borgo San Donnino (fl. c. 1250).

As already indicated, fourteenth-century mystical teaching was dominated by the world-denying mysticism of Pseudo-Dionysius. His works had been translated into Latin in the ninth century by John Scotus Erigena, and from that time they spread through the West. They became a central force behind the mystical writings of the Parisian School of St. Victor (founded 1108), whose devaluation of the world was dangerously dualistic.[4] In harmony with the tendencies of this tradition, the author of *The Cloud,* for instance, issues the following admonition: "One thing I tell thee, that everything that thou thinkest upon is above thee for the time and betwixt thee and thy God. And insomuch thou art the further from God, that aught is in thy mind but only God." And in a frequently quoted passage, he tells his reader: "Look that nothing remain in thy working mind but a naked intent stretching unto God."[5]

The Rhineland mystics teach the same doctrine. According to Eckhart,

So long as any thing is still object of our gaze we are not yet one with The One. . . . Every creature is as a "beam" in the soul's eye since, by its very nature as creature, it is an obstacle to union with God. Thus, so long as anything remains in the soul, it must get outside of itself. Nay more, it should reject even the saints and angels, yes, and the Blessed Virgin, for they are all creatures. The soul should remain in nakedness, without any needs, for God is thus in nakedness and without any need. In other words, it is stripped of matter that the soul attains to God. It is only thus that it succeeds in uniting itself to the Blessed Trinity.

At this point, however, Eckhart goes further; the soul has only reached God, the Trinity, not "beyond and above God" to the "formless abyss and desert stillness" of the naked Godhead; "for the Trinity is only the manifestation of the Godhead. In the pure Godhead there is absolutely no activity. The soul attains to perfect beatitude only in throwing itself into the desert of the Godhead there where there are neither operations nor forms, to bury itself there and lose itself there in that wilderness where its ego is annihilated and where it has no more care than it had in the days before it existed."[6] So wonderful was this experience that Eckhart preaches a cult of contemplation: "One should pray with such energy that he would wish all his limbs and all his strength, his eyes, ears, mouth, heart, and all his senses were straining within him. He should not cease until he seems to have become one with Him who is present and to whom he is praying, namely God."[7] When one has achieved such a state of union, says Ruysbroek, the fruition of bliss "is so immense that God Himself is as swallowed up with all the blessed . . . in an absence of modes, which is a not-knowing, and in an eternal loss of self."[8] Or as Eckhart puts it, the soul is hereafter "buried in the God-head" and "is God Himself" enjoying all things, disposing all as God does.[9]

The soul and God merged into one or "swallowed up" and "lost" in each other—no wonder that some sensed pantheism here. Still we must realize that these writers were trying to find words for experiences far beyond the ordinary. If we would hear anything about mysticism at all, we must allow the narrator a certain extravagance—perhaps a dangerous extravagance—of language.[10] At least we cannot accuse these Dionysian mystical teachers of reducing God to human size and form. To this day they witness that God is, after all, infinitely greater than any of man's inadequate attempts to conceive of, to talk about, or to manipulate him.

As might be expected, the teaching and preaching of these men had a medicinal effect on the cancerous growth of religious symbols and practices discussed in the preceding chapter. Eckhart, for instance, never tired of pointing out that devotion to our Lady and the saints, exercises of piety, and the other "means to obtain Grace," however salutary, can be overrated. A person can become so involved in the means that he never attains the end, union with God; he can become a "merchant," someone who wants to make a deal with God. "What all the external means cannot give you in the course of years, God can grant you in one instant." Even Jesus Christ in his humanity wanted to be only the "way" to the Father. Thus for the true Christian, says Eckhart, there can be only one thing that matters—the Eternal God within him, who is "all in all."[11]

Once due credit has been given to this "holy" iconoclasm, however, one can and must ask how adequately a writer like Eckhart deals with the role of God in history and especially with the Incarnation. There can be little doubt that the master is concerned much more about the birth of Christ in the individual soul than with his actual birth in history.[12] Furthermore, it is disturbing to find that his conception of man's most perfect activity excludes all consideration not only of Christ's humanity, but even of the Trinity. One wonders whether this kind of theological nominalism, which dissociates God as he reveals himself to us from God as he is in himself, is not the most pernicious error in Eckhart's system—although, of course, he did not invent it.[13] Finally, with his conception of a "motionless" Godhead and the techniques required to reach it, what theological support could Eckhart offer anyone—including himself—for a life of apostolic activity?[14]

We have been illustrating and evaluating at some length the Dionysian branch of late medieval mysticism. But there was another branch which, far from teaching a mind-emptying mysticism, thrived on the use of imagery. This was visionary mysticism.[15] As with the Dionysian variety, it was accompanied by both problems and blessings. To begin with the debit side, we need give little further consideration to the aberrations of the pseudo-prophets and mystics like Joachim of Flora and the Brethren of the Free Spirit. There were so many stories of "mystical" visions circulating at the turn of the fifteenth century that the reforming prelate John Gerson was inclined to belittle even the revelations of Bridget of Sweden and Catherine of Siena. A certain woman visionary told him that in the contemplation of God her mind had been annihilated—actually annihilated—and then created anew. "How do you know?" Gerson asked her. "I experienced it," she answered. As if this sort of logical absurdity were not enough, Gerson relates, someone or other was always claiming to have received a revelation that he would become pope. One man in particular believed himself predestined first to become pope and then the Anti-Christ, so that he contemplated killing himself in order to save Christendom![16]

Considering that such fantasies usually issued from uneducated and superstitious people, they are not overly surprising. But what are we to make of all the theological, historical, and aesthetic errors in the visions of this age's genuine mystics, *beati*, and saints? Our Lady, St. Catherine of Siena (1347-1380) believed, revealed to her that she had not been conceived immaculate. St. Vincent Ferrer, who died more than five hundred years ago, declared on the authority of his visions that the end of the world was imminent and believed that he had worked miracles to authenticate his prediction. The details of our Lord's life and death in the visions of St. Elizabeth of Schönau (1129-1164) and St. Bridget of Sweden (1302-1373) clearly contradict each other as well as history. Bl. Lidwina (1380-1433) believed that (without leaving her bed) she travelled nearly every night for twenty-five years to the holy places in Palestine and Rome in order to venerate the relics of the saints. Bl. Henry Suso tells us how all the red and warm blood of the five wounds flowed through his mouth and down into his heart. Alan de la Roche (1428-1475) believed he drank milk from Mary's breast. And finally—although this chronicle could easily be prolonged—Bl. Margaret Ebner (1291-1351) was instructed by the child Jesus "how his holy circumcision was performed" and thought she heard God telling her to nurse the wooden statue of the child Jesus which she kept in a crib.[17] It thus becomes quite clear that the extravagant religious imagination illustrated in the last chapter was just as widespread among leading religious figures as among the people at large.

Nevertheless, it would be wrong to suppose that the influence of visionaries on the Church was entirely detrimental. At times the mysticism of the visionary was a healthy corrective to the world-negating bent of the Dionysian spirit. During much of the fourteenth century, for instance, the Church was rotting from the inside while the vicar of Christ lived on French soil, a pawn in the hands of a French king. In these circumstances, many dedicated Christians felt attracted to a contemplative life which would leave the world to God—or the devil. But the mysticism of Catherine of Siena, far from withdrawing her into herself, thrust her into the role of a prophet who begged and threatened the pope into returning to Rome. Without her visions, Catherine would never have been a "missionary"; clearly hers was a "mysticism of apostolate."[18]

Although they do not issue in so direct a message as Catherine's "Holy Father, go back to Rome," the visions of Dame Julian of Norwich were no less a blessing for the Church of her age;

and because of their greater universality they have continued to inspire subsequent ages. *The Revelations of Divine Love,* based on her "shewings" (visions) of our Lord in his passion, exhibit a notable absence of the customary topics and manner of mystical literature.[19] Julian does not analyze sin and tell us how to eradicate it. She fails to mention the dark night of the soul or the mystical marriage with God and offers no techniques by which the soul can rise to the heights of mystical union.[20] Nor does she talk much about herself; when she does, all that "I say of me, I say in the person of all mine even-Christians."[21] Her notion of God is lacking on the one hand in hyperbolic negation and on the other in the tasteless, repellent imagery of some of her contemporaries. As the following passage shows, her conception is rather "homely," a favorite term with her:

He [God] is our clothing that for love wrappeth us, claspeth us, and all encloseth us for tender love. . . . Also in this [first revelation] He shewed me a little thing, the quantity of an hazel-nut, in the palm of my hand; and it was as round as a ball. I looked thereupon with eye of my understanding, and thought: "What may this be?" And it was answered generally thus: "It is all that is made." I marvelled how it might last, for methought it might suddenly have fallen to naught for littleness. And I was answered in my understanding: "It lasteth, and ever shall, for that God loveth it." And so All-thing hath the Being by the love of God.[22]

But everything in Julian's life and visions was by no means homely. She was in anguish over the evil she saw in the world, and her thoughts keep returning to this problem.

I looked, generally, upon us all, and methought: "If sin had not been, we should all have been clean and like to our Lord, as He made us." And thus, in my folly, afore this time often I wondered why by the great foreseeing wisdom of God the beginning of sin was not letted [prevented]: for then, methought, all should have been well. . . . But Jesus . . . answered: "It behoved that there should be sin; but all shall be well, and all shall be well, and all manner of thing shall be well."

Julian, however, was not satisfied; she puts another question:

"Ah, good Lord, how might all be well, for the great hurt that is come, by sin, to the creature? . . ." And to this our blessed Lord answered full meekly and with full lovely cheer, and shewed that Adam's sin was the most harm that ever was done, or ever shall be, to the world's end. . . . Furthermore He taught that I should behold the glorious Satisfaction: for this Amends-making is more pleasing to God and more worshipful, without comparison, than ever was the sin of Adam harmful. Then signifieth our blessed Lord . . . : "For since I have made well the most harm, then it is my will that thou know thereby that I shall make well all that is less."

Even then Julian was not satisfied:

One point of our faith is that many creatures shall be condemned . . . and methought it was impossible that all manner of things should be well. . . . And as to this I had no other answer in Shewing of our Lord God but this: "That which is impossible to thee is not impossible to me: I shall save my word in all things and I shall make all things well."[23]

In a sense Julian's entire *Revelations* were the answer to her question, centering as they did on the image of the crucified Jesus, the "supreme revelation of God's love in the face of evil in the world."[24]

It is worth dwelling on Julian because she stands in such sharp contrast to the other mystical writers we have been considering. Her vision is cosmic and ecclesial rather than individualistic, Biblical rather than Gnostic. She is at home with the most profound theological questions—the problem of evil and the solidarity of all those saved in Christ. Her *Revelations* are her "gospel to her even-Christians," not only of the fourteenth century but of today as well. Its message rings out loud and clear: "confidence in the Divine love as the ultimate reality of the Universe and the key to its history."[25]

The foregoing presentation of late medieval mysticism beginning with the Dionysian mystics of the Rhineland and stretching to the incarnational mysticism of Julian of Norwich raises theological questions which are far more significant than the historical data we have been reviewing. It has been noted, for instance, that some of the most important and influential mystical writers were probably not themselves authentic mystics. What, then, is a mystic and what is mysticism? Further, can good people—true mystics and saints—have such obviously distorted visions? And finally, what good are these private revelations and visions when, as theologians teach, the Church's revelation has been complete ever since the end of apostolic times?

After encountering several centuries of disinterest if not disdain, "mysticism" is once again becoming a subject for intelligent, or at least heated, conversation. College students are wading into courses on oriental mysticism or practicing Yoga; other people are asking about the latest "prophecies" of Jeane Dixon, the Washington seer, or paying their three dollars to enter a dingy lower-Manhattan theater and witness the psychedelic liturgy of LSD "mystic" Timothy Leary. Such revival of interest in "mysticism" raises additional questions. Is it possible to induce mystical experience by taking drugs? Can a mystic predict the future? What of non-Christian mysticism—can there be genuine mysticism outside the Church?

What follows, then, is an attempt to answer these questions with a brief excursus on the theology of mysticism. Even though this excursus will not be limited to any one mystic or period of mysticism, but will try to encompass the entire mystical tradition, much of the treatment will inevitably depend on the teachings of Teresa of Avila (1515-1582) and John of the Cross (1542-1591). Teresa and John are often considered the greatest of the Church's mystics, not only because of their own mystical experience, but because of their ability to *express* such experience.

To begin with, it is important to state two presuppositions of authentic mystical life. The first of these is moral integrity, the pursuit of a more or less sinless life. Thus one does not expect to find mystics proud and selfish, but humble and charitable. Secondly, mysticism, in the strict theological sense, is not something a person decides to have; it is a wholly gratuitous gift of God. Consequently, there are no "techniques" for *acquiring* genuine mystical experience; one does not induce it by taking LSD, by lying on a bed of nails, by holding one's body motionless for hours and trying to concentrate one's mind on a single, simple idea, or even by methodically and gradually emptying one's mind of all ideas. God gives himself to whom he wills, when he wills, as he wills.[26]

Genuine mystical experience, moreover, is discontinuous with ordinary human experience; even in the order of grace it is something uncommon, extraordinary.[27] Mystical theology in general labors under the supreme difficulty of trying to say something about the ineffable. For only the true mystic knows what mysticism is, and even he cannot communicate this adequately. It is possible, however, to establish the limits of mysticism, first negatively, by distinguishing mystical prayer from ordinary prayer, and then positively, by explicating a common definition of mysticism.

Ordinary prayer has traditionally been divided into four stages. From "lowest" to "highest" (without any implication that the higher are necessarily better or more meritorious), they are as follows: (1) *vocal prayer,* the recitation of a more or less fixed formula; (2) *meditation* or *discursive prayer,* a first stage of mental prayer including meditative reading (or slow recitation of vocal prayers) together with reflection and "affections" (words, sentiments, feelings coming from the heart as a result of the reflection); (3) *affective prayer,* in which reflection becomes simpler and plays a smaller part while the affections predominate; and (4) the *prayer of simplicity* or *simple regard,* in which intuition replaces reasoning, and the affections and ideas, though intense, show little variety and are expressed in very few words.[28]

Once a person passes beyond the fourth stage, he is no longer practicing ordinary prayer, but is experiencing mystical union, mysticism in the strict theological sense often referred to as "infused contemplation."[29] By synthesizing various elements both from the writings of the mystics themselves and from the works of theologians of mysticism, we are able to arrive at the following definition: *Mysticism is the direct and experimental awareness of the presence of God in the depths of one's person.*[30]

The definition demands some elucidation. Mysticism is first of all a *direct* awareness of God's presence, that is to say an unmediated awareness. Ordinary human knowing always involves the mediation of image, symbol, concept, word; in the broadest sense of the term, it is symbolic.[31] Mystical knowledge, on the other hand, bypasses this mediation and is therefore immediate or direct. Secondly, mysticism is an *experimental* or experiential awareness of God. By faith the believer knows that God is present, but unless he is a mystic he does not experience or feel this presence. Thirdly, we speak of an *awareness* of God's presence. Not only does this awareness differ from the knowledge of faith, but, as we have indicated before, it is unlike anything the ordinary person knows as human knowledge. Thus the mystics, struggling to communicate what they have experienced, often make use of metaphorical expressions like the "touch" or the "taste" of God. Fourthly, mysticism is an awareness of *God's presence*. One might be tempted to say an awareness of God himself, so tremendous, intense, and profoundly rich is the experience. And yet there is no question in this encounter of the mystic's really comprehending God. God remains God, the absolute Mystery, even when he gives himself in nearness to man. Hence the mystic seems to experience God in one or other of his attributes—his power, his searing judgment, his mercy and love —or simply as "felt presence." Finally, mystical union takes place *in the depths of the person*. Misleading as it may be to speak in spatial metaphor, it is necessary somehow to indicate that the mystical encounter with God happens in that region of the person where he is most truly himself, unencumbered either by his own image of himself or by other people's images of him.

Although this definition is hopefully broad enough to encompass any and every case of mysticism, it fails to indicate the great diversity among mystics. In an attempt to put some order into this diversity, we can note certain polarities in mystical experience—for example, mysticism of darkness and mysticism of light, theocentric and Christocentric mysticism, Pauline mysticism and Johannine, Dionysian and Ignatian.[32] In the end, however, one is inclined to say with Evelyn Underhill that there are as many different "mysticisms" as there are different temperaments reacting to the one great Reality.[33]

If the reader expected the preceding explanation to provide a criterion for judging the existence of authentic mystical experience, he is apt to be disappointed. True, in regard to the mystic's discernment of his own experience, we have the assertion of Teresa of Avila that no one who has once experienced true mysticism can mistake any other experience for it.[34] But since mystical experience ultimately defies adequate expression even by the most perceptive and articulate subject, nothing he might say about his own experience could be taken by an outsider as intrinsic and direct proof of its authenticity. Consequently, spiritual directors and theologians over the centuries have developed an indirect and external criterion for determining the existence of true mysticism: a significant increase in humility and charity consequent upon the alleged mystical experience.[35] The logic here is not difficult to grasp: it is inconceivable that an untrammeled encounter with the living God at the very core of one's being would not result in an increase in humility and charity.

We turn next in this excursus on mysticism to the complex question of visions (also called apparitions or private revelations). Here, everything hinges on one crucial distinction: visions are not a necessary part of mystical experience, but rather "concomitant phenomena"—something that *might* occur along with mystical union itself. Like ecstacy, stigmata, and levitation, visions are possible reflections and manifestations at the "exterior" of what God is doing in man's innermost being.[36]

Theologians have traditionally divided visions into three types —corporeal, imaginative, and purely spiritual or intellectual.[37] To begin with the last, intellectual visions have to do with conceptual knowledge, but do not involve any conscious imagery.[38] What Julian of Norwich describes as "ghostly shewing" would be an instance of this, as would probably Ignatius Loyola's vision on the banks of the River Cardoner[39] and numerous visions of Teresa of Avila.

There is little more to say about intellectual visions; they have raised few problems. But it has been otherwise with imaginative and corporeal visions. The former exist only in the mind of the visionary, while the latter are seen as physical objects (real persons, places, and things) existing outside the mind. To some this would suggest that corporeal visions are real while imaginative ones are illusory. But the authenticity of a vision cannot be equated with its corporeality. John of the Cross considers imaginative visions more significant than corporeal ones, and Teresa denied ever having had corporeal visions. One can indeed ask whether corporeal visions exist at all. For, as Rahner has shown, the naive equation of visions with ordinary sense perception runs into many difficulties, not the least of which is Teresa's conviction that Christ's glorified humanity has never directly shown itself on earth since the Ascension and the apparition to St. Paul. The impression of reality and accuracy made by the vision is no proof of its objectivity, since this impression is not an immediate fact but a judgment which may be misinterpreting the perception. Moreover, in allegedly corporeal visions, angels often appear, as well as human persons from another world who already possess a resurrected body, together with other people who have not yet risen. Do some of these assume an apparent body just for the moment of the apparition? Then too, how can Jesus appear as a child? Or how explain a past event seen as taking place here and now and, as often is the case, in a manner contradicting both known historical fact and other visions of the same event? How, without postulating innumerable miracles, explain the fact that not all those present at the time and place of an apparition see it? What about the clothes seen in visions—are they too glorified? All these questions lead to the conclusion that most visions are imaginative rather than corporeal.[40]

What, then, of the authenticity of imaginative visions? In order to appreciate the difficulty of the problem, one has only to recall that the content of such visions is often in itself indistinguishable from hallucination. Since an imaginative vision is not itself mystical union with God, it cannot be considered genuine unless it is at least shown to be the result of real mystical experience. Through simple illation, then, an initial criterion for the authenticity of a vision is the increase in humility and charity used to judge the authenticity of mysticism itself.

Nevertheless, if the imaginative element is merely subsidiary to mystical union, then even a genuine vision (as determined by our initial criterion) will proceed largely according to the general psychological laws relating to sensation. And the content of the vision will inevitably be the result both of God's influence and of all the subjective dispositions of the visionary—elements of fantasy, patterns of perception, the historical situation, aesthetic taste, selective attitudes of expectation due to religious training. A prime example of this is St. Margaret Mary Alacoque (1647-1690), for most of the thought and imagery contained in her visions of the Sacred Heart can be found in the earlier published books and traditions of her order.[41]

When, in addition, we recall that the visions even of genuine mystics have been marked by all sorts of distortions and errors, we can appreciate why classic mysticism (e.g., Teresa of Avila and John of the Cross) is generally so suspicious and critical of visions. To repel or disregard even a true vision, it argues, is neither to reject nor hinder what God is directly accomplishing. What is disregarded is merely a reflex, in the sphere of the senses, of God's action in the heart of a man.[42]

Ultimately, only an external authenticating miracle could demonstrate the "inspired" character of a vision. As we are almost always lacking this, it may be helpful to formulate some general conclusions regarding the authenticity of visions. While a certain disposition to grant the divine origin of a visionary experience is quite legitimate, such an experience simply cannot compel one either to accept or reject it in every detail. This is true even when the authenticity of a vision as a whole has been established. It is possible that pure hallucination and genuine visions might occur (at different times) in the same person, for true divine visions use the same psychic mechanisms as hallucinations and occur precisely among persons who show a propensity for experiencing such phenomena. The history of mysticism certainly justifies Poulain's opinion that, even with pious and "normal" people, three "visions" out of four are well intentioned, harmless illusions.[43]

Yet in view of classical mysticism's long-standing devaluation of imaginative visions in favor of pure, imageless mystical union, it is legitimate to ask whether these visions do not have some positive theological significance. In order to answer this question, we must distinguish between purely personal visions and ecclesial or prophetic visions. Rahner defines personal visions as "those the object and content of which solely concern the personal religious life and perfection of the visionary." On the other hand, ecclesial visions are those in which we find "God inspiring a member of the Church with his imperative for the Church in a concrete historical situation."[44] What these ecclesial visions present is already known (or could be) from Scripture and theology; yet they are by no means superfluous. They are neither mere heavenly refresher courses in public revelation nor a Socratic method used by God to lead us to something which could in principle be learned without his help. "What God wishes to be done in certain given circumstances cannot be logically and unequivocally deduced from the general principles of dogma and morals even with the help of an analysis of the given situation."[45] Hence what is needed is a practical, clear imperative for action, and that is precisely what authentic ecclesial visions can provide. To appreciate the theological significance of these visions, we need only adduce the example of visionaries like Catherine of Siena and Margaret Mary Alacoque, whose lives were fundamentally shaped by their visions, and then ask what the Church of their times would have been without them.[46]

A word may be added here about a certain variety of pseudo-prophetic vision not discussed earlier. In this vision, which we might call para-psychological, the seer claims to be able to predict the future. Whether human beings are actually capable of doing this or not is certainly an interesting question; but it is ultimately less important than being able to distinguish this kind of soothsaying, which is purely "natural" or "preternatural," from a true religious and prophetic "word," which comes from God. The former shows the future as present, the latter the future as future. The former usually presents a very clear and concrete but isolated detail or event, a frame or two cut, as it were, out of a long film and thus without a context for interpreting it; the latter gives the *meaning* and religious significance of the future as a whole while leaving the details obscure, since it does not want to interfere with the conditions of man's freedom by offering him a way of avoiding his future.[47]

A final question, which has received little discussion from theologians, is whether true mysticism as we have defined it can or does exist outside of Christianity. Rather than involve ourselves in a lengthy analysis of data from world religions, let us approach the question theoretically. *Can* authentic mysticism exist outside Christianity? If true mysticism, however uncommon, is a culmination of the life of grace in a person, the question can fundamentally be reduced to the possibility of God's revelation and grace, of supernatural faith and charity, existing among non-Christians. While many theologians today want to maintain this latter possibility, the most compelling explanation of it has been advanced by Rahner in his theory of the "anonymous Christian."[48]

Although most men either have never heard the public, objective, verbal revelation of God, or having heard it have passed it by, still God wants all men to be saved. Hence, Rahner speculates, God gives himself to them along with their being, in a (truly supernatural) revelation of which they are aware only in a preverbal, nonobjective way.[49] To this revelation they answer by their lives with a "yes" of acceptance or "no" of rejection which is more fundamental than the one found in their verbal responses of belief or unbelief to public revelation.[50] Putting all this together: if mysticism is the culmination of the life of grace, and if God reveals himself and offers this life of grace not only to Christians but to all men, and if mysticism, like this universal revelation, does not depend on concepts and words, then we must conclude that mysticism can occur among non-Christians as well as among Christians.[51]

Although we have already addressed ourselves to the questions posed by late medieval mysticism and by the current revival of interest in "mysticism," a few summary statements and a final question may be helpful. True mysticism has been too much a part of the Church to be dismissed. Nor is there any reason to do so, provided one keeps to the strict understanding which locates it in an experiential union with God himself and distinguishes it from all other phenomena. In regard to visions, of course, the Church has always exercised greater caution. Nevertheless, it would be unfortunate if we were to let this attitude of distrust hide the important contributions made by ecclesial visionaries in the past or the assistance they may provide in the future. Finally, while granting that the classic, imageless mystics we have discussed may help to purify our ideas of God, we may want to ask them an embarrassing question in response to their long-standing disparagement of visionary mysticism: In view of the Incarnation, can their mysticism of pure spiritual transcendence really be called Christian?

The question is not merely academic. For such purely spiritual mysticism can be Christian only if it conceives itself as a participation in Christ's own emptying of himself through his death on the cross, and only if it acknowledges that the God whom it sets out to apprehend in himself also reveals himself as the Risen Lord who has accepted and transformed earthly existence and, consequently, is more than pure spirit. Because God became man, man himself must realize that any emptying of himself will not be accomplished by practicing pure inwardness, but by the real activity which is called humility, service, and love of his neighbor. That is, one must descend together with Christ—"lose" his soul—not directly to God, who is above all men, but in the service of one's brethren, in whom Christ also reveals himself. A failure to take all the implications of the mystery of Christ with utter seriousness easily leads the mystic into the trap of mere self-absorption and sheer imageless nihilism.[52] To this extent, there is a close parallel between the mystical tendency to undervalue the Incarnation and the more general tendency in spirituality to rank any kind of "worldly" activity entirely secondary to a life of pure contemplation. It is to this problem that we shall address ourselves in the next chapter.

Chapter VI

THE COST OF ENGAGEMENT

Some Thoughts
on Prayer and Action

AT SEVERAL POINTS in the preceding chapters we have alluded to the difficult and important problem of uniting prayer and activity in and for the world. It is probably too pessimistic to say that from the time of the Fathers of the Church until well into the Middle Ages there was no suitable spirituality for those Christians who remained in the world. At least it is clear that serious-minded Christians of the early centuries tried to live their lives in a way that resembled monastic life as closely as possible. Although they may have retained their positions in the world, they focused all earthly interests as directly as possible on God because they believed that only by doing so could true holiness be achieved. The basic concept of spirituality at this time was, as we have seen, an overwhelmingly negative one which rejected the world and attempted to discover the divine in the solitary recesses of the desert where rigorous asceticism and contemplation could be pursued without interruption.

Even though in the West monasticism underwent important modifications, this contempt-for-the-world attitude continued to predominate, practically overshadowing the existence and validity of other spiritual principles. It is difficult to underestimate the significance of this outlook for the simple reason that spirituality in the West was truly fashioned by the monks. Many bishops had previously been monks and continued to be so even after their episcopal consecration. The monks had educated the princes and, as a result, the whole of Christendom. As Yves Congar has pointed out:

> Thus medieval Christendom was brought under strong monastic influence by the historical conditions of its development and by its own inner logic, which was to bring this world's affairs under direct and strict control by the ends of eternal salvation. It was shot through with a spirituality that was deeply monastic in its inspiration, well expressed by the Cistercian principle, "He to whom God is enough lacks nothing"; it reflected the characteristics of the monastic state, the referring of this life to the other, lack of regard for earthly things for their own sake and in themselves.[1]

The mendicant orders, it is true, tried to break out of the monastic mold. But in spite of their thoroughly positive appreciation of Christian service in the world, the mendicants' own growth and internal difficulties forced them back again into a more or less monastic framework. The futile attempt of the people to impose a religious interpretation on their most ordinary and insignificant activities is another sign of this desire to reconvert the increasingly secular world into a monastery.

It would be rather obnoxious, not to say historically false, to claim that the monks were not engaged in strenuous activity, or that contemplatives are not active in their own way. The very ideals of a genuine contemplative life included the apostolate through prayer, sacrifice, and the radiation of holiness as an essential duty. At the same time, there can be little doubt that the rhythm of their cloistered lives was thrown out of balance, if not often turned topsy-turvy as the activity of the monks increased. Even for the mendicant orders the crucial problem was to show *how* man's supernatural union with God was to be achieved outside the cloister and simply by means of one's apostolic engagement with the world. The challenge, in other words, was to discover how activity which was profane by nature could sanctify souls and unite them with God.

Certainly the task of developing a theology of action was complicated by the way in which medieval theology generally viewed the "world." "In the theological and spiritual literature of this period," Alfons Auer remarks, *"world* means the God-centered totality of visible and invisible realities—the creation of God, the goodness and beauty of which are so often enthusiastically praised. In the spiritual literature, however, this doctrinal concept of the world is considerably overlapped by a one-sided emphasis on its evanescence and frailty, which have experienced an extreme intensification in the sinful disordering of the world."[2] Such a pessimistic attitude was undoubtedly aggravated by a certain decadence of the time, a gloomy evaluation of the contemporary religious situation, and severe catastrophes like famine, plague, devastation, and war. Perhaps a stronger motive for adopting a contempt-for-the-world attitude was the need for peace and security. The logic involved was deceptively simple: possessions, pomp, and inordinate desire cause man numberless troubles; contempt for them would free him from many worldly burdens and open to him a safer path to salvation. But in the end, the world-denying spirituality of the Middle Ages was the natural consequence of medieval society—a society at once completely Christian in idea and institution, yet often only nominally so in practice—and the consequence of a fundamentally static culture in which the world made few demands on the individual's spiritual resources. In such a context "sincere Christianity" could only be seen as a matter of going beyond the natural and ordinary, setting the spirit over against the secular. The Middle Ages thus tended to a transcendent type of religion, despite a human, even anthropomorphic, idea of God.

Of course, the medieval period was not entirely bleak and pessimistic. The theological truths of man's origin from God, his destiny to reflect God's image and to rule in the world, his calling to communion with Christ and his final fulfillment in the glory of heaven were the common property of the entire Middle

Ages. Some Christian mystics, as we have seen, taught man to look for the traces of God in the world in order to find its Creator. And medieval symbolism is unthinkable without a candid respect for creatures, even though it too quickly made a person shy away from recognizing their intrinsic value. The medieval Christian had also learned to understand the world as a gift and a task from God. He actively perceived his profession as a calling, and this emerging sense of profession was being cultivated in guilds and crafts long before the theologians pondered over their teaching on vocation.[3]

Nevertheless, if one attempts to comprehend the thrust of the total religious consciousness and experience of the time, the goodness of creatures was surely overshadowed by the reality of man's fallen nature. The world presented a danger which became acute in the disaster of sin. Sinfulness appeared to be the ruling characteristic of the contemporary era in salvation history. Man had to be protected from the fascination of the world; and the best way to do this was to focus on the darker side of the world, to screen one's eyes from the world's allurement by fixing them squarely on God. In a profound sense, then, one of the great achievements of the Middle Ages became its very limitation. No other age has been able to achieve such blending of the earthly and heavenly kingdoms into a single universal order with the temporal realms directly ordered to the spiritual reality of the Church and even subjugated to spiritual ecclesiastical regulation. But in the long run, this attempt of medieval Christianity to subjugate and sacralize the temporal order amounted to a practical denial of the already existing radical unity between God and the world effected in creation and redemption, and herein lay its failure.

God, after all, has not created two realities which need subsequently to be harmonized. Rather he has constituted the whole of reality distinct from himself, to which he communicates himself; as a result there exists between God and his world a fundamental unity which precedes any differences which might arise from it—such as the difference between the sacred and secular orders. If we want, then, to formulate the relation between the supernatural order (the saving action of God) and the natural order (the created world), we can just as correctly speak, as Karl Rahner has done, of the supernatural order of redemption *within* the created order or of the created order *within* the supernatural order of redemption.[4] A failure to recognize this unity of the secular and the sacred—even if it be unconscious—inevitably affects one's understanding of the spiritual life. On the one hand, such a separation made it possible for Thomas Aquinas and subsequent theologians to formulate a "worldly spirituality" alongside the monastic spirituality which focused exclusively on God —a spiritual approach designed for men who continued to have obligations toward the world and who were irrevocably inserted into the world. On the other hand, the acceptance of a dichotomy between God and the world necessarily resulted in a situation in which temporal matters were not adequately considered either to possess inherent value in themselves or to be fashioned according to their own laws. There still remained, in other words, a certain *ambiguity* toward the world, and this issued in a pervasive ambivalence toward activity in the world and the relationship between such action and the life of prayer and individual union with God which had been the hallmark of monastic spirituality.

In order to make this point as clear as possible, it will be helpful to focus on two pivotal figures in medieval spirituality: Thomas Hemerlien of Kempen, whose inspirational work, the *Imitation of Christ,* "remains to all time a lasting record of human needs, human consolations, the voice of a brother who, ages ago, felt and suffered and renounced,"[5] and the learned Dominican Thomas of Aquin whose theological treatises constitute a masterful harmonization of traditional Christian values with the natural wisdom of the Greek, Arabic, and Latin philosophers. Just as the *Imitation* has long influenced spirituality, traditional discussions of the spiritual life and the relation between prayer and action have been strongly influenced by Aquinas' treatment of these subjects.

We have referred, in an earlier chapter, to the rise of the Canons Regular and their desire to unite a quasi-monastic religious life with a life of active ministry in the world. Their importance cannot be underestimated either for the contribution they made to Christian life at large or for establishing a climate which facilitated the growth of the mendicant orders. One of the groups to emerge from the ranks of the Canons was the congregation of Windesheim, established in 1386 under the influence of the vigorous and popular preacher, Gerard Groote, the founder of the "Brethren of the Common Life." Into one of the houses of this congregation, Mount St. Agnes, there entered in 1400 the monk Thomas a Kempis, who had been educated in the schools of the Brethren at Deventer. There Thomas lived for seventy-one years and, among his other labors, compiled his *Imitation of Christ*. Historically, Thomas' work is the last and, in some respects, one of the best defenses of the ideals of the monastic world. For us it is important to note his abandonment of the merely negative side of renunciation and yet his unequivocal expression of contempt for the world.

Even a cursory reading of the *Imitation* would provide apt illustrations of the obvious and repeated occurrence of the theme of renunciation. "A soul that loves God despises all things that are less than God." "A true lover of Christ, and a diligent pursuer of virtue, does not search after comforts." "Let me not be drawn away with various desires of anything whatsoever, whether worth the having or otherwise."[6] Not only had Thomas inherited and assimilated the usual monastic view of self-denial, but he knew that there could be no spiritual life where some degree of negative asceticism was not found. Although there are times when this negative approach to renunciation is too heavily weighted, the real core of a Kempis' message is much more positive: no abandonment, self-mortification, self-crucifixion, without a holy passion of love, can bring us to our goal. "If you are to find free access to Christ, then you must learn how to despise everything else." Or again, "Never be idle or vacant. Be always reading or writing or praying or meditating, or employed in some useful work for the common good."[7] Clearly, for Thomas, this "common good" could no longer be restricted to the monastic community.

But perhaps the strongest impression that one takes away from reading the *Imitation* is its individualistic attitude of isolation from the world. One can go through the book from beginning to end and not detect even a suspicion that there are millions of souls to be converted and saved. When one recalls that the author was a Brother of the Common Life, a congregation dedicated to the same type of tireless preaching, teaching, and social labor as were the mendicant orders, the irony of omitting the social dimension of spirituality cannot be overlooked. What was the active apostle to make of Thomas' advice: "Keep your friendship for God and his holy angels, shunning the acquaintance of men. . . . Fly the tumult of men as much as you can. . . . We seldom return to silence without prejudice to our conscience. . . . 'I never yet went out among men,' said the philosopher, 'without feeling less of a man when I came home. . . .' It is better to hide yourself away with an eye to your soul's welfare, than to neglect one's self to work even miracles."[8] How far this is from Paul's self-imposed admonition: "Not that I boast of preaching the gospel, since it is a duty which has been laid on me; I should be punished if I did not preach it" (I Cor. 9:16)!

The *Imitation* was far more than a single book. It represented an entire movement. And whatever our judgment is of it today, no one can dispute its significance in spiritual literature. The book itself represents a collection of maxims, prayers, uplifting exhortations and colloquies drawn from different writers of the period and from the depths of a Kempis' own soul. This collection first consisted of one small work, to which three others were subsequently added. Thus combined, they formed the *Imitation* as we know it.[9] For this reason it formed something of a compendium of spirituality for at least a large segment of people in the later Middle Ages.

One of the most positive features of the spiritual approach of the *Imitation* is certainly its simplicity. It insists on inward renunciation, humility, patience, mutual support; these virtues, combined with due observance of the monastic rule, bring peace to the heart, make the true religious a perfect follower of Christ, and raise the soul to the dignity of the mystical spouse of the Word. Part of the general popularity of the work can also be attributed to its anti-intellectual appeal, which came at a time when many were reacting strongly against the highly speculative theological writing of a decadent scholasticism. Toward the end of the fourteenth century, as we have seen, there developed a very pronounced return to affective spirituality—tentative and unsystematic, aiming solely at providing simple devotional practices rather than inquiry and intricate reasoning into the mysteries of God and the spiritual life. As the *Imitation* warned: "If men would only use as much diligence in rooting out vices and planting virtues as they do in proposing questions, we should hear less about sin and scandals, less about lax behavior in religious houses." Or again, "What does it avail you to discourse profoundly of the Trinity if you are void of humility and, consequently, displeasing to the Trinity. After all, learned talk does not save a man or make a saint out of him; only a life well lived makes him dear to God. For myself, I would sooner know what contrition feels like, than have to define it."[10] Theories, then, should be put aside in order to strive to live with fervor. It is only in this way that we bring about conversion in ourselves and help others to reform.

Our concern in citing these passages from the *Imitation* is mainly to illustrate the climate which cherished it, rather than to criticize its approach. In terms of its principal themes, the author clearly intended to foster an intimate union with Christ, especially through the Eucharist; he praised detachment from all earthly realities and a steadfast love of the cross; he saw public opinion, passing comforts, and human suffering entirely from the vantage point of eternity; and he attempted to point out the obstacles confronting man's spiritual growth. In developing these notions, a Kempis proposed no theory of the spiritual life and certainly no theology of activity in the world. To this extent, the *Imitation* aptly serves to demonstrate the failure of the spiritual theology of the period to develop an understanding of the world in a way which does more than allow for engagement as a part-time endeavor or as a distraction; in so doing, it represents the swan song of a system whose effective work in the world was rapidly waning and whose days were numbered.

The second figure to concern us is Thomas Aquinas. Here we

must move the clock back almost two centuries to the time of the great religious syntheses of Catholic doctrine and before the onset of the decadence and caviling which so unnerved Thomas a Kempis. The topic of spirituality was included within these synthetic works, since it did not as yet constitute a distinct branch of theological reflection. In the *Summa Theologiae* of Aquinas, the subject is found a little everywhere, but principally at the end of the treatise dealing with the pursuit of the theological and cardinal virtues. Is it not, Thomas argues, by the practice of virtue that we attain to perfection and, if it please God, reach contemplation and rapture? For our own purposes it will be sufficient to concentrate on Thomas' discussion of the state of perfection and the contemplative life to discover his approach to spirituality and the way in which he foreshadows the climate of opinion we have been considering. For although Thomas differed in time and temperament from a Kempis, he gives evidence of a similar ambivalence toward the place of activity in the world and its relation to the spiritual life, even if his tone is more moderate and his approach more flexible.

Like other thirteenth-century theologians, Thomas connects spirituality with the virtue of charity—that charity whose excellence and efficacy the *Imitation* extols in such poetic terms. "Every being," he says, "is perfect when it attains its final goal. But charity unites us to God, the goal of all human life, a truth expressed by St. John's words on him who abides in God and God in him. Hence charity constitutes the life of Christian perfection."[11] Thomas then distinguishes three forms of Christian life: the contemplative life, the active life, and the apostolic life. Contemplation studies divine truth, action serves our neighbor, preaching and teaching give to our neighbor the fruits of our own contemplation.[12] It is important to probe this threefold distinction more deeply if we are to grasp Thomas' understanding of the relation between prayer and action and its implications for spirituality.

Thomas begins by asserting that human life, looked upon from the spiritual point of view, may be fittingly and adequately divided into the active life and the contemplative life.[13] Gregory the Great, he notes, perceived symbols of these two lives in the wives of Jacob: Leah, who was fruitful, represents the active life; and Rachel, the contemplative. The real proof offered for this assertion, however, is the duality of man's intellectual activity: he strives to understand truth by use of his contemplative intellect; he employs himself in external activity by reason of his practical intellect. What, then, does Thomas mean by active life and contemplative life?

Life in its totality is the active life if it is ordered principally (although not exclusively) to external activity.[14] The practice of moral virtue belongs here, especially prudence which has as its object the reasoned ordering of one's moral life. According to this twofold notion of action, therefore, Thomas harmonizes both the ancient Greek and the patristic understanding of activity; action is not only external activity in general, but moral activity as well. For Thomas, every free act of a man in a given situation has some moral significance.

Contemplative life, on the other hand, is principally ordered to the understanding of truth, especially to the understanding of divine truth. But contemplation is also directed to the consideration of the works of God through which we must ascend to the contemplation of God himself and includes such practices as reading, prayer, meditation, and reflective study. The pursuit of the moral virtues, obviously, does not belong to the essence of the contemplative life because the end of contemplation is the consideration of truth. These virtues do, however, retain a strong link to the pursuit of contemplation because they eminently dispose the soul for contemplation of God. "For the act of contemplation, wherein the contemplative life essentially consists, is hindered both by the impetuosity of the passions which withdraw the soul's attention from intellectual to sensible things, and by outward disturbances."[15]

The basic difference, therefore, between contemplation and action lies in the *interior* life of an individual; and this distinction hinges, in turn, on the double function of his intellectual faculty. The kind of active life which most concerned Thomas was the struggle to overcome defects and to regulate one's moral life so as to be disposed for contemplation. A person's exterior life—the work he engages in, the observable manner of life he leads—is activity also; but these aspects of the active life spring from the interior life and are conditioned in their effectiveness by the individual's moral virtue and his practice of contemplation.

If at first glance these definitions seem quite clear and acceptable, we may become slightly uneasy when we read further in Thomas' discussion: "Nothing prevents certain things being considered more excellent in themselves, whereas they are surpassed, in some respect, by other things. Accordingly, we must say that the contemplative life is *simply* more excellent than the active."[16] How is this to be understood? "To the contemplative life," comments Thomas, "chiefly belongs the contemplation of divine truth, since such contemplation is the whole end of human life. This is why St. Augustine says (*De Trinitate* I, 8) that 'contemplation of God is promised us as the end of all our actions and the eternal perfecting of all our joys.' It will only be perfect in the future life when we shall see God face to face, which will render us perfectly happy."[17] Does Thomas' definition, then, consider contemplation a purely intellectual process as the Greek philosophers did? Aristotle proposed eight reasons for the superiority of contemplation. Contemplation pertains to what is best in man—his intellect; it is more continuous, more delightful, makes man more self-sufficient, is loved more for its own sake, consists in leisure and rest, involves man in divine things, and pertains to what is most proper to man—his intellectual activity. Thomas accepts these arguments, corroborates them theologically with examples from Scripture, then goes on to add one more of his own: contemplation will continue even in eternity.[18]

The problem here is twofold. In the first place, despite the buttress of Scripture, this is Greek, not Christian, thought; as such it can justify the mystical contemplation of the Mohammedan (*mushāhada*) just as well as the prayer of the Christian. Thomas' fundamental proof, from which all the others more or less derive, is that the intellect is the most noble and essentially characteristic faculty of man. But since the intellect is concerned with spiritual knowledge, intellectual contemplation is the act and perfection of man according to his highest tendency—and the highest possible human activity. Secondly, no attention is given to the fact that intellectual knowledge as such is ethically unrelated to perfection. If moral value is constituted by a free, personal act of the individual, then the moral worth of any endeavor derives more from man's will than from his intellect. Christian perfection does not mean perfection of the understanding but perfection of love. Greater knowledge can surely lead to a deeper, more mature personal orientation to moral values, and so would contribute to an increase of love. But knowledge is only the preparation for perfection. It does not lead to it of its own intrinsic necessity. It is quite possible, after all, for a person to devote himself to a study of God's own revelation without making a personal commitment and self-surrender to it and, consequently, without any supernatural profit. If, then, there is any validity to Thomas' proposition that, simply considered, the contemplative life is superior to the active, it must be because the contemplative life is understood not in the intellectual sense alone, but in the *religious* sense, as concerned with personal acts of faith and love.

Obviously, this is what Thomas intended. He knew, for example, that a religious order is different from a scholarly society organized for the purposes of philosophical and theological study, that it is organized essentially with religious values in view. He also knew that, for a Christian, perfection primarily consists in love. Love, therefore, was the beginning and end of the contemplative life; it both incites to the knowledge and contemplation of God and is, in turn, the goal and fruit of contemplation. "Contemplation," he declares, "befits man according to his nature as a rational animal—the fact that all men naturally desire to know, so that they delight in the knowledge of truth"; but contemplation is also delightful, "because of its object, insofar as one contemplates that which he loves. . . . Since, then, the contemplative life consists chiefly in the contemplation of God, of which love is the motive, it follows that there is a delight in the contemplative life, not only by reason of the contemplation itself, but also by reason of God's own love."[19]

In fact, two essentially diverse strains of thought overlap one another in Thomas' evaluation of contemplation: its superiority over any other human activity because of its intellectual aspect, and its value proportioned to the degree of love. But since love, according to the first line of thought, is extrinsic to the essence of intellectual contemplation, then it follows that intellectual contemplation, as such, remains without supernatural value for perfection. It follows from the second argument that this contemplation, which should become the all-informing principle of a life striving for holiness, is something entirely different from purely intellectual activity. It acquires its superiority not because it is contemplation, but because it most completely expresses one's love of God above everything else. In the end, then, Thomas' contemplation is *religious* contemplation, which considers love not only as its source and goal but as intrinsically constituting it through personal acts of surrender to God in faith and love. But inasmuch as this distinction between intellectual and religious contemplation is not perfectly clear in Thomas, his discussion of it remains indefinite and has led to many conflicting interpretations of his thought—the all-too-common fate of most synthesizers, no matter how eminent or learned.

If Thomas ultimately justifies the superiority of contemplation sometimes from its intellectual and sometimes from its religious worth, where, we might ask, does the active life of involvement in the world derive its value? Here we must move beyond Thomas' treatment of contemplation and the state of perfection to his discussion of the various kinds of religious life. Contemplation and action differ "according to the different occupations of men intent on different goals: the one (contemplation) is occupied in the consideration of truth, the other (action) is directed toward external work."[20] Action, moreover, embraces two distinct, but related, aspects: the pursuit of moral virtue which directly disposes one for contemplation, and activity in and for the world. Leaving aside, for our purposes, a detailed consideration of the practice of moral virtue, the value of worldly activity clearly arises from the dictates of charity. The contemplative life "seeks to devote itself to God alone and belongs directly to the love of God; the active life, which ministers to our neighbor's needs, belongs directly to the love of one's neighbor."[21] Apart from this systematic ordering of contemplation to the love of God and action to the love of one's neighbor, which tends to oversimplify the interrelations of the two and thus bring everything into a false light, we find Thomas further distinguishing two different types of activity. The first, exemplified by preaching and teaching, proceeds from the fulness of contemplation, whereas the second consists of entirely outward occupations like alms-giving, receiving guests, caring for the poor and the sick. Although contemplation is generally superior to activity, the works of contemplation are thus superior not only to merely outward activity (except in cases of extreme necessity), but even to simple contemplation itself. The reason for this hierarchy is simple: "For even as it is better to enlighten than merely to shine, so is it better to give others the fruits of one's contemplation than merely to contemplate. . . . Accordingly, the highest place in religious orders is held by those which are directed to teaching and preaching. . . . The second place belongs to those which are directed to contemplation, and the third to those which are occupied with external actions."[22]

It is especially interesting, at this point, to notice Thomas' notion of contemplative prayer and its function in the active life, as well as the way he applies it to prove the superiority of the "mixed life" as the best type of religious life. Aside from any unconscious interests he might have had in justifying the style of his own Dominican order, he certainly places a higher premium on the charity value of contemplation than on its intellectual orientation, thus demonstrating his notable Christian concern with contemplation as a religious act. Just as important, however, is the fact that he appraises activity in the world primarily from its contemplative element, not from the intrinsic value of apostolic work itself. The fact, then, that Thomas preferred a mixture of contemplation and action to a purely contemplative life, and all the more to a completely active one, does not alter his acceptance of the basic superiority of contemplation over action. For him, an active life which is derived from the fulness of contemplation belongs in the realm of the contemplative life, but rises above pure contemplation insofar as others are given to share in the overflow of one's own contemplative resources. Hence, the perfect active life, as exemplified in the apostles and their successors, presupposes a plenitude of contemplation, which itself advances by the gifts of knowledge, understanding, and wisdom, all of which make faith more penetrating and attractive.

If we were to summarize our textual sketch of Thomas' consideration of prayer and action, the first point of importance would be his distinction between the interior life of an individual and his exterior or observable manner of living among his fellow men. In the ancient Christian writers until and including Thomas, the two terms, contemplation and action, seldom or never refer primarily to the observable manner of living. They designate the intellectual and volitional life of an individual.[23]

Secondly, in Thomas' understanding as well as in the usage of other ascetical writers of the time, the active life and the contemplative life designate successive but interacting stages of growth in the interior life of a Christian seeking spiritual growth, whether he be a religious or a layman. The active life is the earlier stage where, seriously beginning his pursuit of living spiritually, he struggles against sin and imperfections in himself and both learns and practices the moral virtues and the exterior acts which spring from them. Activity thus comprises the two stages of spiritual growth which were later named "the purgative way of the beginners" and "the illuminative way of the advancing." The contemplative life, on the other hand, is a higher stage where the Christian practices chiefly the theological virtues, especially charity, and under its inspiration works of love that witness to it. Among these manifestations of charity one often finds a growing desire to withdraw into solitude in order to achieve undistracted contemplation of God.

Thirdly, the terms active life and contemplative life come not from Scripture but from Greek philosophy. Jesus' own ideal of the Christian life was put quite simply: "You must love the Lord your God with all your heart . . . and your neighbor as yourself" (Luke 10:27; Matt. 5:48). As Christian writers attempted to communicate this doctrine they employed terms, concepts, and a general outlook drawn from Greek philosophy. The Alexandrians, prone as they were to use allegorical interpretations of Scripture, found in Martha and Mary apt symbols of the active and contemplative lives discussed in the Greek philosophical tradition. Thomas and the medieval theologians accepted this tradition with little or no qualification and used it as a basis for evaluating various types of strictly religious life. Yet it is far from certain that, by his words to Martha, Christ intended to instruct us about the Greek distinction between the active life and contemplative life, or about their comparative importance.[24]

On the positive side, one cannot ignore the fact that Thomas did consider the world and activity in the world as possessing some value of its own. Although the theology of the twelfth and thirteenth centuries stressed the dependent and relative nature of the created world, Thomas placed considerable importance on the virtue of magnanimity, and from this standpoint, which perhaps seems today rather restricted, he approached the question of the value of life in the world. Magnanimity, in Thomas' precise use of the term, consists in man's ability to act and to develop himself through participation in the affairs of life. Within this context, as R. A. Gauthier has pointed out, the ground was prepared for a genuine spirituality of commitment to the world.[25] Without denying the primacy of the supernatural order or the relative autonomy of worldly affairs, Thomas considered that this virtue of magnanimity would issue in a sensitivity for the genuine human greatness which is to be found in all earthly realities. In this way Thomas partially succeeded in replacing an unbalanced spirituality, which overemphasized the divine, with one truly human, which dignified the very worldliness of the world. Magnanimity would shape the type of man society demands; it would inspire people with a strong enthusiasm for human tasks, with a sense of initiative, energy, and especially confidence in man's power and techniques, which alone are capable of assuring the accomplishment of human tasks.²⁶ For Thomas, then, God established everything in its substantial form and still maintains it in existence. But once created, the world stands on its own foundations. To have grasped both these ideas was, indeed, an outstanding accomplishment, especially when one remembers that medieval Christianity was dominated by other-world and hierarchical ideas, and that the prevailing contempt-for-the-world attitude prevented most Christian thinkers from seriously considering the intrinsic worth of anything secular. For the medieval Christian, consequently, the world was, as far as possible, completely subordinated to the Church.

From what has been said, it is clear that to describe Thomas' contribution to the prayer-and-action discussion as simply monastic would be an oversimplification. Although unaware of its implications, he did make an honest attempt to work out elements of a spirituality which gave evidence of real appreciation of the world. On the whole, however, his attempt to integrate these actions into his over-all synthesis was not successful, especially in his treatment of the nature of contemplation and its relation to action. In the end, despite definite advances beyond the traditions he attempted to harmonize, he demonstrated the same kind of ambivalence toward earthly activity that reached more extreme expression in the *Imitation*. It is one of the tragedies in the history of spirituality that, instead of following the direction forged by Thomas in his treatment of magnanimity, spiritual writers focused more on his theory of contemplation and thus reverted to an outmoded Augustinian outlook in which the dynamism of the world and commitment to its tasks were of only secondary value because of a false and exaggerated conception of the exclusive might and wisdom of God. Moreover, when we probe into the spirituality of the Christian laity during this period, we discover that the monastic-ascetical ideal of perfection still remained dominant.²⁷

From our outline of some of the historical factors involved in the problem of prayer and action especially during the Middle Ages, as well as from the previous discussion of the nature of mysticism and the evolution of the monastic ideals in the East and West, we have posed questions that are as disturbing as they are complex. But the questions and the climate in which they arose must be grasped if we are to become sensitive to the challenges of spirituality in a way that does not lose sight of the problems as they originally emerged. Part of the difficulty in finding creative solutions to contemporary issues lies in our facility for overlooking their historical dimension. As the monk left his cloister, as the friars became more deeply engaged in activity in and for the world, the former structures erected to foster and protect those desiring a more intensive spiritual life no longer justified the kinds of things religious people did. At the same time, men keenly felt the need of a spirituality which was not modeled, for the most part, on the religious orders.

It is virtually axiomatic to say that theological reflection follows on the experiences of men. The problem of the relation between prayer and action is, at root, a theological problem which must be faced on theological grounds. By the end of the Middle Ages, the theological problem was not much different for the mendicant orders than for the laity. A spirituality which was ambiguous and, to a degree, even hostile toward the world, a spirituality which was lethargic and incompetent in secular matters—even though many religious and laymen still made significant contributions to the Christian life and to the world—needed a change of direction. The Christian found himself more and more in the world. He was not only surrounded by it, but felt it deeply within himself. He realized that he had been placed there by God to accomplish definite tasks, that he must answer to God, and yet that he was threatened by evil. How, then, could he realize his Christian existence in this situation? To this question he had to have an answer. And the answer would be found in new insights into the nature of spirituality, into a theology of earthly realities, and into a deeper appreciation of the value of action in the world.

Chapter VII

FINDING GOD
IN ALL THINGS

IT HAS LONG BEEN CUSTOMARY for historians to designate the year 1500 as the beginning of the modern world. Arbitrary as any such designation must be, one can find convincing evidence for selecting this date as the beginning of a new age in the history of the West. By the turn of the sixteenth century, learning and the arts, geography and astronomy, social structure, economics, and politics, as well as religion and the Church itself, had assumed or were about to assume radically new forms. The scholar tired of arid speculation about God and his angels turned to the study of man, to the great sources of humanism recently recovered from the ancient world of Greece and Rome. While Renaissance art exalted European man's image of himself, explorers like da Gama and Columbus and astronomers like Copernicus were immensely expanding his picture of the world and the universe in which he lived. Such expansion was of considerable moment in the face of Europe's rapid growth in population since the Black Death. Society had become more complex and more organized; rulers consolidated their power, joining cities and duchies into nations; money and banking played a larger part in shaping the structure of the new states. The Church, with now only a shadow of its medieval political prowess, had for years been a pawn in the hands of French kings; and currently the popes were more interested in the political advancement of their families and in the renaissance of art than in the rebirth of faith and morals in themselves or in the Church. In short, by the year 1500, God and his Church had become much smaller and man and his universe much larger.

Into this new world, in the castle of Loyola in the Basque country of northeastern Spain, probably in the year 1491, was born a new man of God. His parents had him baptized Inigo, but in later life he used the name Ignatius, probably after the great teacher and bishop of Antioch who gloried in martyrdom for the name of Jesus. Although as the youngest son he was destined for a clerical career and hence was tonsured at an early age, young Inigo was not noted for his piety. He spent his adolescent years at court and dreamed of winning honor in the eyes of noble young ladies through military exploits. He was "much addicted to gambling and dissolute in his dealing with women, contentious and keen about using his sword."[1] His impetuosity once led him into some delinquency which the prosecuting magistrate judged to be grave. Nevertheless, he did prove himself a good and loyal soldier of King Charles V. On May 20, 1522, while vainly defending the castle of Pamplona against an invading French army, he was struck by a cannon shot that wounded one leg and shattered the other.

During a long convalescence at Loyola he asked for books of chivalry to pass the time, but the only books available were Ludolph of Saxony's *Life of Christ* and a collection of saints' lives. From these, Ignatius learned a new kind of chivalry and heroism, and he discovered that different thoughts had different effects on him: while his worldly meditations charmed him at the time he yielded to them, afterwards they left him dry and ill at ease; but when he fancied himself rivaling the saints in serving Christ, these thoughts consoled him not only while he dwelt on them, but even afterwards left him happy and content. As he continued to recuperate, Ignatius also spent long hours looking at the heavens and stars, and from these reveries he drew great courage to serve Christ. As he understood it, this service consisted in a jour-

ney to Jerusalem barefoot, followed by a life of continual penance. He also thought of living in a distant Carthusian monastery where he would be unknown, even though he feared that
this kind of life would restrict his desire for great penance. While
his penchant for pilgrimage and penance was to undergo modification as he matured, even at the very beginning of Ignatius'
interior life important traits appeared which would remain characteristic of his spirituality: the dominant idea of outstanding
service to Christ, emphasis on imaginative contemplation, self-
analysis, and the attentive control of what went on within him.

In March of 1522 Ignatius left Loyola. After vowing perpetual
chastity, he spent an entire night in vigil before Our Lady's
statue in the Abbey Church of Montserrat. For a short time he
received spiritual direction from a Benedictine monk there; but
soon he retired to the nearby town of Manresa, where he cared for
the sick, participated with great devotion in the daily liturgy,
and spent long hours in penance and prayer in a deserted cave
outside the little city. The fact that Ignatius remained at Manresa nearly a year indicates that this was a period of capital
importance in his spiritual life; here the converted soldier, still
very plain and coarse even in his desires to serve God, was transformed into a truly interior man and a master already expert in
training and directing souls.

While the beginnings of Ignatius' days at Manresa were relatively calm in their austerity, there soon followed a period of
stormy alternations of desolation and consolation, a tempest of
intensive scruples which swept him on to the temptation of sui-
cide, and finally a series of signal graces through which he
emerged a "new man." These graces concerned certain spiritual
illuminations he received regarding the nature of the Trinity,
"the manner in which God had created the world," the "humanity of Christ," and "how Jesus Christ our Lord is present" in the
Eucharist; they culminated in the great "intellectual vision" on
the bank of the River Cardoner in which, although no images
were involved, he saw and understood many things, spiritual as
well as those concerning faith and learning. This took place with
so great an illumination that these things appeared to be some-

thing altogether new. He could not point out the particulars of
what he then understood, although they were many, except that
he received a great illumination in his understanding. This was
so great, that in the whole course of his life right up to his sixty-
second year when he wrote of this experience, "if he were to
gather all the helps he had received from God, and everything he
knew, and add them together," none of this "would equal what
he received at that one time."[2]

While the exact nature of the favors related in the passages
which Ignatius dictated toward the end of his life in his cautious
and halting style is not stated explicitly, one thing strikes us at
once. Unlike so many other mystics, Ignatius came away from
these experiences not merely an interior man, but an apostle.
Service of God after the example of Christ was not a consequence
of his mystical life, but its very object. His view was extended
beyond a self-centered consideration of sin, practices of extreme
penances, and dreams of entering a Carthusian monastery or of
going on barefoot pilgrimages. His imagination and heart had
been captured by the world around him viewed in a perspective
of apostolic service; the result was an absolute conviction that the
"Eternal Lord of all things" was calling Ignatius to join him in
restoring the whole created universe to his Heavenly Father.[3] It
was precisely this orientation which he attempted to incorporate
into the first draft of his *Spiritual Exercises,* and in the light of
such experiences he continued to revise the *Exercises* during
the next twenty years of his life.

The next phase of Ignatius' spiritual development consisted of
his pilgrimage to Jerusalem. The journey had the effect of expanding still more his tender devotion to the humanity of Christ
and to the mysteries of Jesus' earthly life. Because of the hostility
of the Turks and the unsettled political situation Ignatius stayed
in the Holy Land only a few weeks. Sailing back to Europe with
a heavy heart, he reflected on what he should do now that it was
clear God did not wish him to remain in Palestine. Finally decid-
ing to study for a time in order to be able to help souls, he
embarked (at the age of thirty-four) on a long academic course,
first at Barcelona, Alcala, Salamanca, and then at Paris (1528-

1535). Unfortunately, we have no exact information about the nature of Ignatius' interior life during these seven years, though we do know that several times he was imprisoned and questioned by the authorities of the Inquisition, who were suspicious of his teaching and spiritual direction. With complete confidence in the source of his knowledge, he remained unperturbed in the midst of these trials and each time was exonerated of the charges against him.

In August of 1534, after obtaining his master of arts degree, Ignatius and six companions, among them Francis Xavier and James Lainez, vowed to live in poverty and chastity and go to the Holy Land; if this pilgrimage became impossible, the group would offer their services to the pope. Finding their journey to Palestine blocked by the war between Venice and the Turks, the little band headed for Rome. Just outside the city, in a small chapel at La Storta, Ignatius was accorded a second great vision. He saw God the Father and Jesus carrying his cross, and heard himself given by the Father to Jesus as co-worker.[4] From this vision came the conviction that the companions should form a permanent body to be called by the name of Jesus. Three years later the Society of Jesus was officially approved by Pope Paul III (1540) and in the following year Ignatius was (unwillingly) elected superior general. Thus while his companions travelled all over Europe and to the farthest corners of the world, he spent the last fifteen years of his life directing the vast missionary enterprise with thousands of letters and writing the *Constitutions* of the order. While these *Constitutions* were written in a form different from that of the *Spiritual Exercises,* they were filled with the same spirit and embody the same revolutionary vision.

Although contemporary scholarship has laid to rest some of the more obvious misconceptions of Ignatius' character—the "soldier saint" deploying his battalions to conquer the Protestant leviathan, the harsh taskmaster wielding his power over his subjects, the champion of the "iron will" approach to spirituality—we must carry on a further process of "demythologizing" if we would appreciate the unique contribution of the man, both what is true innovation in his teaching and what he borrowed from others.[5]

It is often assumed that Ignatius' genius lay in the invention or popularization of methodical mental prayer or "meditation." It is true that methodical prayer—understood as mental prayer undertaken for a specified length of time each day and focusing on material arranged beforehand into carefully organized points—did not exist before the fifteenth century.[6] Nevertheless, by Ignatius' time it was widely used in the Low Countries and especially in Spain as an instrument of reform; the supposition underlying the practice was that religious communities of the "mixed life" needed method and discipline in their prayer in order to combat the distractions of the world. Ignatius merely adopted this already existing prayer technique for his *Spiritual Exercises;* but, as we shall see, he never intended this detailed regime to be used as a paradigm for one's daily life.[7]

Similarly, it is assumed that Ignatius invented the idea of "spiritual exercises," a highly organized program of set subjects for meditation, arranged in careful psychological progression and designed to lead to the reform of one's life. Actually, such a program of spiritual exercises had been developed by Garcia Ximenes de Cisneros, Abbot of Montserrat, before Ignatius was born; it is entirely likely that Ignatius made such a course of exercises under one of Cisneros' disciples when he first came to Montserrat.[8] If we look at Ignatius' own spiritual exercises, we find that it is not their overall structure, so much as their content, which is peculiarly his own.

This content, which God the "schoolmaster" taught Inigo the "rough and uncultivated little boy" through the mystical illuminations of Manresa, has been called the "Ignatian Vision of the Universe and of Man."[9] This vision is marked by a sense of the greatness of the triune God as seen in his activity in history. The Ignatian God is a God who acts, who has accomplished and continues to accomplish the great deeds of creation and redemption.[10] The central event of God's intervention in human history is the coming of Christ to inaugurate God's kingdom. Thus the central place in the Ignatian universe is occupied by Christ, and it is important to note that this is the risen, living Christ, who continues to accomplish his Father's mission in the Church to this day.[11] Opposed to the history which God fashions in Christ and his Church, there is also the progressive growth of evil in the world. For Ignatius sees the world as the stage of a dramatic conflict in which the apostle by the power of Christ liberates men from spiritual captivity.[12]

To this vision of the universe with its sacred history, Christocentric history, and history in conflict, there corresponds a certain conception of man. The Ignatian man is a person seized by the grandeur of the divine works, who is therefore incapable of attaching ultimate importance to anything else.[13] "I have ascertained," wrote Ignatius' secretary Polanco, "that he [Ignatius] desires above all men capable of doing something great for the love of God."[14] The Ignatian man is thus a magnanimous worker with God. But his magnanimity is directed and channeled through obedience. Since God is present and acts in this world through his Church, cooperation with the Church and obedience to it is man's way to union with the mysterious and holy divine will. Finally, because the Ignatian man must abandon his own will and yet lead a life of activity in the world, he is a man who seeks God in all things. Casting off the last traces of Neo-Platonism and surmounting the prayer-action dichotomy of previous Christian spirituality, Ignatius affirms that union with God is essentially a union of love where correspondence to the divine will is more important than psychological techniques; it is therefore a union which can be achieved no matter what the circumstances.

The revolution in spiritual thinking and practice initiated by Ignatius of Loyola consisted, then, in a shift of emphasis in the idea of God—where he is, how he acts in the world, and how he might be found. It should not be surprising that these notions would lead to a new approach to spirituality and a different understanding of the relation between prayer and action. To Ignatius, the spiritual life was not, first of all, a problem of prayer or activity, but of a fidelity to God which demanded fidelity to divine tasks. If previous writers conceived of the spiritual life as a union with God principally through interior prayer, Ignatius, so impressed with God's continuous saving action in the world, was convinced that a person could achieve union with

God in action. He worked on the principle that to unite one's will and action with God's own saving will was to find God; to cooperate with this will even in total activity was to be *totally* united with God. In Ignatian spirituality, then, contemplative prayer is subordinated and ordered to the active and apostolic life. Perfection is to be realized in action guided and impregnated with love. The object of the spiritual life is simply union with God; and this union can be achieved both in prayer—in the traditional sense of contemplation—and in action, by uniting one's will to the will of God. We must now sketch these ideas in more detail, as well as the presuppositions which underlie them, both from the writings of Ignatius and those of his closest companions.

Although Ignatius never denies the legitimacy or the necessity of prayer, it is certainly true that one finds little explicit mention of it in the *Constitutions* which he wrote for his new Society. Nowhere does he describe in what it should consist. The *Spiritual Exercises,* of course, is a whole series of meditations, contemplations and vocal prayers which Ignatius required his followers to make, but as we have seen, the basic form of these exercises had been in use before, even though the content he gave them was the result of his own unique vision. When Ignatius does discuss prayer in the *Constitutions,* he makes it quite clear that complete freedom should be allowed to those who had been fully admitted to the order. Even Jesuits in training (scholastics) were not to give much time for formal prayer.

Although Ignatius left no direction for the personal prayer of his followers and set no limits to it, he did enunciate the universal principle that prayer and bodily penances must be governed and limited according to the demands of apostolic work and obedience. There is definite indication, in fact, that he maintained a certain attitude of distrust toward purely formal prayer. Action was what Ignatius wanted his followers to be interested in. Activities which withdrew one from explicit attention to God, if undertaken out of love of God, not only were equivalent to the union and recollection of contemplation, but could be even more acceptable:

Regarding the charge of temporal affairs, although to some extent they may appear to be—and even are—distracting, I have no doubt that your right intention and the direction of all of you to the divine glory do make your work spiritual and very pleasing to his infinite goodness. For distractions undertaken for his greater service and in conformity to his divine will interpreted by obedience, not only can equal the union and recollection of deep contemplation, but may even be more acceptable as proceeding from a stronger and more fervent charity.[15]

It seems clear, then, that Ignatius' thought regarding prayer had two important aspects: his focus on the action of God in the world, and his emphasis on union with God through which the individual joined his will to God's will—a principle of union parallel to the union of mind and heart in formal, "contemplative" prayer. Certainly Ignatius was not opposed to prayer. But what mattered most was this union with God, and this, he maintained, could be found in any activity whatever.

When, moreover, Ignatius proposes the twofold goal of his Society—the salvation and perfection of one's own soul and the salvation and perfection of the neighbor—his idea is no longer that such perfection be achieved in the quiet of contemplation in such a way that others will then be able to share (as Aquinas had put it) the overflow of light and grace. The trouble with the medieval treatment of the relation between prayer and action was that it furnished the individual with a prefabricated ideal of holiness acquired through pure contemplation, then sent him out into the world to apply it. Since he was fully formed to begin with by contemplation, involvement with the world (or with concrete activity in the world) could not add anything positive; its only effect was to dilute, to compromise, to corrupt. The problem here is that such "withdrawn" contemplation or "undistracted" prayer really cannot be attained in an active life without a certain schizophrenia; that it leads not only factually but inevitably to the image of the spiritual life satirized as a long downhill slide from the peaks of contemplative fervor to the sheol of worldly activity. This image accords well, of course, with the medieval world-picture of history as a waste, a secular desert, a painful interim between the lost Golden Age and the future Kingdom, and of life as a temptation, a threat, a danger—almost anything but an opportunity.

For Ignatius, however, contemplation and action were to penetrate one another to perfect unity so that apostolic work for the salvation and sanctification of others was the informing principle of one's life and, consequently, the principle of one's striving for Christian perfection. The basic dimension of human living and acting, therefore, was not ignored or reduced to a secondary position. Ignatius saw clearly the need for human experience in the world as the ground not only of knowledge but of that spontaneous affection without which any "spiritual" love becomes thin and unsubstantial.

Now, Ignatius was never a mere theorist. Most often what he had to say was not based on traditional teaching, but on a personal experience which found its guarantee in the inner certainty which accompanied it. In this context it will be useful to quote from an observation of Jerome Nadal, who was in close contact with him for many years and to whom Ignatius entrusted the task of promulgating the *Constitutions* of the new order in many parts of the Society:

Although this is not the time to treat of prayer, there is a fact which I do not wish to omit. Father Ignatius had received from God the special grace to rise without effort to the contemplation of the Most Holy Trinity and to repose in it a long time. Sometimes he was led by grace to contemplate the whole Trinity; he was transported into it and united himself to it with his whole heart, with intense sentiments of devotion, and a deep spiritual relish. . . . If such prayer was granted to Ignatius, it was a great privilege and of an entirely different order. But he likewise had another privilege which made him *see* God present in all things and in every action, with a lively sense of spiritual realities: *contemplative in the midst of action,* or according to his ordinary expression: finding God in all things. Now this grace which illumined his soul was revealed to us as much by a kind of brightness which emanated from his countenance as by the enlightened sureness with which he acted in Christ. We were filled with admiration for it, our hearts were much consoled by it, and we felt as though the overflow of these graces was descending on ourselves.[16]

When we juxtapose this comment of Nadal with Ignatius' writings, we find three uses of the term prayer: (1) formal prayer and ordinary contemplation, that is, contemplation on the mysteries of Christ or our redemption; (2) the spirtual attitude which enables a person to find God even in the thick of the most absorbing activity; (3) a mystical dimension with which Ignatius was clearly favored in all his prayer. Leaving aside the mystical aspect, we can at this point accurately speak of prayer as a particular and definite "exercise" of the spiritual life and prayer as one's continuous union with God in action.[17] A life of explicit prayer is necessary, especially in fostering a person's faith-commitment and love of God, his familiarity with God, which must animate and sanctify his whole life. But explicit prayer, as Ignatius makes clear, is no longer the highest end of a contemplative life. Such formal prayer is rather an exercise of that conviction and disposition which is not limited to the time of prayer, but fills up the whole active life. And because it is not an end in itself, but —in a properly understood sense—a means to an end, it is limited by this end: action performed with a pure intention for the love of God.

From this it is clear that perfection is determined not by the extent of such "exercises" of prayer and abnegation—as important as they are and as much as they are repeatedly emphasized by Ignatius—but by the love-inspired execution of all our actions in God. This kind of motivation demands that, with the greatest possible purity, we love God in all creatures and all created reality in him. This is to find God in all things; and the essence of any union with God is always the commitment of personal love:

Let all strive to have a right intention, not only concerning their state of life, but also as regards all particulars, seeking sincerely in them always to serve and please the divine Goodness for its own sake, and for the very special blessings which he first bestowed on us. . . . And let them seek God in all things, removing themselves as far as possible from the love of all creatures that they might bestow their whole affection on the Creator, loving him in all creatures and them all in him, according to his most holy and divine will.[18]

In the end, Ignatius proposed a thoroughly action-oriented spirituality—a spirituality of active service for the kingdom of Christ. In outlining the structure of his order, he mentions all the forms of priestly-apostolic work as well as a style of life which would guarantee the greatest possible freedom of action for such work. There is no mention of contemplation as the heretofore recognized goal of one striving for perfection. There is mention only of action for the glory of God. Ignatius thus developed a spirituality which provides a theoretical, theological support for apostolic work and explains how one engaged fully in action is no farther from God than the contemplative at his prie-dieu. He might, in fact, be closer.

Our factual discussion of Ignatius' approach to spirituality, especially his view of the relationship between prayer and action, necessarily leads to a deeper question.[19] Is it not, for example, a complete inversion of objective values to consider that prayer (contemplation) functions primarily as a servant of action? Religious contemplation, and thus interior prayer, constitutes man's acknowledgment of and surrender to God *par excellence;* as such, it represents the absolute zenith of human life. In the traditional evaluation of contemplation and action, interior prayer could never be considered a relative thing—ordered as a mere means to the goal of action—for Christian perfection essentially consisted in contemplation. Accordingly, every action was more or less sharply evaluated as an approximation to or defection from this enterprise. Although the defection was justified either because of the practical necessities of social activity within the Church or because it was a communication of the fruits gathered during contemplation, the essential characteristic of the spiritual life still remained its contemplative component. How, then, can prayer be legitimately subordinated to activity?

Any attempt to answer this question must first of all consider the intrinsic nature and value of the goal to which contemplative prayer is ultimately referred in an active life. Emerich Coreth has rightly pointed out that as long as human perfection is estimated as the perfection of pure interiorness of the spirit as opposed to the exteriorness of action, then perfection remains a thing of the

individual alone; to pursue this perfection demands the surrender of all human associations in order that the soul might attain
its goal of communion with God alone.[20] But such a separation
between the interior and exterior life of man is unsound. If
exterior activity is action produced by the total human person
and not a self-estrangement of the spiritual interior of a man,
then only such activity can express that rich fullness of life
which, from the pure love of God and of the neighbor, places at
God's disposal all its activity and works with all its strength for
the salvation of souls. In apostolic work of this kind, interior and
exterior, intention and activity, are united, and in this unity the
whole commandment of love given by Christ is fulfilled. In this
fulfillment, and not in an isolated love of God alone, consists the
sanctification of one's own self. By the same token, work for
the sanctification of others is not only the highest development of
the love of neighbor, but also of the love of God, insofar as all the
toil and anxiety of work is undertaken for the love of God as a
surrender of oneself entirely to the plans or wishes of God in
order to cooperate in his redemptive mission in the world.

Within this context, then, we concur with the opinion of
Aquinas that the apostolic life is the highest type of life; but we
disagree with him in assigning the reason. It is not because apostolic contemplation is more perfect than pure contemplation, but
because activity embraces in a unity both the interior and the
exterior—the love of God and the love of neighbor—and brings
them to their highest development in an external act which is
animated by the interior conviction of this two-dimensional
Christian love. This notion of action surely presupposes that the
unselfish conviction of love is, both interiorly and exteriorly, a
life-giving power actually penetrating every act with the greatest possible force. And this is precisely the goal which interior
prayer and the contemplative impulse serves: contemplation *in
the midst of* action.

We are now prepared to explain whether and to what extent
contemplation can be placed at the service of action without
foolishly inverting the right order of things. We are talking,
obviously, not about a purely intellectual enterprise, but about

religious contemplation—an interior act of personal surrender to God. Two things need to be emphasized.

First, action for the sake of God is a form of glorifying God that is, as we have described it, the most complete expression of the love of God. God's glory is achieved essentially in a free personal recognition of the creature-Creator relationship which finds its most apt reflection in an attitude of love. This attitude reaches its perfect realization, not in a pure "interiorness," but in the unity and totality of interiorness and exteriorness—inner conviction and exterior action enlivened by this conviction. Hence, union with God reached in prayer loses nothing of its value it if is ordered to the perfection of activity. The attempt to find this harmony between prayer and action by inverting the relationship—that is, by subordinating action to prayer—too easily leads to the denigration and abandonment of action altogether, to denying any positive value to experience in the world. Concrete activity then contributes nothing but the exterior context (in the terms of scholastic theology, the *materia disposita*) to the ideal of holiness through contemplation. In such a perspective there is nothing to be said *theologically* about the existential order; there is only activity which "applies" the illuminations achieved in prayer to those who have not been so enlightened.

Besides this theological impasse, however, such a perspective also results in a spiritual and psychological dead end. For how large a dose of prayer is needed to sanctify action? If regular reception of the sacraments, a short daily examination of conscience plus morning and evening prayers are not sufficient to help a person be more deeply motivated by the love of God, then is one to ask for an hour of private prayer? And if an hour is not long enough, would it be good to suggest two hours? And if two hours do not obtain better results, there would be little left but to spend the entire day in prayer and try one's best to avoid discouragement![21]

It should be clear, then, that interior prayer is not *completely* subjected to the goal of action. Prayer does not consist in speaking with God merely in order to be more effective in working for souls. The meaning of prayer lies rather in ever striving after an expressly new actuation of one's whole attitude toward God—an attitude that cannot be restricted to the time of prayer alone, but which should penetrate and transform one's whole life. Since this is a personal attitude toward a personal God, it can be properly actuated only by a deliberate personal acceptance of intimacy with God. To this extent formal prayer is absolutely necessary in every Christian life. But insofar as prayer is an attitude which should determine the whole course of life, it remains essentially ordered to a sanctifying permeation of all our activity. The more this attitude does infuse one's life, the less is a definite time of prayer necessary in itself. The *ideal,* in other words, is that one's life be so entirely ordered to God, saturated and filled with him, that nothing of this union is lost, even amid the most strenuous activity with men and things of the world. Rather, prayer becomes the unique atmosphere in which a person lives and acts. To the heart filled with God, all things speak of him. And it is not just a question of orienting one's will to this end; it is a question of *spiritual experience* where God is "tasted" in everything.[22]

Although this kind of prayer represents a state of highest sanctity, Ignatius' conception of it is quite simple. As a basic spirituality, it is valuable not only for religious but for anyone who is striving for union with God in every aspect of his life. For what Ignatius recommends is a simpler kind of prayer which considers the omnipresence of God with special emphasis on his immanence in persons, situations, and experiences. If Nadal's phrase, "contemplation in the midst of action," is used, contemplation must not be taken in the Neo-Platonic sense of purely intellectual contemplation, since it is a fundamentally religious act. Nor is the term merely equivalent to what we have designated as religious contemplation or formal interior prayer. We get a clue to its meaning from the *Constitutions* of the Society of Jesus, where Ignatius speaks of the "union and familiarity with God" which must be present in action as well as in prayer.[23] Contemplation is the response and gift of this union; it clearly stands over against explicit, formal prayer, in the sense that it is surely actuated and realized in formal prayer but is not restricted to it.

Contemplation is a sensitivity which enables a person to meet God present and active in the world, in history, and in the activities of men. In the midst of action, such a person may sense that what he is doing is God's work, that God is present and active in him and in the situation. It is precisely this ongoing awareness of God's activity here and now that Nadal refers to as "contemplation in the midst of action," or Ignatius calls "finding God in all things."

It is understandable that the language of sense experience should frequently recur in the description of this kind of prayer and, along with it, the indication that there exists a spectrum of religious experience in which one finds God in all things. At one end there is the basic union of man's will with God's will accompanied by the simple conviction and satisfaction that "I am doing what God wants me to do." At the other extreme is the great mystical experience of Ignatius himself—the constant felt awareness of the Presence of God which is an infused gift, a perfection of the virtue of faith. The "ability" to so meet God in everything is, then, the manifestation of one's union with God; the different levels at which this awareness can be found are as various as the degrees of one's union and familiarity with God. It would be imprudent to think that a person could go very quickly to God through creatures. What Ignatius actually describes is an idea of consummate perfection, of a soul so totally filled with God that everything leads to him. Such spiritual insight is generated *between* the moment when the *created world* is an obstacle to union with God and the moment when it becomes a means to finding him. It is at the time of this breakthrough that a person begins to "love God in all creatures and all creatures in God."[24] Both formal prayer and practices of penance can bring an individual closer to this awareness, but these merely prepare for, and to some extent are the conditions for, union with God; the manifestation of this union is the ability to find God in everything. Formal prayer and penance, moreover, guide the prayer of apostolic action, while the prayer of apostolic action roots formal prayer in reality and prevents it from becoming merely speculative.

Before we close this part of our treatment of Ignatius' spirituality, we must mention two crucial presuppositions which underlie his vision and without which one runs the risk of completely misconstruing his doctrine. In discussing Ignatius' approach to prayer we have concentrated on what we feel were his truly revolutionary contributions to the history of spirituality—elements which help both to resolve the prayer-action controversy described in the preceding chapter and to open the genuine possibility of a spirituality of the world, a spirituality of activity available for either the professed religious or the Christian layman. In order to fill out this picture of Ignatian doctrine, however, a word needs to be said about his theology of the Cross and about his attention to God *beyond* the whole world. Both these propositions will require some comment.[25]

There can be little question that Ignatius' spirituality is a spirituality of the Cross; and in this characteristic is revealed his inner continuity with the universal stream of Christian piety before him. As he writes in the introduction to the *Constitutions:*

Lovingly let us direct our minds to this fact—for this it is which has great, even decisive weight before our Creator and Lord—how much all growth in the spiritual life depends upon our rejecting utterly and not merely half-heartedly all that is an object of the world's love and longing, and our accepting—even demanding—with the whole power of our soul that which Christ our Lord loved and took upon himself. . . . Those who walk thus in the spirit and the true imitation of Christ have only one love and burning desire: to wear the robe and the sign of Christ out of love and reverence for him. If it were possible, without offending the Divine Majesty and without sin on the part of another, they would wish of themselves to bear the sufferings of insult and calumny and injustice, the treatment and consideration which is shown toward fools. All this because they have only one desire: following and being conformed to Jesus Christ, their Creator and Lord, wearing his robe and his mark, which he wore as an example to us for the sake of our salvation, in order that we might imitate and follow him in everything that our strength in his grace allows him who is the true way leading man to life.[26]

In his own life, in his piety, and in the spirit which he transmitted to his followers, Ignatius is consciously and clearly taking over and continuing that ultimate direction which determined the life of the religious orders before him. With his companions, he bound himself to God by vows of poverty, chastity, and obedience. And with them, he necessarily assumed the attitude of radical renunciation which characterized religious spirituality from the time of the hermits of the desert. As Rahner comments, "Ignatius stands in the line of those men who existentially flee into the desert in a violent *fuga saeculi,* even though it may be the God-forsaken stony desert of a city, in order to seek God far from the world."[27] For although Ignatius held firmly to the view that God can and must be encountered through creatures, he also saw quite clearly that God has no need of creaturely service. He is greater than all the means by which we think we can serve him. His grace is never obtained by our efforts alone; it remains always his free gift.

The committed Christian is the man who dies *into* Christ. He takes upon himself the Lord's renunciation, he is clothed in his garment—a fool for Christ's sake, the man for whom enjoyment of and engagement in the world have been submerged by his desire to see the reign of Christ established here and now in his situation. The lesson of the Cross, to which Ignatius incessantly returns, is as simple as it is direct: where men fail, God's grace can still triumph; his power is made perfect in infirmity. The Cross is thus the annihilation of merely created goodness, the squandering of human resources, the foundering of human hopes, and the ultimate in terms of suffering. Christ in his nakedness is reduced to creaturely impotence, and it is precisely here that man's redemption is achieved.[28]

Behind the apparent worldliness of Ignatian spirituality, then, there always lurks a profound devotion to the Cross. In Christ's passion Ignatius finds the supreme victory of grace. His deepest longing is to be with Christ, to wear the garments in which he was clad, and to suffer for his sake. A spirituality which spoke only of self-fulfillment, involvement with the world, apostolic efficiency and success, would be profoundly un-Ignatian, not to say decisively un-Christian. Ignatius' thought does not admit for himself or his disciples any active work or even joy in which the world and God, or time and eternity, are totally reconciled in amicable harmony. There can be, in other words, no question of an acceptance of and openness to the world by which man first takes his stand in the world by striving for the fulfillment of humanity, and then also waits for happiness with God after completing his tasks and leading a moral and relatively holy life. Only if a man has first submitted himself in faith to God's revelation of himself in a suffering Jesus Christ and committed himself to his Cross and apparent foolishness, can God accept in grace also man's service of the world. Once a man has placed himself under the Cross and has died with Christ, once he has entered into the obscurity of faith and the ecstacy of love, only then—to express it in the bold conception of Karl Rahner—can every act which is good in itself, and therefore meaningful within the world, be supernaturally elevated by grace so that its aim and meaning extend beyond its immediate significance and into the life of God himself.

Such considerations obviously lead to the second presupposition underlying Ignatian spirituality to which we have already referred: Ignatian piety is a piety toward the God who is beyond the world as well as within it, a God who freely reveals himself to man and gives man the possibility of genuinely accepting the world for what it is. A grasp of this proposition will give us the ultimate reason for a spirituality of the Cross and the basic justification for Ignatius' emphasis on prayer as "finding God in all things."

If one of the hallmarks of the Ignatian vision is that God must be sought in the way he appears to us in the mirror of the world, it is nonetheless true that this discovery of God has a distinctively double character.[29] First, we acknowledge God as the ground of the world, as the ultimate ground of everything we meet. But we come to know him as the free, personal, eternal being who is the God *beyond* the world and all its limitations, so that the world does not properly and completely express what he is.

God is, in other words, more than a God according to our image and likeness, who merely lets men increase and multiply and blesses them when they subject the earth. For this kind of God would be nothing but what we could know of him by natural means; therefore, he would be nothing but the horizon remaining always in the distance, watching and approving humanity as it developed according to its own proper laws. He would, in short, be nothing but the divinity of the world. But God is more than this. He has broken in upon man's existence and has shattered the world; he has revealed himself in Jesus Christ. And the ultimate meaning of this revelation is a calling of man out of this world into the life of God, the personal life of the Being exalted above the whole world in inaccessible light.

Thus God brings himself face to face with man and makes a demand which calls him out of the pre-established order of things and gives rise to the possibility that God might issue commands which are not, at the same time, the voice of nature. In this way, renunciation of the world and the abandonment which the Cross involves go essentially further than the merely natural fulfillment of the existential tasks demanded of man. All Christian mortification, as Rahner has written, has progressed beyond the struggling self-mastery of man trying to find himself; "it is already, the primitive Christian *Didache* prays, 'allowing the world to pass by' in order that grace may enter."[30] Christianity, then, is essentially a kind of flight from the world; it is the commitment to the personal God who freely reveals himself in Christ—the God of grace who is not the fulfillment of the immanent craving of the world for its completion, even though it brings about this completion in a supereminent way.

To summarize the two presuppositions we have been considering: Ignatius approaches the world from God, not the other way around. Only because he has delivered himself in the lowliness of an adoring self-surrender to the God beyond the world and to his will is he prepared to obey his word, even when he is sent back into the world which he had found the courage to abandon in the foolishness of the Cross. Because God is greater than everything, he can be found apart from all things—in flight from the world; because he is greater than everything, he can also come to meet man anywhere—in the midst of the world. For this reason Ignatius acknowledges only one law in his restless search for

God: to seek him in everything. And this means to seek him in that spot where at any particular time he wants to be found.

Thus, the dialectic between flight from the world and acceptance of the world found from the beginning of the evolution of the monastic ideal and repeated in the two medieval concepts of contemplation and action recurs with new emphasis in the spirituality of Ignatius. Action as well as contemplation is adherence to the God who is the goal of Christian existence, therefore to the God beyond the world who yet has freely entered into the world and there continues to accomplish the great deeds of salvation. We should now be in a better position to understand the formula of Ignatian acceptance of the world. For Ignatius seeks only the God of Jesus Christ—the free, personal God whom he encounters either in prayer or in activity. So he is prepared to seek him alone, but also everywhere—especially in the world—in contemplation in the midst of action.

We have not been able to touch on many questions which would have to be included in a more detailed investigation of what has been said—particularly how this Ignatian outlook which, after all, is primarily that of the religious could be expanded to embody a properly lay piety. But enough has been said to bring our historical analysis a step further and to provide at least the basic outline for subsequent development. To some extent every Christian has the ineluctable vocation of entering into the world and its work with the strength born of his superiority to the world, sent by him with whom we are united in the one spiritual life.[31]

Such an affirmation of the world would be founded neither on a naive optimism nor on an establishment of the world as the center of our lives. Involvement in the world springs from our conformity with him whom we have joined in that flight from the world expressed in the foolishness of his Cross. Once we have found the God beyond, then all previous seclusion breaks into the world where we meet God in any place he chooses to show himself, where we work as long as day lasts, immersed in the work of our time, yet praying with the Book of Revelation: "Come, Lord Jesus" (22:20).

Chapter VIII

THE LOGIC
OF CHRISTIAN
DISCERNMENT

RESEARCH INTO THE SOURCES of Ignatian spirituality, particularly into the structure of the *Spiritual Exercises,* has brought to light an important finding. What is most characteristic of Ignatius' vision, and what, from the saint's own personal spiritual experience, represents his most striking contribution to Christian asceticism, is his discussion of the influence of various psychological determinants—"good and evil spirits"—on an individual's spiritual growth. It is easy to show that the directions for discerning these "spirits" during the first and second weeks of the Exercises hold a central place in the structure of this program, at least in the mind of Ignatius, if not always in the Exercises as they are commonly presented today. For, as many commentators feel, the Exercises have only one principal aim: They are intended, by means of meditation, examination of conscience, silence, mortification, and prayer to produce in the retreatant a condition of interior sensitivity in which he experiences the influence of forces both good and evil; as a result of this sensitivity the retreatant is able to determine his state of life according to the unique personal "call" of God or to find the means best suited to unite him more closely to God in a state already chosen.[1] Provided this structural kernel of the Exercises is preserved, they remain specifically Ignatian exercises, even if the director makes certain modifications in the content of the meditations. But if this dimension of discernment is absent, not even the most dogged adherence to the details of the individual meditations will be productive of the Ignatian spirit and vision.

As a guiding focus of the Exercises, the Rules for Discernment bear the unmistakable impress of Ignatius' own experience. They derive from the saint's attempts to unravel "different spirits and thoughts" as he lay in bed at Loyola recuperating from his battle wounds and read through "a *Life of Christ* and a book of the *Lives of the Saints* in Spanish."[2] Again at Manresa his alternate experiences of consolation and desolation made him aware that, from the beginning, the way by which God was causing him to advance was a way apart—one in which he was instructed less by men than by the experiences he underwent and the lights he received.[3]

But however personal and biographical the reference, it is equally plain that such experiences and their pastoral application are deeply rooted in the mainstream of tradition. Certainly Ignatius did not need to be consciously aware of his sources. Authentic tradition has its own life and can be exposed to critical judgment only with difficulty. It is a living bond which binds generations together, an atmosphere which supports an individual without his needing to be aware of it. For our purposes, however, let us attempt to sketch the patterns of this traditional teaching on discernment. Then, after delineating some necessary definitions and distinctions, we will take up Ignatius' own treatment of the influence of good and evil spirits, discuss several problems involved in interpreting his doctrine, and finally offer some reflections on the use of discernment today.[4]

The essential elements of Ignatius' theme of good and evil spirits that influence men are apparent from the very beginning of the Old Testament. The story of man's fall in the Book of Genesis (3:1–8), along with the metaphysical and psychological background of temptation, sin, and the deceits of the tempter, depicts the situation with exquisite vividness. Here, perhaps more clearly than anywhere else in Scripture, the need for "spiritual realism" is evident; the third dimension of God and spirits is not only accurately described, but is inseparably interwoven into the experience of Adam and Eve. The narrative attributes sin to the free choice of man in his primitive condition, when he was not yet subject to the burden of sin and evil desires.[5] Man is indeed tempted by agents outside himself, and what distinguishes the serpent from the rest of God's created animals is its greater cleverness and deception. The narrative affirms that man has the power to resist temptation, and the fine psychological insight of the story shows both the devices of the tempter and the reasons why man yields.

As we move further into Israelite history, it is clear that the ability to discern the spirit of God speaking and acting in their midst is a constant concern of God's people. The Patriarchs walked along obscure paths, but they discerned with lucid judgment that God was guiding them because he was always true to his promises. In the time of the prophets, the Israelites were confronted by a more complex challenge: the need to choose between false prophets and God's true spokesmen; thus, they sought criteria to help them distinguish the genuine from the counterfeit. Personal sincerity and conviction, irreproachable conduct, and even the working of signs did not suffice to authenticate a prophet's claim or exclude the possibility of delusion. God's people looked for something more: doctrinal harmony with their traditional religion, whose core was the stern challenge that had first given them existence as God's covenanted people. "I will be your God and you will be my people" (Exod. 19:34). I will be your savior, Yahweh had promised, but you must abide by my terms of salvation. The true prophet was the one who chastened the people by his preaching, who did not dilute God's message. Finally, Jewish theology, as is evident in the noncanonical books of the century before Christ—especially in *The Testament of the Twelve Patriarchs*—developed the ideas of good and evil spirits intensively, and even exaggerated and cheapened them with fantasy.[6]

In New Testament times men were called upon to recognize God's Spirit at work in Christ's activity, message, and person. His parables were intelligible only to those who could discern in them the imperatives of God's new kingdom. His miracles were signs only to those who were not blind to God's love. His death and resurrection were the ultimate challenge to perceive the power of God intervening in man's history.

Among New Testament writers, however, it was Paul who laid the foundation of later tradition with his fully developed teaching on dominions and powers, as well as with his insistent exhortation to watchful struggle against the evil powers of darkness (Eph. 6:10-20). For Paul, the ideal Christian existence is a progressive realization of that divine sonship to which all men are called by the Father. "Everyone moved by the Spirit is a son of God. The spirit you received is not the spirit of slaves bringing fear into your lives again; it is the spirit of sons, and it makes us cry out, 'Abba, Father!' " (Rom. 8:14-15). Paul's whole ascetical ideal, in fact, demands attention to the workings of the Holy Spirit, who directs and aids the adoptive sons of God to an ever deeper awareness of their relationship to the Father. The immediate, concrete means to this filial obedience is the love of all men as our brothers. It is essentially through this experience of solidarity with one another that we can, by the grace of Christ, experience the supreme truth that God is our Father. When the Christian arrives at a perfect awareness of these relationships, he has no need of any law to indicate how he must act or to coerce him into so acting, for he is entirely influenced by the movement of God's Spirit.[7]

Among post-apostolic writings, the *Didache* and the *Shepherd of Hermas* provide the first elements of a doctrine on discernment of spirits. A further step was taken by Origen whose detailed rules for judging inner experiences read almost like a preliminary sketch of Ignatius' Rules for Discernment.[8] Origen's ideas became the common property of eastern monasticism and were further developed in Athanasius' *Life of Anthony* and the works of Evagrius of Pontus. Here, God's activity among men was depicted in terms of a cosmic battle in which graphic antithetical descriptions of the diverse effects of good and evil spirits serve to forewarn and forearm the unsuspecting Christian. Through Cassian, these ideas became current in the monastic writings of the West, though with notably different emphasis. The grace of discerning spirits in genuine spiritual experience of consolation and desolation has been transformed into the virtue of discretion, which ultimately is nothing more than prudence and tact.[9]

In the Middle Ages, Bernard indicated how to distinguish the vain spirit of the flesh, the world, and the devil from the movements of the good spirit. Thomas a Kempis contrasted the different motions of nature and grace. Others, such as Denis the Carthusian, distinguished divine, angelic, diabolical, and natural movements in man's soul. In accordance with the doctrine proposed centuries before by Aquinas, these authors limited angels and demons to direct action on man's sensitive faculties and only indirect action on his intellect and will, reserving immediate action on man's soul to God alone.

Far down this stream of tradition we find Ignatius. Probably the immediate link with Ignatius' teaching is provided by a Kempis and the other writers of the so-called *Devotio Moderna,* as well as by Bernardine of Siena (1380–1444). Like Ignatius, Bernardine was convinced that the Kingdom of Christ was under siege by the forces of Satan as Jerusalem and Babylon intermingled in the quarrelling church of the fifteenth century. While Bernardine's influence on Ignatius was not immediate, the relationship—both in thought and expression—between Bernardine's emphasis on discernment of spirits and Ignatius' more elaborated teaching is too close to be passed over without mention. On the other hand, the high esteem in which Ignatius held the *Imitation of Christ* strongly suggests that this is one of the more important sources of the spirituality of the Exercises. This dependence, however, would seem to extend only as far as their literary formulation is concerned, since it is unlikely that Ignatius realized, when he had his first spiritual experiences at Loyola, how close he was to the spirit of the *Imitation* or how far he was to develop and alter its perspective.

Two conclusions are evident from this brief historical survey:

Religious men have always been concerned with the ability to distinguish the activity of diverse spirits; and they have met this need by formulating criteria and rules in terms intelligible to their contemporaries. What Ignatius contributed to traditional teaching on discernment was his own fundamental vision, elaborated in the preceding chapter, of finding God in all things. The discernment of spirits is simply the persistent putting into practice of that supernatural concrete logic of discovering the will of God through the experimental test of consolation and desolation. This affective logic is inseparably connected with Ignatius' basic synthesis of contemplation in action which is the hallmark of his spirituality.[10]

Before gathering together some of the more important texts which deal with discernment, we must admit that the whole enterprise of discerning spirits is likely to strike the contemporary Christian as highly dubious. Modern science attributes to physical and psychic causes most of the impulses formerly ascribed to God, angels, and demons. Quite simply, Ignatius took over from the Judaic, patristic, and medieval traditions the idea that these supernatural agents more or less regularly invade human consciousness, evoking virtuous or sinful inclinations.[11] Discernment was needed to identify the source of these impulses. Building on this received doctrine, Ignatius applied the techniques of discernment to the process of making important choices. This was his proper contribution. If modern readers are compelled, at least to some extent, to "demythologize" Ignatius' doctrine, his essential insight must not be lost.

For while the problem of spiritual choice has always been difficult, it has become enormously more complicated for contemporary man. In previous ages man lived comparatively close to nature, in a relatively homogeneous cultural environment. His field of choice was narrow and, even within that field, custom and tradition often played the determining role. But modern society has greatly mastered the forces of nature and environment. Man lives in a culturally pluralistic society, in which a bewildering number of world views compete for his allegiance. Social structures are rapidly changing; venerable precedent is no longer unquestioned. Modern man thus anxiously gropes for a method and a logic which can help him find the course of action which is right for him as a unique person in ever-changing specific situations. This need is felt with special urgency by earnest Christians in the spiritually momentous decisions of their lives. How can they find the will of God?

By viewing Ignatius' personal emphasis on discernment against the background of the traditional teaching already presented, and by not attempting to camouflage his often dramatic vocabulary, we hope to bring out the precise meaning of what the *Exercises* says on "diverse spirits" and on the influence of these good and evil spirits on the soul. Hopefully, an understanding of Ignatius' technique will be useful not only in our appreciation of the development of spirituality, but also in our own struggle to acquire the art of finding God's will.

As one opens the book *Spiritual Exercises,* the first reference to discernment occurs almost at once, in the Introductory Observations written for those engaged in giving the Exercises to others. Here Ignatius dwells on the theme of discernment more frequently than on any other. The length of the weeks into which the retreat is divided, for example, should depend upon how far the retreatant is "disturbed and tried by different spirits."[12] When these "spiritual motions, such as consolations or desolations" are absent, the director should be suspicious that the retreatant has not begun the exercises with proper seriousness.[13] For Ignatius, obviously, the experience of desolation is something more than purely physical or psychological weariness or depression. Not only does he exclude natural explanations, but he expressly takes into account a *third force.*[14] Under the disguise of tiredness and depression, it is the "enemy of human nature" who approaches and capitalizes on the introversion brought on by solitude. The director's task is to uncover the deceits of Satan and to safeguard the retreatant from misguided choices.[15] Thus, Ignatius considers the vigilant control of all these inner experiences so important that he refers to the Rules for Discernment from the start; and even though the Rules themselves are to be found only at the end of the book, they are an essential factor that threads its way through the whole book.

The director, consequently, can carry out this task only if he is "faithfully informed about the various disturbances and thoughts caused [within the retreatant] by the action of different spirits."[16] This kind of knowledge is more important for the outcome of the Exercises than knowledge of "private thoughts and sins" (i.e., those not inspired by other spirits). Thus, it is not necessary for the retreat director also to act as confessor; but he cannot fulfill his true function without some insight into the spiritual stirrings which take place in the retreatant. Moreover, the director's principal task is not to provide material for meditation; this can be supplied by a book or by passages from Scripture. It is primarily the director's power of discernment which determines the genuine fruit of the Exercises. In fact, it may be said that a good deal of the criticism directed against Ignatian spirituality in our day is justified precisely because of a neglect of this discernment of spirits on the part of those who give the Exercises.

A review of the passages already cited reveals the necessity of distinguishing several kinds of interior movements which a person may experience. Ignatius speaks, for example, both of "various spirits" and "various thoughts." Are these spirits simply our representations and feelings? The answer is given early in the *Spiritual Exercises* where "three kinds of thoughts" are distinguished.[17] Thoughts of the first type are "strictly my own, and arise wholly from my own free will," that is, they spring from my innate powers of mind and affection. The other two "come from without"; they are produced by intelligent powers outside the person and may be good or evil. If good, the operating agent is God or one of his spirits; if evil, it is the devil in one form or another.

Consequently, two kinds of discernment are logically demanded in the spiritual life. We should be able first to distinguish our native thoughts and sentiments from those produced by forces outside ourselves and, among the latter, to recognize the difference between inspirations that originate with God and temptations which come from the devil. The first discernment is perhaps less important, since all our interior movements are subject to the influence of God and are never completely isolated from the contrary activity of the devil. On the other hand, it is highly practical to be able to judge between the outside agents operating on our minds and wills, in order to know whether to welcome or to resist them.

Moreover, in speaking of "movements" of the soul, we can refer to those which precede a deliberate action of the will—those involved in the actual choice itself—and those which follow. The discernment of spirits which concerns us most properly refers to the *antecedent* motions of mind and will which, in a sense, impel me toward good or evil. It makes considerable difference whether these impulses are from God or the devil. Without forcing the will, they solicit my consent; consequently my decision, for or against a given impulse, will be objectively good or bad insofar as the spirit which suggested the choice was divine or diabolical. In a subordinate way, the movements which *follow* an act of human choice are also worth discriminating as valuable signs that my choice was correct or not—to repeat and confirm the decision if it was correct or if wrong to change or revoke it.

Ignatius, then, is very far from holding the view that the whole matter of human choice can be discussed in psychological terms. As a believer, his position is one of "spiritual realism"; for him, reality is not confined to the space-time world of sensible or even psychological experience. He knows that the influence of supernatural powers is so adapted to the rhythm of our interior life that it will often be difficult to distinguish between the "natural" and "supernatural" or how these components blend in a single experience. Certainly logic and psychology have a place in discernment. But if a person were to think these two disciplines sufficient, his judgment in the realm of the "spirit" would be flawed; the recognition of the "third dimension" is essential.

Once this has been grasped, the danger of confusing spiritual direction with psychotherapy is more easily avoided. In psychotherapy the natural value of psychic health is at stake; in spiritual direction, values of the supernatural order become the critical determinants.[18] The psychotherapist is concerned with the integration of individual and social relationships in the order of nature; the spiritual director is concerned with nothing less than leading the Christian to "completed growth in Christ" (Eph. 4:13). Of course, a good spiritual director must have understanding and experience in the sphere of healthy and disturbed psychic states; he must at least know enough to acknowledge the limits of his competence and, when necessary, to refer an individual to a psychiatrist. But even the best psychiatrist is usually disinclined to undertake the task of spiritual direction, if only because a new dimension is involved which implies a break in continuity with the natural order.

If a director expects, however, that Ignatius' Rules for Discernment will provide him with a fully developed science of good and evil spirits, he will be disappointed. The faces of these spirits remain hidden; only their effects on one's interior experience are revealed and criteria set down by which their origins can be discovered. Ignatius lays great stress on the fact that a person's spiritual constitution and level of experience must be known in order to judge the processes taking place within him. The indications vary, according to whether the man is a "beginner" or not. With these preliminary definitions and distinctions in mind, we turn to a more detailed description of the Rules for Discernment themselves.

Ignatius, we will recall, groups these Rules into two categories. The first are more suited to the earlier, purgative, stages of the spiritual life, and correspond to the type of meditation presented in the First Week of the Exercises—considerations of man's absolute dependence on God, the fact of his sinfulness, the eventuality of death, and the continual presence of God's mercy. The second set of Rules pertains more to man's increasing union with God, and correspond to the meditations of the Second Week of the Exercises—considerations of the call of Christ, the spiritual combat, and contemplations on the life of Jesus. Of more importance than this division of the Rules, however, is Ignatius' remark that it never depends on the will of the retreatant which of the two groups of Rules he should take up. The director must be concerned that someone who is "spiritually" still in the First Week should not read the Rules intended for those who have made greater progress. He is convinced that a premature use of the second group of Rules is not only useless but positively harmful. In other words, priority is assigned to the insight of an experienced spiritual director who knows that all truth must be adapted to the dispositions of the learner; this adaptation depends, in turn, upon the arrival of the opportune moment.

According to Ignatius' Rules for the First Week, one who lives under the spell of serious sin is tempted by the evil spirit to remain in a deceptive peace.[19] Satan places before his eyes sensual pleasures and gratifications, weaves before him a tapestry of illusions, and tries to distort his judgment on the seriousness of life. By chaining him to the realities and objects of sense willed for themselves alone, the spirit of evil thus increases a man's powerlessness to rise above the visible and tangible and tries to make him believe there is nothing beyond. To prevent him from desiring and relishing the things of God, Satan invites a man to focus attention on what is earthly, in order that he may seek to satisfy himself with this alone. If a man allows himself to be taken in by this artifice, he experiences a certain superficial peace. Yet remaining beneath this peace is a feeling of sadness. This is the sadness by which the good spirit makes a sinner unsure, restless, and shakes him out of his satisfied calm.[20]

But when a man has seriously begun to free himself from sin and to direct his life toward God, it is the evil spirit who instils in him all kinds of worried and anxious thoughts. Here, the evil spirit tries by sadness and scruples to make progress burdensome and to maintain the soul in weary depression and resignation. In such a case, according to Ignatius' Rules for the Second Week, it is a sign of the good spirit when the heart is generous and courageous, when peace and consolation flow into the soul.[21]

When a man, in other words, has broken the chains of sin with the help of grace and goes forward with the freedom of the children of God, deep inward joy and cheerfulness are signs of the good spirit. Joy is the principal sign of the presence of Jesus, because the Spirit is the overflow of love come down to us. Dwelling in our hearts, divine charity shows itself as a flood that wants to spread over our whole being to spiritualize it, to communicate

that lightness of soul which makes it possible for man to ascend
to God. This kind of spiritual tranquility is in no sense compar-
able to idleness. It is, on the contrary, the ordering of a man's
living forces, all his human powers, to the love of God. It is the
supreme harmonizing, the complete response, of all that he is.
And it is from this harmony that peace comes. Ignatius defines it
as "all interior joy that invites and attracts to what is heavenly
and to the salvation of one's own soul by filling it with peace and
quiet in its Creator and Lord."[22] Thus, God's love which comes
from on high immediately makes a man rise up toward God, but
at the same time God bends toward man anew to fill him with
his love and peace.

It would indeed be a mistake to think that we can establish
ourselves in this kind of spiritual consolation once and for all,
even if we submit fundamentally and consistently to God's
Spirit. For although true consolation clearly originates from God,
it is not his only way of dealing with us. He often allows desolation and sadness to alternate with consolation in our lives. It is
this lesson which Paul once labored to teach his community at
Corinth. His reproaches have saddened them, but this suffering
was good, he tells them, because it resulted in their conversion.

But to tell the truth, even if I distressed you by my letter, I do not
regret it. I did regret it before, and I see that my letter did distress
you, at least for a time; but I am happy now—not because I made
you suffer, but because your suffering led to your repentance. Yours
has been a kind of suffering that God approves, and so you have come
to no kind of harm from us. To suffer in God's way means changing
for the better and leaves no regrets, but to suffer as the world knows
suffering brings death [II Cor. 7:8–11].

The desolation brought by Paul's just reprimands might have
provoked among his correspondents a refusal to recognize their
fault, might have enclosed them within themselves and resulted
in spiritual slavery and death. The Corinthians, on the contrary,
have acknowledged their sin, repented, and have been flooded
with a joy that has reflected back on the apostle. Thus, three
factors stand out as indispensable criteria for discerning the spirit

of God: peace, joy, and freedom of spirit. On the other hand, whatever disturbs true peace, impedes joy, and checks freedom cannot come from God.

Yet a warning must be given at this point. The evil spirit is a liar. He knows how to assume "the appearance of light" and thus counterfeit the good spirit. He speaks of great and holy things, but only to conceal his real intentions. Then he leads man forward, step by step, first to an atmosphere of ambiguity and obscurity and finally to open sin.[23] Therefore, it is of fundamental importance that a Christian should notice how the movements of the spirit develop within him over a period of time. Many things in the beginning seem harmless or even admirable; suddenly they are transformed and a man becomes aware that the devil has made a fool of him. A good start does not guarantee unambiguous growth in the spiritual life.

For Ignatius, in other words, no genuine discernment is possible at a single moment. A succession of experiences which point to a definite goal is necessary, for the forms assumed by joy and sadness are reciprocal. The more the spirit of Jesus reigns in us, the more energy Satan puts into his attack. In other words, the two influences (the spirit of Jesus and the spirit of Satan), which may be difficult to distinguish at the starting point, become increasingly differentiated until they can be recognized quite clearly. The spirit of evil, after all, is capable during a period of desolation of offering false comfort; at such a moment it is impossible to discern the true nature of this consolation. For example, the believer who today listens to the account of the crucifixion can understand clearly that Christ overcame Satan on Golgotha. At the actual time, however, all appearances pointed to the contrary interpretation, since by murdering the Messiah the primitive design of the devil was accomplished.

There is another dimension of the process of discernment which deserves our attention. If we are to make progress in the discovery of God, spiritual intelligence is just as necessary as mortification and surrender to God. As he concluded the parable of the unjust steward, our Lord deplored the fact that "the children of this world are more astute in dealing with their own kind

than are the children of light" (Luke 16:8). In the meditation on
the Two Standards, one of the central meditations of the *Exercises,* Ignatius fills out the description of the tactics of Satan
which he outlines in the Rules for Discernment.[24] The purpose
of this meditation is to reveal how "the enemy of human nature"
concentrates on those who are striving to give themselves wholly
to God. For Ignatius, the decisive remark is that the evil spirit
attracts and tempts men even with things which are themselves
indifferent, that is, in no way sinful. The fact that the meditation mentions possessions and concern about fame is conditioned
by the age in which Ignatius lived and should not be understood
in any exclusive sense. The evil spirit's aim is to limit men's
freedom by holding before them the illusion of greater freedom,
only to lead them gradually to his side.

Although up to now we have discussed the Rules for Discernment as a whole, our comments have focused more on the Rules
for the First Week and the discernment of desolation. The strat-
egy of the evil spirit who attacks under the appearance of good is
also a major theme of the second group of Rules. Here, Ignatius
offers only succinct hints with little development, confining himself to the essential. Yet it is clear that no matter how aware
Ignatius is of the danger to spiritual progress which comes from
Satan, he is far from being afraid of the evil spirit. On the
contrary, Ignatius knows that the devil is ultimately cowardly
and powerless.[25] All his strength derives from human anxiety
and stupidity by which, to borrow Augustine's phrase, "men
enter the realm of the chained dog."

The person for whom Ignatius intends his second set of Rules,
however, is no longer enslaved by the realities and objects of
sense, desired solely in and for themselves. His gaze has been
lifted to the Creator, and his spiritual choices no longer focus
merely on the sinfulness or non-sinfulness of a given course of
action. Such a man has freely admitted that obedience is due to
the Spirit of God. He has, moreover, encountered the person of
Christ and responded to his invitation to build God's kingdom
on earth. Thus to confess Jesus Christ is to conform ourselves to
him, to strive to follow him in order to imitate and love him

better. Undoubtedly we can be mistaken as to our sentiments and intentions if we are satisfied with professing faith in Christ with our lips alone; but if we strive to raise toward him all the powers of our mind, allow ourselves constantly to be drawn by him, our sluggishness of mind and our selfish inclinations will be unmasked. It is in this perspective that Ignatius proposes the second group of Rules for Discernment. Through the gaze we bring to bear on Jesus Christ, a judgment for or against Christ is effected and we have to recognize the conformity or nonconformity of our sentiments with the Word made flesh. To acquire this kind of spiritual intelligence, it is not sufficient to follow the course of our own thoughts. We must refer ourselves to the fullness of light given to us in Jesus Christ and to his spirit who speaks in us, which, more adequately than our own efforts at lucidity, will separate the chaff from the good grain.[26]

As in the first set of Rules, Ignatius points out that it is in our reactions of consolation and desolation that we are able to discern the will of God in our regard: "Meditating on the life of Christ our Lord, let the retreatant consider, when he finds himself in consolation, in what direction God is urging him and similarly when he is in desolation."[27] On closer analysis, however, it would seem that the more difficult aspect of discernment at this stage concerns our experiences of consolation. The interpretation of Ignatius' treatment of consolation has long aroused keen interest among commentators on Jesuit spirituality. Because of the controversies involved, it may prove useful to probe the issues in more detail.[28]

Consolation, as we have seen, can be caused both by the influence of God and by the influence of Satan, although the actual result of such consolation is different depending on the source. The good spirit consoles for the progress of the soul, "that it may advance and rise to what is more perfect" in God's service.[29] The evil spirit, on the other hand, consoles for the contrary purpose, "that afterwards he might draw the soul to his own perverse intentions and wickedness."[30] At the same time, it is characteristic of Satan to assume the appearance of "an angel of light." He begins by suggesting thoughts of his own. He will, for example, suggest holy and pious thoughts that are entirely in conformity with the soul's striving for sanctity; afterwards, he will little by little draw the soul into his own hidden snares and evil designs.[31]

The most unmistakable sign of the spirit of God, however, is that God's action alone "can give consolation to the soul without any previous cause."[32] What Ignatius supposes is that God's grace of consolation as a spiritual reality is experienced as an element in consciousness. But this grace is not so clearly experienced as to enable us, by simple introspection, to identify it as such. How can we single out the impulses which are truly from God? This is the crux of the problem of discernment in the second set of Rules. What Ignatius suggests is that one can find in his own experience a privileged type of consolation which is incontrovertibly divine in origin and which can then be applied as a criterion and prototype of all other movements of God's grace.

Such self-validating consolation can be described in terms of two attributes: the one negative, the other positive. On the negative side, Ignatius describes it as occurring "without any previous perception or knowledge of any subject by which the soul might be led to such a consolation through its own acts of intellect and will." On the positive side, the soul finds itself "wholly drawn to the love of His Divine Majesty."[33]

But these attributes themselves give rise to difficulties. Are we to understand the expression "consolation without any previous cause" as a sudden experience whose divine origin is clear, inasmuch as God alone can act immediately on man's will? Modern depth psychology would consider this a questionable assumption at best, since the effect could just as easily be attributed not to grace but to purely natural causes working through unconscious motivation.[34] There can be little question that the mere suddenness and unexpectedness of an experience of consolation can hardly afford solid evidence of a special intervention of God. When one reviews Ignatius' remarks, however, it becomes clear that the main feature of this consolation is not its negative attribute, its "uncaused" nature, but its positive characteristic—

that the soul finds itself wholly drawn to the love of God. As Ignatius described it in a letter to Sister Teresa Rajadella, whose spiritual director he was: "It frequently happens that our Lord moves and urges the soul to this or that activity. He begins by enlightening the soul; that is to say, by speaking interiorly to it without the din of words, lifting it up wholly to his divine love and ourselves to his meaning without any possibility of resistance upon our part, even should we wish to resist."[35]

When God so takes hold of a soul, "it is inflamed with love of its Creator and Lord, and as a consequence, can love no creature on the face of the earth for its own sake, but only in the Creator of them all."[36] But even this consolation can be realized in various degrees. Short of the level of properly mystical experience, it can happen that finite objects present in our consciousness become almost transparent and practically fade out before the transcendence of God. In such an experience no deception is possible. The content is immediately given. Since nothing finite can make itself present as infinite, the divine origin of the consolation is indubitable.

Since we have arrived at the heart of Ignatian discernment, we must dwell on this topic of consolation a bit longer. It seems necessary to emphasize that the experience of consolation, as we have described it, is a free and gracious self-communication of God and not a Promethean act whereby man effects a confrontation with the divine. There is no such thing as natural mysticism or any kind of psychological projection that can sufficiently explain this type of consolation. Rather, as Rahner has pointed out, the Christian experience of consolation and joy usually comes at moments of self-renunciation, and it attracts the soul to poverty, humility, suffering, and even martyrdom.[37] To find fulfillment in suffering, delight in poverty and humiliation, life in death, is not given to man, at least in the long run, apart from the commitment of faith. The attraction is so patently from above that the believer can only acknowledge it with deepest gratitude. At such a moment the Christian knows that the Holy Spirit himself is at work; he experiences the hour of grace.

But once we have granted that this "uncaused" consolation is self-validating as the gift of God, there still remains the task of applying it to our task of choosing concrete courses of action in everyday life. The basic directive which Ignatius gives to someone attempting to find the will of God in a situation where several alternative choices are possible is that there exists, between the person who is gratuitously drawn in pure openness to God and the possible object of his choice, a basic *affinity*. That is, the "right" decision for a particular individual will be one which leaves intact the consolation of pure union with God, and even intensifies it, rather than one which weakens or destroys it.

Thus, a person's ultimate decision that this particular choice is God's will for me, here and now, depends upon the perdurance of the effects of pure consolation during the entire process of decision-making. This perdurance can be discovered by a process of prolonged experimentation. Ignatius describes one such process in the first part of his *Spiritual Journal,* regarding his deliberations about the poverty to be practiced by the churches operated by Jesuits. Should this poverty exclude all fixed income, not merely for the support of the professed members of the order, but also for the expenses of divine worship in the churches attached to Jesuit houses?[38] For forty days Ignatius himself made use of all the counsels he gives in the *Exercises* for discerning spirits and making a good decision—for finding God's will on some given point. What pervades this whole deliberation is the testing of inner movements which are carefully noted down from the first day. On February 2, for example, he writes of experiencing an abundance of devotion and "tears," all of which incline him more toward possessing "nothing." It is the same on February 3, 4, 5, 6, and 7. Finally, Ignatius offers to God his resolution not to accept any possession for his churches, and notes down in approbation the graces and consolations which he received. In conformity with what he recommends in his Rules for Discernment, he is not content with any kind of indication, but in these experiences he desires to find a good deal of light that this decision is from God. He asks for light earnestly, and urges his mediators (Christ our Lord, the Blessed Virgin, the angels and saints) to intercede that God might confirm his decision with clarity. After he passes through darkness, confusion, and temptation, this supplication comes to an end on March 12 through a last outpouring of light and one irrevocable decision punctuated by the word *Finido* written in bold letters.[39]

Another example from the second part of his diary reveals how the same method of discernment can be applied to smaller matters. On March 14, amid great interior consolation, a thought penetrates Ignatius' soul: "With what reverence and respect he should pronounce the name of God in the Mass." It also occurred to him that he should not desire this consolation itself, but rather the experience of respect and reverence for God which seemed to underlie it. When he yielded to his feeling of respect which, he thought, came not from himself but from God, this only served to increase his devotion and inner joy. Consequently, his conviction grew "that this was the way which the Lord wished to show me, since on the preceding days I perceived that he wished to show me something. So well did I perceive this that in saying Mass I persuaded myself that for the good of my soul, I ought to place a higher value on this grace than on all the others that had preceded it."[40] This gift of infused respect continued through the following days; the words "respect," "reverence," and "humility" recur explicitly every day from March 14 to 17. On March 30 his lights bear upon the element of love contained within this feeling of respect; not from fear but from love should the respect arise.[41] On April 4 he notes that "if one does not obtain this loving respect, he must seek the respect of fear by thinking about his faults, in order to arrive at the loving respect."[42] This last observation was undoubtedly suggested by the fact that on the preceding day, April 3, he did not have any strong feeling of consolation before, during, or after Mass, while on April 4, he could note an abundance of joy, intellectual insight, and interior peace.

This kind of self-analysis and experimentation, however, was not the only method Ignatius proposed for ascertaining God's will in a given course of action. Often enough the compatibility of the object of choice with the soul in its total self-surrender to God will best appear in a kind of "play-acting" in which the person imaginatively places himself within the situation which he is thinking of entering.[43] For example, a man considering the basic vocational choice between marriage and the religious life might imagine himself actually engaged in one or the other state of life in order to judge eventually whether the prospective choice so harmonizes with his own inner religious orientation that he experiences "peace, tranquility, and quiet."[44]

A careful reading of the *Exercises* makes it clear that Ignatius proposes his treatment of discernment—especially the discernment of consolation—within the context of making spiritual choices, that is, of finding and choosing God's will in the concrete situations of everyday life. As Ignatius comments regarding matters about which a choice should be made: ". . . if a choice in matters that are subject to change has not been made sincerely and with due order, then if one desires to bring forth fruit that is worthwhile and most pleasing in the sight of God our Lord, it will be profitable to make a choice in the proper way."[45] For Ignatius, the "proper way" will always involve the use of the Rules of Discernment. But this is not as simple as it might appear.

Once the nature of discernment has been understood, it would seem easy to define spiritual choice as rejection of the spirit of evil and the acceptance of the spirit of good. But in order to grasp the significance of such terms, it is necessary to consider three different occasions for making spiritual choices which Ignatius places at the heart of the *Spiritual Exercises*. In essence, these times of decision correspond to three different levels of man's existence: his direct relation to God, to himself, and to the world. Human liberty, after all, extends far beyond mere deliberation. It shows itself in the results it achieves and the objects it chooses; it operates as a force capable of transforming the world into the image of Jesus Christ. And ultimately it appears as a pure relationship with God who created man's freedom within him. This would seem to be the thinking behind Ignatius' pointed remark about the motives for making spiritual choices: "My first aim should be to seek to serve God, which is the end, *and only after that,* if it be more profitable, to have a benefice or marry, for these are means to the end. Nothing must move me to use such means, or to deprive myself of them, save only the service and praise of God our Lord, and the salvation of my soul."[46]

The first time of choice, as explained by Ignatius, occurs "when God our Lord so moves and attracts the will that a devout soul without hesitation, or the possibility of hesitation, follows what has been manifested to it."[47] The second time is identified as one in which "much light and understanding are derived through experience of desolations and consolations and the discernment of spirits."[48] The third time is "a time of tranquility, that is, a time when the soul is not agitated by different spirits, and has free and peaceful use of its natural powers."[49]

It is clear, upon reflection, not only that these three occasions are specifically different, but that a person in either the first or third situation has little need to employ discernment of spirits. In the first instance, for example, God makes known directly what he wants us to do; we are confronted with a special disclosure whereby God makes known his mind in such a way that the range of alternatives open to us is spontaneously restricted. This disclosure, in practice, comes down to a private revelation, such as we read of in the lives of certain saints (e.g., Catherine of Siena or Margaret Mary), when they were divinely called to various tasks which they could not have discovered without a special revelation. In the third instance, on the other hand, God's will is communicated by the objective order of creation viewed in the light of faith and reason. In other words, as we apply the principles of abstract ethics and the general moral imperatives of the Gospel and the Church to a concrete situation (e.g. whether or not to accept a new job or undertake a particular project), it is possible to ascertain the general will of God in our regard.

For the person who finds himself in the second type of decision-making situation, however, there is no special revelation of God to enlighten him, nor can the general principles of Christian living help him to make a proper decision. Where is he to turn? According to Ignatius, God's will on this occasion must necessarily be grasped through a perception of one's own spiritual orientations, the movements he experiences in his own soul through which God speaks to him as a concrete person by virtue of his own positive individuality. Perhaps an illustration will help to bring out the perplexity of this second time of decision.

In his famous lecture, "Existentialism Is a Humanism," Jean-Paul Sartre attempts to expose the inadequacy of Christian ethics to resolve a decision-making situation when, in our terms, the third time of election is not possible.[50] As an illustration he proposes the case of a pupil of his who, during the Nazi occupation, was anxious to decide whether he ought to leave and join the Free French Forces or stay home with his mother, who very much depended on his presence. Christian doctrine, Sartre remarks, could say nothing to this young man, torn as he was between the conflicting demands of patriotic generosity and filial devotion. No priest could settle the problem, for everything depended on which priest he consulted. In the last analysis, the student would be responsible for the choice of his own counselor, and the counselor's answer would be as arbitrary as the student's own. "I had but one reply to make," says Sartre; "you are free, therefore choose—that is to say, invent. No rule of general morality can show you what you ought to do: no signs are vouchsafed in this world. . . . We ourselves decide our being."[51]

What Sartre here expresses is the feeling that in many of the truly vital decisions of actual life, universal norms, whatever their abstract validity and binding force may be, afford no adequate guidance. Nor can reliance on the advice of others relieve the individual of ultimate responsibility for his own actions. It is, after all, the person himself who decides whether to follow the direction of others and whose directions he shall follow. What Ignatius would say to this man is that his course of action can scarcely be discovered except through a process analogous to the second occasion for making a decision—that is, through the discernment of his own experiences of consolation and desolation as he considers whether staying home or joining the Free French Forces would more promote the service and praise of God. Ignatius' insistence would be, in other words, on the personal and subjective dimension of God's movement within him.

There can be no doubt that Ignatius sees such subjective criteria—for example, personal sensitivity to consolation as well as the interior perception of harmony between one's openness to God and the concrete object of choice—as the principal indices of discernment. But if this subjective experience, made intelligible by discernment, is to be linked with our whole selves, if it is to see the presence of God active in history and in the universe, it must go out from itself. If discernment resulted in pure introspection, the analysis of thoughts and sentiments would inevitably tend to make us forget the world. Since it puts us into relationship with God, we are, from the very center of ourselves, projected outside so that we can no longer be content with a God who can be felt by the heart; rather, we find ourselves turned toward creative interest in others and to the objectivity of our work in the world with a keener penetration and a wider vision.

It is not surprising to find, therefore, that Ignatius associates with these subjective criteria certain objective manifestations such as an increased love of God, love of neighbor, growth in humility and a spirit of penance, as well as an unqualified obedience to the Church. These objective manifestations of God's spirit are important precisely because we can so easily be deceived by our own perception of reality. The tree is judged not merely by the quality of its seed but also by the fruit it bears. If we keep this in mind, much ambiguity as to the direction and value of our thoughts and sentiments may be removed.[52] It will be helpful, then, to reflect briefly on two of these manifestations of the spirit of God: love of neighbor and submission to the Church.

We have already demonstrated that, for Ignatius, joy is the principal sign of the presence of the Spirit within us, because the Spirit is the overflow of God's love come down to us. As the angel announced to Zachary, "Your wife Elizabeth is to bear you a son and you must name him John. He will be your joy and delight and many will rejoice at his birth . . ." (Luke 1:13-14). Later in the Gospel, on the occasion of Jesus' going up to Jerusalem, the same connection is made between the experience of joy and the

presence of the Spirit: "It was then that, filled with joy by the
Holy Spirit, [Jesus] said, 'I bless you, Father, Lord of heaven
and earth . . .' " (Luke 10:21). But what joy does in our hearts to
make known the presence of God's spirit, fraternal charity effects
in a visible fashion. In both instances it is a question of the
upsurging of divine love—always unpredictable and always
awaited—which seeks to show itself in works and manifest God
to the world in a way which men will have to recognize.[53]

The first Epistle of John, implicitly a treatise on the discernment of spirits, often returns to the importance of this love of
neighbor as a manifestation of the action of the Spirit: "Anyone
who claims to be in the light but hates his brother is still in the
dark. But anyone who loves his brother is living in the light and
need not be afraid of stumbling; unlike the man who hates his
brother and is in the darkness, not knowing where he is going,
because it is too dark to see" (I John 2:9-11). The justification of
this principle is simple. "Anyone who fails to love can never have
known God, because God is love" (I John 4:8). True love comes
only from God, and unless a person is continually open to the
loving action of God's Spirit, he simply will not have the power
to love others. Charity is thus a daily finding of the Spirit who
renews himself in us so that the obstacles that separate us from
our fellow men may be surmounted and an understanding created that we could neither imagine nor develop purely on our
own initiative.

As the love of neighbor is spread abroad, it extends to an ever
ascending movement which bears us and our brothers toward our
common origin which is Christ. As Paul reminds us, divine charity which has come down toward us in Christ ascends again with
him toward the Father after having united those who claim the
same faith and the same baptism. If Christ gives us a new commandment whose execution will enable his true disciples to be
recognized, it must group us together in a common confession of
belief and commitment to possess "the mind of Christ" (I Cor.
2:16).

Hence the upsurging of love that unites us with our neighbor
and with Christ also builds up the Church into a harmonious

dwelling. Another objective manifestation of our subordination to the Spirit is thus our obedience to the Church of Christ, in the correspondence of our thoughts and sentiments with what the Church teaches.[54] That is why John writes: "Children, you have already overcome these false prophets, because you are from God and you have in you one who is greater than anyone in this world; as for them, they are of the world, and so they speak the language of the world and the world listens to them. But we are children of God, and those who know God listen to us; those who are not of God refuse to listen to us. This is how we can tell the spirit of truth from the spirit of falsehood" (I John 4:4-6). The Church is the new humanity that restores all men to the Father in Christ. The consolation of the Spirit of God should thus lead us to deeper respect for the law of grace established by the Creator and Redeemer, of which the Church is the chief agent and guide here below. Conversely, desolation corresponds to a resistance, in one way or another, to that force of the Spirit which seeks to establish the universe anew.

The enlargement of this perspective enables us to apply the same principles of discernment to everything which touches our own personal spiritual lives. In regard to penance, for example, Ignatius explains that we can be tempted not to do enough "because we are too much concerned about our bodies and erroneously judge that human nature cannot bear it without becoming seriously ill."[55] But, on the other hand, he also points out that a person should recognize he is practicing excessive penance if "in this abstinence he has not sufficient strength and health or is less disposed for spiritual exercises."[56] The spirit of evil is thus the master in us if we are incapable of submitting ourselves to penance, but this spirit is equally in control if by our penance we disturb an equilibrium that we should respect because it is necessary for action. Therefore, when our body resists penances we want it to undergo, we can ask ourselves if this comes from the fact that we are asking too much of it, or not enough. The fact that we are freer and more active to follow the Spirit of God and discern his will means that we are open to his influence.

Our brief digression on the objective manifestations of the

Spirit has focused on certain aspects of the theological virtues—charity expressed in brotherly love and the acceptance of guidance and salvation from the Church as an extension of Christ's action to our own time and place. But these and all objective signs of the presence of the Spirit are in danger of remaining purely formal and external if they do not lead to dialogue with God. Thus, we return to the major thrust of Ignatius' Rules for Discernment: that the surest way to find God's presence and his will is by the path of interior experience. Through the experience of our own meeting with God and the consolation he brings, we discover the intervention of the Spirit who transforms our existence, slowly opens broader horizons, and awakens us to more receptive understanding.

Before drawing this chapter to a close, it will be helpful to focus attention on one crucial question implicit in our preceding treatment of discernment: Does Ignatius imply, as Sartre's story might suggest, that God's will is actually determined by human choice and can be frustrated because of man's resistance to the Spirit? A strong case can be made to support the view that Ignatius' teaching on discernment, even though he did not consciously formulate the implications of his position, presumes that the problem of finding or determining God's will ultimately depends on a person's sensitivity to the stirrings of God both within himself and within the situations of everyday life. Let us be more specific.

Among the various indications of God's creative will which comprise the raw data of discernment, there is, first of all, the expression of God's will which comes in his sustaining of all the dynamic orientations of a person or group of people at a given time. Every human being is being sustained right now by the creative act of God with the potential, the understanding, the aspirations he finds within himself. All of these elements of human consciousness provide certain indications, certain pointers, which correspond to concrete situations in which we find ourselves—what we might generically call the needs of the situation at a given time.

Recall Sartre's story of the young man torn between the desire to stay with his ailing mother and his conflicting desire to join

the Free French Forces; here we find both the above manifestations of God's will illustrated. The boy's conflicting aspirations
form one source of influence, the specific needs of his mother and
of his country constitute another. Christian revelation provides a
perspective to these moral demands in that it raises kinship loy-
alty and patriotism to the level of filial devotion and fraternal
love as specific means to express love and service of God. Nevertheless, as Sartre rightly observes, Christian rationality alone cannot solve the dilemma. More insight can come from weighing the
specific urgency of each situation. But can it be said with certainty that the greater good demands defense of one's country,
that this single man's contribution to the French resistance
movement is so important that his mother's health and safety
must be forfeited?

Obviously, in addition to the two manifestations of God's will
already mentioned—the person's own desires and the needs of
a given situation—we must add a third, the influence of good
and evil spirits. Admittedly, this is the most nebulous aspect of
all. A Christian trying to discern what really is the most Christian course of action for him to take reflects upon everything that
he knows in the light of the life situation which is his; but in this
reflection he is also moved by the Spirit of Christ. Here we encounter a factor which cannot be completely rationalized; it simply cannot be delineated in the same way as the other elements
operating in a situation. If we follow Ignatius' lead, we look for
an experience of "felt-compatibility" with one course of action or
another which, as one prays and reflects, brings peace—a certain
"felt-ease" with this way of going about things. For Ignatius, in
other words, even after going through all the pros and cons involved in choosing anything, one still must take the matter to
prayer in order to find out whether or not there is peace, whether
or not this action "fits." One can more easily embark on this kind
of creative decision-making, however, and through it determine
the will of God, on the supposition that one has broken away
from a false understanding of some kind of pre-arranged plan
that must be discovered at the pain of perhaps not fitting in with
what is taken to be the will of God.

In this connection, we might consider the question of a priestly or religious vocation. Here, primary weight cannot be given to objective and universal norms which are subject only to the decisions of ecclesiastical authority. While these norms are significant, it is clear that no man is apt for the religious life unless he is called to it by the grace of God. Such a call cannot be simply equated with good health, intelligence, and moral character; still less can it be ascertained by objective psychological questionnaires. The individual vocation can scarcely be determined except through a process of discernment—attention to the personal and subjective dimension of the action of the Spirit. In practical terms, this means that if two men experience God's invitation equally before the same concrete situation and in the face of the same alternative courses of action, and one of them chooses not to follow God's inspiration, the man who rejects the grace did so even though he had the same power to accept it as the other man, and even though he was just as much loved by God as the other man who freely chose to follow a religious vocation.

In both cases, man's freedom and responsibility are manifest. For although God extended an invitation to each man, he did not prevent the one from ultimately refusing him. Certainly such a refusal cannot be equated with "missing one's vocation"; nor can it imply that because of a single missed opportunity, a person's relationship with God will be stigmatized from that moment on. In an extremely restricted sense, of course, the man has passed up a religious vocation. But to suppose that this single decision will "ruin" the rest of his life would be to devaluate God's knowledge and power, to attribute to him a human, piecemeal way of understanding and planning.

But what of the man who seeks to discover God's will (for example, whether to marry, to enter a religious community, to join the Peace Corps, to seek a particular employment) and, even after a long process of honestly attempting to arrive at a decision, is still unable to find any clear manifestation of how he can best serve God? Here, one would have to conclude that, *for this man,* God's will is simply not antecedently determined; it is to be determined by the man's free choice. In this sense, one can agree with Rahner that such a man does not "miss his vocation" and that, for him, the virtue of discernment lies not in the objective course of action chosen, but in the very process of choosing under the desire and the constant orientation he has to discover God's will.[57] For this man, God's will is manifested precisely in the options open to his free decision and not in any one specific alternative.

Because of the emphasis Ignatius places on man's freedom and the necessity of being sensitive to the influence of his spirit, the problem of discernment ultimately comes down to the interpretation of interior spiritual experience. Through this experience the roots of human liberty and the intervention of the Spirit are made clear. It is this Spirit that transforms our dreary existence, slowly opens broader horizons, and awakens us to deeper understanding of ourselves, our neighbors, and the world. Many are the Christians whom sensitivity to the Spirit leads to unexpected changes in their lives, to a deliverance from miseries which they thought they would have to retain until death, and to an inner peace which nothing can disturb. By the process of discernment people come to discover that the dialogue with God is effective. The existence of the Spirit is no longer merely asserted by them in blind faith; it is grasped as a reality, more certain than the things and people that they can feel and touch.

For the man of today, the recognition of the action of the Spirit is a challenging enterprise. At a time when science and technology have desacralized the universe and man no longer sees the world as a mere reflection of God's power, prayer is a most wonderful field of religious experience—we might almost say of experimentation "to know the most holy will of God."[58] Certain lights, certain consolations are there experienced; they seem to fade away and then return to become more definite and imperative. Particular aspects of the life of Christ exercise an ever-growing charm. A person can vary his efforts, the method, or the subject of his prayer. But if the Spirit is guiding him in a particular direction, he ought to yield even to the point of overcoming all hesitation. The will of God then takes on a clarity, all the more indisputable, since the soul will be more interiorly prepared to perceive it. Dryness or repugnances which are experienced in

prayer also have the value of signs, whether they indicate that the
Spirit is not drawing in this direction when the soul remains
desolate, or whether this desolation is a necessary purification or a
specially exacting presence of God.

Within this context, we can understand the high spiritual
value of what Ignatius called "repetition," which consists in re-
using a particular subject for prayer in order to review "those
points in which we have experienced greater consolation or desolation or a greater spiritual appreciation."[59] It is a method of
confronting the Spirit himself, the better to see the goal he proposes to us by his action. Such repetitions of prayer make us
relive the moments of the greatest graces and thereby strengthen
their effect. They will also have the result of gradually simplify-
ing our prayer by making it less discursive; still more, they will
contribute to the revelation of God's activity in us and the influence of his will.

It is even legitimate to say that we have a duty positively to
interrogate the Spirit, to go over again certain subjects of reflection or of prayer, to modify them, to wait for grace to bring
about certain new or already experienced sentiments which
might enlighten us about God's will, which is the object of our
search. "We may," says Ignatius, "present one view to God our
Lord today, and another day, another view; as for example, one
day the precepts, and another the counsels, to observe in which
our Lord gives greater signs of His Divine Will, just as one would
present different dishes to a prince and observe which one it is
that pleases him."[60] Or again, when he invites a man to penance,
Ignatius advises him now to do more, now less, and to await
enlightenment from God, for in these varied experiments God
"often grants each one the grace to understand what is suitable
for him."[61]

For Ignatius, however, it is not only in prayer that one dia-
logues with the Holy Spirit. Every human situation becomes a
spiritual encounter. God's will is manifested much less by imperatives of conduct worked out in advance than by our inner response to his Spirit, the fruit of which is the result both of grace
and human psychology. For this reason, the examination of con-

science made at regular and short intervals becomes a privileged moment of inner docility, a means of encouraging the activity of the Spirit and of insuring our fidelity. The "examen" is more than a private courtroom in which we indict ourselves for our sins and negligences; it is a school for discerning the action of God in our everyday lives. We observe where our thoughts during the day come from, where they lead, what they demand. This understanding of the "examen" goes beyond a mere cataloguing of our failures so as to free us "from all inordinate affection" and selfishness.[62] Rather, it is an exercise of perfect submission to the Spirit.

Connected with the use of discernment in prayer and in the actions of one's everyday life is the relationship of discernment to the practice of religious obedience. While this application of discernment would seem more relevant to those living under a vow of obedience, there are important ramifications here for the general problem of authority, decision-making, and obedience within the Church.[63] Without doubt, the Second Vatican Council has brought about a change in the image of authority in the Church. The Church is no longer conceived simply as a hierarchical institution, but as the people of God in which all—from pope to layman—contribute their part, in their own way, to building up the whole. Certainly the pope still appears as the visible head of the Church. But he appears less as an isolated ruler over against the mass of Christians and more as the head in whom the whole Church expresses itself and makes itself heard. He is the spokesman, together with the body of bishops to whom he is collegially bound, of the entire Church giving expression to the stirring of the Spirit within the Church.[64]

Just as the pope is no longer to be thought of except in relation to the episcopate, so each bishop is no longer confined to his own bishopric, but bears responsibility for the whole Church. By the same token, the Church is also unthinkable without the responsible cooperation of the laity. The Council established theologically that the Holy Spirit works in the whole Church and not just in the hierarchy. The Church thus exists as a community in which the salvific will of God for man becomes manifest and which, as a whole, must feel itself responsible for the salvation of mankind. The Spirit, consequently, can use everyone in the Church for the working out of the mysterious plans of God. Because all can be bearers of the Spirit and can be called to the unfolding of the good news and to the work of saving others, all must be open to the action of the Spirit and co-operate in the process of discerning the direction in which the Spirit is leading.

The decisive emphasis of this new understanding of authority, therefore, is that, first and foremost, the Church in all its members reveals the truth of Christ, makes him known, and mediates his life. Since religious orders are themselves part of the Church, structures of authority and obedience within these groups cannot fail to adopt the Church's changing styles of government.

Outsiders often have the impression that religious enter their orders to obey, to give up their own will, to renounce their freedom. Such an intention would be perverse, for if a man really wanted to renounce his freedom, he would be denying that very capacity for self-determination and responsibility that makes him the person he is. Unfortunately, such a misconception of religious obedience finds all too many examples to support it: The religious is thought of as "the staff in the hand of the old man who wields it" or as "a corpse" which one can push about at will. According to this understanding, the general execution of the religious order's will starts with superiors who, in the manner of a secret political cabinet, seek to legislate for their subjects. Because these commands come from superiors they automatically are viewed as the mysterious biddings of God for our time; by carrying out these commands "blindly" the subject is supposed to feel securely united to the infallible will of God.

But this style of governing belongs to the Church of the past, which was conceived as absolutely centralized, and in which the middle ranks of bishops and priests had little, and the laity nothing at all, to say about it. Historically, of course, people did not bind themselves together in religious groups to obey, but to serve the Church in a special way. As a result of this common desire they worked out possible outlets for their commitment. Later they chose from their group a superior, because a community cannot last without a firm organization. But the superior is not an individual authority set apart from the religious community; he is an expression of the community's concern and responsibility for the service of God and men. For this reason the superior does not lead a life alongside of or over against the community, but in its midst so that he can be a real expression of the action of the Spirit in that community. Apart from this unity of a religious order or from the common process of discernment carried out by the total community, obedience seems as arbitrary as papal directives and magisterial pronouncements which are given without reference to the common beliefs and common life of the Church.[65]

The relationship between superiors and subjects, therefore, is primarily a spiritual relationship, analogous to the union of love between Christ and his Church. In this way, obedience cannot be conceived of merely as a legal relation between a superior who exercises power and his subjects who have to obey. For according to this notion of obedience, the will of the superior has the force of an expression of one man's power and obedience is no more than a response to this expression of power. Such an understanding would assume that no one is responsible except the bearer of authority and that those under him feel no inner obligation to the Church or to the particular work of the Church in which they are engaged.

True obedience, on the other hand, means that a religious order perceives itself as a community which has in its superior a head in whom the common life and salvific will of the whole expresses and proclaims itself through mutual discernment of the action of the Spirit. In a very profound sense, the recovery of this understanding of obedience is the most crucial problem facing religious groups today: How will a community with a common will flourish again in the Church? If here and there, at least, one finds groups who enter into mutual discernment and arrive at this will, then religious orders have a future.

Our treatment of Ignatius' teaching on discernment began with a summary of the tradition which he inherited and then attempted to explicitate his analysis of the movements of the good and evil spirits, to show the ways in which they influence our experiences of desolation and consolation, and to indicate certain objective manifestations of the Spirit of God in our religious attitudes and everyday life. We also probed the more involved questions of the meaning of Ignatius' understanding of consolation as well as the related issues of spiritual choice, the importance of personal spiritual experience, and certain applications of discernment.

The man who submits to the pedagogy of discernment will, as we have seen, pay very close attention to the touches of God within him, more or less repeated, more or less certain, more or less decisive. He will be neither surprised nor disturbed at them. Experiencing feelings that he knows come from God, he will slowly familiarize himself with this kind of interior reality. He will learn to recognize them in himself. In his activity as well as in his prayer he will be open to these different movements of fear or love, humanity or confidence, ardor or peace. Little by little his fidelity will turn into submission as he increases in wonder and love for the Spirit who, living in him, communicates the infinite riches of God himself.

Because of the subtlety and complexity of interpreting these actions of the Spirit and because of the ever present danger of self-deception, discernment is best carried out in dialogue with a spiritual counselor who enters into the process and brings to it more objectivity than a person himself can often muster. It is especially through this kind of personal relationship between the director and the individual that emotional balance, acceptance of oneself, trust in others, and true freedom and openness to the Spirit can be achieved and deepened.

It is thus that the spiritual man is, in his spiritual effort itself, a living being who participates in the fullness of God. His inner life has no false stability which becomes fixed and hardened like death. His life is rather an extremely varied history, marked by divine encounters which he himself cannot regulate. To one who has begun to experience such effects of the Spirit, a strained and mercenary generosity is no longer sufficient. Being at home with God's action within him, he submits in happy attention to the movements which transform his prayer into a real dialogue and his activity into an alert service where toil is absorbed in love.[66]

To respond to God in this way is first to allow him to love us freely as he understands it, without setting before him objections about our limitations and helplessness. If God loves us, it means that he chooses us although he knows us, that he prefers us such as we are and not such as we might be. So to accept God's will which offers itself to us today amounts to allowing ourselves to be chosen by him, and allowing him to choose in us what he wants us to effect. We shall do his work in truth when we content ourselves with allowing his love to indicate the direction we should take and to give us the strength to go forward. Such an attitude is both utterly passive and completely active. It is the utter passivity of the soul who is the "bride." But it is also the supreme activity of renouncing all selfish initiative in order to accept only those impulses which come from Christ. In this abandonment and commitment there is more strength, more passion, more courage and determination than in heroism, for we have renounced all attempts to obtain salvation by our own efforts.

In the end, then, discernment of spirits is intrinsically linked to the kind of spiritual orientation we described in the preceding chapter. To seek God in all things is to seek his will. To love him in everything is to do his will. As Teilhard has written, "God is as out-stretched and tangible as the atmosphere in which we are bathed. He encompasses us on all sides, like the world itself. What prevents you, then, from enfolding Him in your arms? Only one thing: your inability to see Him."[67]

Chapter IX

SPIRIT VERSUS TRADITION

A Case Study in
the Development of Spirituality

OUR PRECEDING REFLECTIONS on the history of Christian spirituality have led us to trace the development of asceticism from its formal beginning in the deserts of the East, through the evolution of Western monasticism and the inauguration of an urban spirituality by the friars of the Middle Ages, to the complete break with monastic tradition carried forward by Ignatius Loyola. We now turn our attention to a subject as intriguing to the student of spirituality as it is demanding of discretion and responsibility on the part of the narrator—the problem of the *internal* history of spirituality within the various styles of asceticism we have considered so far. For whether our preference lies with the ideals of the desert, Benedictine monasticism, the mendicant friars, or with Ignatius' "seeking God in all things," the problem of separating the spirit of the founders from the traditions which developed after their deaths becomes central. As the problem takes shape, it often points to a critical confrontation between two or more important personalities in the history of a religious group; and even in the present "historical era" there are few who know how to distinguish between a historical question of fact and a personal judgment of value. One has only to recall the distinctively different approaches of Pachomius and Cassian, Benedict and Bernard, Francis of Assisi and Brother Elias, Ignatius and the second and third generations of Jesuits represented by Francis Borgia and Claude Aquaviva, to understand that questions about the authentic spirit of religious founders and the authentic transmission of that spirit in the religious groups they organized are far from academic.

This is neither the time nor the place to enter into lengthy discourse on the manifold and far-reaching implications of religious renewal considered as a speculative theological issue. Indeed one of the central aims of the present book is to chart some of the historical factors which contribute to our current attempts to delineate a spirituality for our time. In this search for renewal, however, it is not too far from the mark to suggest that the problem of authenticity is crucial. Somehow or other we must bring ourselves up to date without losing our heritage from the past; we must adapt without sacrificing those essential elements in the tradition of Christian spirituality which give us our identity. This is a difficult and delicate task and we have no special preliminary assurance that we shall be successful at it. Quite frankly, we need all the help we can get from whatever sources are available.

In light of this pressing concern over the fundamental spirit of the great innovators and the authentic transmission of that spirit to their followers and through them to us, we propose to examine the early history of Jesuit spirituality in some detail.[1] We turn to this investigation not as an exercise in spiritual propaganda, nor for edification and exhortation, but in order to help us understand the problem of authenticity as it emerges in the history of a single religious group. The reasons which prompted our selection of Jesuit spirituality should be clear: understandably, the authors are more familiar with the Jesuit tradition than with any other; furthermore, Ignatius' *Constitutions* have formed the backbone of many subsequent religious congregations as well as the inspiration of a large number of those chiefly concerned with developing a spirituality for laymen.

We have already seen that Ignatian spirituality is characterized, in the first instance, by an interior disposition of soul by
which one's union with Christ—and responsiveness to his Spirit
—is oriented toward action undertaken for God's greater glory.
This union with God in all things finds its concrete manifestation in an unflagging allegiance to God's will as this is determined through the discernment of spirits; by embracing God's
will the Ignatian man is thus committed to serve "the Eternal
Lord of all things." From the opening consideration of the *Exercises* to its conclusion, the question of union with God and
commitment to his service remains a central leitmotiv. It is the
teaching of the "Principle and Foundation" that man is created
to "praise, reverence, and serve God." The meditation on the
"Triple Sin" poses the challenging questions: "What have I done
for Christ? What am I doing for Christ? What ought I to do for
Christ?" In considering one's basic spiritual decisions, "the first
aim should be to seek to serve God"; and in the "Contemplation
to Obtain the Love of God" the retreatant is reminded in clear
terms that "love is shown more in deeds than in words." What
Ignatius has done, then, is to identify finding God in all things
with finding how, in all things, one might *serve* Christ. What
stands out in full light in the whole of his spirituality is "the
thought of a distinguished and enthusiastic service, the thought of
the will of God to be fulfilled on a grand and magnificent scale."[2]

As a religious institution, the Society of Jesus incorporated this
service theme of Ignatius. Significantly, the first "Formula of the
Institute" of the Society, written by Ignatius in 1539, begins with
the words: "Whoever wishes to serve under the standard of the
cross in our Society, which we wish to bear the honored name of
Jesus, and to serve our sole Lord and the Roman Pontiff his
Vicar on earth. . . ."[3] God is thus served by fulfilling his will,
which is most surely discovered in and through the Church. By
adhering to the Church, Ignatius' Society would adhere to Christ,
and by doing the will of Christ in this world it would do the will
of the Father in heaven. The service which the Society would
render was concrete, specific work on behalf of Christ and his
Church. Thus, Pope Paul III in his bull of recognition, *Regimini*

militantis ecclesiae (September 27, 1540), remarks that Ignatius and his companions have banded together "to dedicate their lives to the perpetual service of our Lord Jesus Christ, to our service, and to that of our successors."[4]

Looked at from this point of view, the character of the Society of Jesus becomes clearer. Since Ignatius conceived the Society as an instrument of service, the *Constitutions* were drawn up in such a way that the structure of the new group would be flexible, mobile, and adaptable to any kind of work which the crisis of the times demanded. Obviously, the monastic props of stability and self-sufficiency were eliminated from his arrangement of things. The *Constitutions,* therefore, prescribed neither the recitation of the canonical hours in choir, the imposition of regular and obligatory bodily penances, the acceptance of ecclesiastical dignities, religious exercises in common, nor government by monastic chapter. The members of the Order were to conform in the external manner of their lives to the local diocesan clergy. They wore no distinctive habit, nor were they required to spend their lives in one residence. Both in principle and practice the break with the past was sharp and decisive. So novel was Ignatius' conception of the Society, in fact, that some ecclesiastics of the day refused to recognize it as an authentic religious order.[5]

Such movement away from the old traditions of religious life also meant a break with traditional forms of prayer. The vision which Ignatius wished to impart to his followers was to see God in all things. This practical attitude, as we have seen, embraced an entire theory, not of presumptuous mystical aspirations, but of simple faith and awe before the omnipresence of the "divine majesty." Considering that in his discussion of prayer Ignatius' imaginative creativity is most striking, it is indeed ironic that this very aspect of his teaching was one of the first to be modified by subsequent generations of Jesuits. Before discussing these later changes in the Ignatian spirit, however, it will be helpful to narrate in some detail Ignatius' own teaching on prayer.

The first instruction on prayer which Ignatius intended for all those who wished to enter his Society was to be given during the Spiritual Exercises, which each candidate made for a period of

thirty days (more or less). Here the man was carefully instructed
in a systematic approach to the spiritual life which included
meditation and contemplation as forms of mental prayer. He also
came to know other methods of prayer which had their own
functions in the spiritual life, such as vocal prayer and the
thoughtful reading of Scripture. Actually, the mental prayer
which the *Exercises* taught was never intended by Ignatius to be
a permanent, universal pattern for all his followers. As an instrument of initial conversion, it formed a beginning for one's life in
the Society, not a fixed program of prayer. In the mind of Ignatius, in fact, there was to be no general obligation to meditate
daily according to the method of the *Exercises* or any other
method. No specific type of prayer was either prescribed by Ignatius himself nor introduced into the Order during the first thirty
years of its existence, for such regulations would have meant
erecting barriers to the natural dispositions of the individual and
to the influence of divine grace. As a master of the spiritual life,
comments historian Robert McNally, "Ignatius stands not on the
side of rigid system, regulation and law, but rather on the side of
the human person and his individual liberty, the peculiar needs
of his heart and mind and body."[6]

Ignatius thus looked on prayer as a species of life, something
organic that must be nurtured carefully under the inspiration of
grace and its own inner laws.[7] It was not a mental exercise to be
pursued mechanically according to some set form. Every individual's prayer-experience was unique, and the history of his growth
in continuous prayer was different from everyone else's. Thus
Nadal wrote of Ignatius: "In contemplation he found God as
often as he devoted himself to prayer; nor did he think that a
definite rule or order was to be followed, but prayer was to be
made in various ways; and in meditation God was to be sought
now one way, now another."[8] In another place he writes:

Let Superiors and spiritual fathers use this moderation with which, we
know, Father Ignatius was quite familiar, and which, we believe, is
proper to the Society, that if they know that one is making progress in
prayer with good spirit in the Lord, they do not prescribe anything for

him, nor interfere with him, but rather strengthen and animate him that he might advance in the Lord gently but securely.[9]

Such statements from Nadal as well as from Ignatius could easily be multiplied. Nowhere do we find a passage which changes the meaning and spirit of the above texts. In Ignatius' concept of the spiritual life, prayer was not an end but a means to developing the perfect servant of God. It is only logical, then, that prayer and contemplation, since they are means, should only be employed according to the needs of each one.[10] Religious idealist that he was, Ignatius could bequeath to his followers only the highest norms.

In the text of the *Constitutions* we find the fundamental flexibility of Ignatius' teaching on prayer developed in more detail. He begins with the principle that no single spiritual program is obligatory on all. For Jesuits who have finished their period of formation he judges that

. . . since it is certainly expected that these will so advance in the way of Christ our Lord that they will be able to race along it, to the extent that physical health, and the external works of charity and obedience will permit, it does not seem in those things which pertain to prayer, meditation and study, nor in the bodily exercise of fasting, vigils, and other practices, which concern the austere chastisement of the body, that any rule is to be set down save that which discreet charity will compose for each, provided that the confessor shall be consulted and, where there is doubt as to what is best, the matter be referred to the Superior.[11]

The thought contained in this quotation is based on three presuppositions: that the experience of the Spiritual Exercises which initiated the Jesuit's religious life terminated in a reformation, a conversion, and a commitment to the service of Christ; that this experience deepened through the Jesuit's formation and training; and that the formed Jesuit is a spiritual man engaged in an active apostolic life. The last point is crucial. For Ignatius, the weakening of bodily strength and the lessening of the works of charity and obedience which result from involvement in arduous ascetical practices and long prayer, distract from that service to which the Society is committed. Thus, the prayer life of the formed Jesuit must be realistically conceived in terms of his apostolate. Because the Jesuit is a "spiritual man," no specific norms are to be set down regarding his practices of prayer and asceticism.

To repeat, such teaching is intelligible only because Ignatius conceived prayer as a means for the service of souls.[12] In the basic provisions regarding the prayer life of the Society which Nadal as Ignatius' legate drew up for Jesuits in Spain we read: "All must make this the goal of their prayer and spiritual life in the Lord: to find God in all their apostolic endeavors and occupations, taking the way of the spirit only, accustoming themselves to activate the spirit and devotion in all tasks, and making use of the afterglow of meditation and its habitual attitude—as much as the weakness of our nature will allow. . . . The Society regards it as an imperfection to have to withdraw much in order to pray."[13] Most characteristic of all, however, is Ignatius' own statement: "If he [Ignatius] had his way, all his spiritual sons would be like the angels, who no longer have any concern for themselves, but ever keeping God in mind, are totally preoccupied with the salvation of men."[14]

How Ignatius interpreted his fundamental prayer principle in practice is clarified by the fact that no letter of his is known in which he recommends long prayer. On the contrary, many of his letters set limits to extended prayer and point in the direction where prayer and work become one. In all this, of course, the *spirit* of prayer was taken for granted. Actually Ignatius faced a zeal on the part of his followers that needed restraining rather than encouragement. Thus, he instructed the scholastics at Alcala to cut their time of prayer in half. He urgently pleaded with Francis Borgia to do the same. The Spanish provincial Antonio Araoz had to reduce his prayer time by two thirds. When, as early as 1549 (i.e., nine years after the Order's founding), some Jesuits alleged that a reform was necessary and insisted that it was to be effected by means of longer periods of prayer, Ignatius treated the suggestion with stern coolness.[15]

For Jesuits in training, however, Ignatius set down more detailed specifications; in addition to daily Mass, a total of one hour of prayer was required of which the first part was to be given to vocal or mental prayer in the morning, the second part to two examinations of conscience.[16] The first half hour was generally devoted to the Little Office of the Blessed Virgin or other vocal prayer (for example, the breviary or rosary) or, at the discretion of one's spiritual director, to mental prayer if a scholastic or brother showed the proper maturity for it.[17] Beyond these requirements, no visits to chapel in common, no litanies or other periods of prayer in common were allowed—any more than the chanting of the office in choir.[18]

But would not the life of prayer suffer under such conditions? Ignatius' justification was clear and direct:

Over and above the spiritual exercises assigned, they [the scholastics] should exercise themselves in seeking out the Lord's presence in all things, . . . since it is true that His Divine Majesty is in all things by His presence, power, and essence. And this kind of meditation which finds God our Lord in all things is easier than raising oneself to the consideration of divine truths which are more abstract and demand something of an effort, if we are to keep our attention on them. But this method is an excellent exercise to prepare us for great visitations of our Lord even in prayers that are rather short. Besides this, the scholastics can frequently offer to God our Lord their studies and the efforts they demand, seeing that they have undertaken them for His love to the sacrifice of their personal tastes, so that to some extent at least we may be of service to His majesty and of help to the souls for whom He died.[19]

Comparing this quotation with others already cited, we see how entirely consistent was Ignatius' understanding of the length and method of prayer, as well as of the nature of apostolic work and study. For Ignatius, work and study were not merely exterior tasks. They presupposed charity, obedience, and selflessness in those so engaged. But besides these personal qualities, work and study were also sacramental in character; they provided points of encounter with God and possessed a mysticism all their own. The encounter with God in prayer stretched beyond the limits of formal meditation into the concrete realities of everyday life. The totality of human activity thus became a discovery, rooted in charity and obedience, of God in all things. So much for Ignatius' ideas on prayer.

We come now to the subsequent development of his teaching within the history of the Society of Jesus. To some extent changes were inevitable. For if it is true that, as the Order grew in numbers, some of the members found Ignatius speaking a bit over their heads, then at least when the training of young religious did not coincide with his ideas, certain adjustments were bound to take place. What direction these modifications took is clear; who was responsible for them is, in the end, unimportant.

The beginnings of what was eventually to constitute a shift in course reach back to the time of Ignatius himself.[20] Many members of the Order in Spain, especially those belonging to the spiritual circle of Gandia, felt ill at ease with Ignatius' interpretation of the apostolate and ·its relation to formal prayer; they admitted a certain uneasiness in defending the religious style of their founder against the reproaches of older religious orders.[21] Such reactions were perfectly intelligible in the Spanish environment of the Protestant Reformation and Catholic Reform, where religious life flowered with an almost unmatched brilliance, and the propensity for long prayer was especially pronounced. Most of the older orders had devised elaborate programs of prayer and penance which concretely expressed their inner fervor and devotion. Few of the early Jesuits in Spain could escape these influences. As members of a new order whose rule refrained from prescribing either a fixed quantity or method of prayer, obligatory penances, or communal religious duties, they naturally felt inferior in the face of the asceticism of the day. More than once, even while Ignatius was in charge of the order, the Spanish provinces moved in the direction of obligatory penance and prayer for their members.

When in 1554 Nadal visited these houses to introduce and explain the order's *Constitutions,* the Spaniards found him not entirely unsympathetic toward their views. When Nadal returned to Rome, he even argued their position with Ignatius in order to gain some concessions at least for those who had already undertaken additional prayer and penance. As Nadal himself recounts: "The vehemence with which I argued the case displeased Ignatius; yet at the moment he said nothing. The next day, however, he sharply rebuked me in the presence of the most respected fathers, and from then on he did not make much use of my services."[22] "Never," said Ignatius, "will anyone dissuade me from holding that one hour of daily prayer is sufficient for someone in studies, provided he practice abnegation and self-discipline; for such a man prays more in a quarter hour than a selfish, undisciplined person in two hours. Still, when anyone experiences desolation or is undergoing some interior crisis, he can be permitted longer periods for a while."[23] According to Gonçalves de Camara, who was present at this encounter between Ignatius and Nadal, Ignatius betrayed "both in his facial expression and in his speech such resentment and unusual agitation that I was amazed. . . . His concluding remark was: 'A truly self-disciplined man needs only a quarter hour of prayer to be united with God.' "[24]

At the same time that the Spanish Jesuits were feeling the pressure for increased prayer from their religious contemporaries, another tendency was developing among the rank and file of the order. Already the fervor of the first days of the foundation had cooled, yielding to religious tepidity. The primitive spirit of the Society—its charity and spirit of prayer—seemed to be disappearing.[25] As time passed, the need of renewal and renovation grew stronger. From the generalate of Francis Borgia (1565-72) until the death of Claude Aquaviva (1615), the Society's administrators were continuously occupied with discovering ways of restoring on all levels the pristine spirit of the first days. Highest on the list of priorities for renewal was the prayer life of the order. Ultimately, the Society found its method of reform not so much in implementing the *Constitutions* of Ignatius as in supplementing and revising them.

Ignatius died in 1556. The First General Congregation of the order convened shortly thereafter, and with it came the first

formal attempt to regularize Jesuit prayer. To those who proposed such a change the Congregation's answer was decisive: the
Constitutions are to be preserved and no determination is to be
added which is not already found in them.[26] But the Spanish
provinces were not to be put off so easily. Despite the explicit
decree of the Congregation, they retained a continuous hour of
obligatory prayer—a situation for which Francis Borgia was responsible.[27] Consequently, by the time of the Second General
Congregation, which was to elect Borgia third general of the
order, the fathers had to deal with a custom contrary to the
Constitutions within the most powerful provinces of the Society.

Given such a situation, there was an understandable sense of
urgent expectancy regarding the position this Congregation
would take. Borgia was elected general on July 2, 1565, and it
did not take long for the controversial question to come up.
Several days' discussion elapsed before the assembled fathers
could agree that the general, prudently using the power they had
entrusted to him, might increase the time of prayer, "after taking
into account persons and nations."[28]

The care for the minority—specifically the north European
provinces—evidenced by this last qualification seems never to
have been taken seriously. In cold fact, the majority had succeeded in changing the position of the Society on the question of
prayer. The shift was due not so much to the direct influence of
ideas and movements outside the order, although some fathers
did appeal to such reasons. Nor was the change due only to the
fact that the training of young religious in the order's largest
provinces had taken place under Borgia's influence and had been
partially controlled by persons who considered Ignatian spirituality simply as a new patch on an old monk's-habit.[29] For even
those who lived according to the original spirit of Ignatius had
tended to lose some of their assurance in the face of the actual
situation. In the end, "the superiors of the Society believed they
noted more and more how the ideal—so dear to Ignatius—of
continual union with God and of purity of intention which he
expected his sons to realize in all their activity was hard to attain
for the vast majority, unless the spirit renewed itself day after

day in long periods of meditation."[30] It took Borgia only one month after the close of the Congregation to use his new power to issue a set of regulations for prayer to the whole Society; he required all Jesuits to make one hour of prayer each day.

The difference between Borgia's new regulation and the original tradition of the *Constitutions* lay not so much in a prolongation of the time to be given to prayer, as in the uniformity of the obligation imposed on all—even the formed Jesuit. With this move a fundamental Ignatian principle was abandoned and the way opened to further regulations for the spiritual life. In contrast to this basic reorientation, the change regarding the time for prayer seems slight. The half hour of morning prayer was lengthened to one hour over and above Mass and the examination of conscience. Outside Spain, however, this hour did not have to be continuous. In Italy, France, and Germany, one quarter of the hour was at first shifted to the evening and added to the examination of conscience. But when the forthright German Jesuits admitted that they usually fell asleep during this period, the general took this opportunity to enforce the continuous hour of morning prayer that had, in the meantime, been introduced in Rome and elsewhere.[31] The original Ignatian tradition actually remained most alive in the Rhineland Provinces, which submitted a petition for the "restoration of the *Constitutions*" in the next two General Congregations (1573 and 1582), but with no success.[32]

In 1581, the Fourth General Congregation elected a thirty-eight-year-old Neapolitan, Claude Aquaviva, fifth general of the Society. Aquaviva's generalate lasted thirty-four years—the longest in the history of the order—and was marked by a concentrated effort to renovate and restore its depleted spirit. Following Borgia's lead this Congregation made it a matter of law that every member, both scholastic and formed Jesuit, make one hour of prayer every day in addition to the two examens of conscience and attendance at Mass. Although the decree did not say that the hour had to be in the morning, that it had to be continuous, or that it had to be a particular kind of prayer (mental or vocal), the writings of Aquaviva clearly conceive it as a continuous hour of mental prayer (meditation). As with Borgia, the historical climate of the period is also important for understanding Aquaviva's emphasis. This was the time when Teresa of Avila and John of the Cross were instructing their spiritual charges in meditative prayer and the stages of mysticism, and when Charles Borromeo was urging the same form of prayer on his priests. Nevertheless, the impact of Aquaviva's writings can be assessed by the fact that even to this day the hour of morning "meditation" is considered by many to be not only an authentic tradition of Ignatius, but almost a measuring rod of Jesuit asceticism.

In summary, then, a review of the developments in the prayer legislation of the Society of Jesus in its early history indicates the following: (1) the distinction which Ignatius drew between religious in training and formed religious was put aside and the same norm was now introduced for all; (2) the half hour of prayer in the morning was extended to a full hour and, through other additions, the time for prayer in general was almost doubled; (3) at least implicitly, a full, continuous hour of mental prayer became the rule; furthermore, because of Borgia and Aquaviva's predilection for meditation, the way was prepared for the priority, even the supremacy, of this method of prayer.

The preceding description of the developments in the early prayer tradition in the Society raises the perplexing question of how this historical data is to be interpreted. At the outset it would seem entirely justifiable to say that, as the order expanded, a certain regularizing of the practices of the first Jesuit generation was desirable and even necessary if the Society was to function as a coherent totality. Clearly, the conditions which underlay Ignatius' rule for the Society's prayer no longer obtained. Ignatius' view of the spiritual life had been extraordinarily high, perhaps too idealistic for the general run of mankind; the basic principles which he taught were meant for a chosen elite. Yet, by Borgia's time the requirements for admission into the order had been lowered to meet the needs of a growing number of colleges administered by the Society, and as the training of young Jesuits was less resolutely oriented in the directions indicated by Ignatius, the greater was the number for whom Ignatius' idealism—if they knew it at all—seemed unattainable. It can be freely granted, then, that both Borgia and Aquaviva, as well as the Second and Forth Congregations, faced serious problems which they felt could only be solved, or at least mitigated, by the ascetical prescriptions they provided. Moreover, these men had full authority to act; their decrees in the matter of prayer are part of the law of the order to be observed by all its members.

But a further question can be posed with regard to Ignatius' *Constitutions* and their historical development. Even when one grants that the enactments of Borgia and Aquaviva served to shift the basic direction of Ignatius' teaching on prayer, should one also concede that the changes introduced were actually a providential and therefore authentic and irrevocable development of Ignatius' original spirit? In other words, are we so to insert the idea of divine providence into our story that Borgia and Aquaviva, as well as the Second and Fourth Congregations, become agents of divine providence more important than Ignatius himself? The question, obviously, is a crucial one, and its ramifications extend far beyond the case study we have been considering. For if the particular style of evolution which the Society of Jesus underwent during these years was so definitive, then the Jesuit today cannot appeal over it to the founder's original conception or to the guidance of the Spirit in our own time. Indeed, then any particular form which the general development of spirituality takes could be made irreversible by attaching the "providential" label to it.

For the historian, however, the use of the concept of providence as an explanatory category is an intrusion; it constitutes a kind of *deus ex machina* since it both removes the concept or practice under discussion from control by historical method and effectively insulates it from any criticism or revision.[33] It is indeed difficult to see why the historian of spirituality can be allowed to use this notion of providence when his colleagues in biblical exegesis and Church history have long ago been forced to abdicate whatever prerogatives they may once have claimed for it in their explanations of scriptural inspiration or the history of the papacy. It is simply not accurate to imply, as some have done,

that the developments in the Jesuit order from Ignatius to
Aquaviva are similar to the development from Ignatius' rude
days at Manresa to the full flowering of his spirituality in Rome;
nor is it justified to equate the development of Jesuit spirituality
with the evolution of the apostolic Christianity of the first century to the grand Catholicism of the fourth and fifth. The development of spiritual tradition should never be automatically
treated as a sacred principle. As the theologian Henri de Lubac
has remarked, "To call purely human things divine is even more
blasphemous than to utter a cry of revolt against One who is
falsely alleged to be their eternal warrant."[34] Such an appeal to
Providence, therefore, can be criticized on many grounds.

Of course one might also explain what happened under Borgia
and Aquaviva simply as the routinization of Ignatius' original
spirit; but probably the truth lies somewhere between the two
extremes of "providential" and "routinized." One can accept, in
other words, the development which took place in Jesuit history
as practically inevitable under the influence of historical circumstances without necessarily claiming that it was irreversible. It is
hardly open to question that a certain regularization of a religious charism will always be needed in a large and diversified
group; but it is also indisputable that this regularizing can take
different forms and be subject to rather penetrating revision
from time to time. A tradition may be authentically united to its
original spirit, but at the same time authentically manifold in
its articulation in history. For this reason it is important to discuss, as we have done, some of the particular intellectual, cultural, and religious currents which prevailed during this period
in Jesuit history. Not to do so would be to leave the impression
that the patterns of thought and feeling of the Counter Reformation, the Baroque Era, and the flowering of Spanish mysticism
swept by the Jesuits without influencing the seemingly homogeneous flow of their traditions.

Thus in reflecting on the Society of Jesus, or the history of any
religious group, it is rather disconcerting to find interpreters apparently assuming that, because the Spirit is always offering his
guidance to the Church and its leaders and because the Jesuit

superiors were sincere and prayerful men, trained in the Jesuit tradition, they were by these very facts successful in capturing Ignatius' meaning and in translating it into forms which presumably explored all its potentialities. Subsequent religious leaders are products of their own times, formed by a very definite milieu; this seemingly obvious fact poses for them, as for those who inherit their insights and formulations, an interpretative problem of the first magnitude.

But if the original significance of the great spiritual innovators is not to be determined from the later practices of their followers, neither is it to be restricted by ancient traditions. Our concern in this chapter, therefore, with "Ignatian" in contrast to "Jesuit" spirituality is not born out of an artificial antiquarianism. Rather, it is motivated by the conviction that in the course of history brilliant and original insights are often lost under the pressure of momentary need and kept hidden by the weight of tradition. Ignatius' teaching on prayer, at least in what touches on the regularization of its quantity and method, is one of those forgotten insights which is only recently being recovered and implemented. There is no question, then, of forsaking a tradition, but of rediscovering the original spirit which inspired the tradition.

In setting down his principles on prayer, Ignatius showed a remarkable boldness of judgment and liberality. But with respect to the quantity and method of prayer prescribed for the whole Society, Ignatius had already explicitly precluded any change in the text of the *Constitutions*. On the other hand, he respected the individual religious and his needs to the extent that he did not wish to exclude the possibility of changing general norms in favor of particular needs, even to the extent of allowing this or that one more time if it should be needed. But the sources do not show that Ignatius intended or would have approved a basic displacement of the spiritual program which he outlined in the *Constitutions*.[35]

What, then, are we to understand by "tradition" in spirituality? How are we to judge it? In order to put this admittedly complex question in perspective, it will be helpful to review some of the themes implicit in the previous chapter on discernment of spirits. God's revelation to us, like all personal revelation, is a self-disclosure, and belongs necessarily to the present—any present moment.[36] The primary revelation of God to the world is the self-disclosure that he makes in and to his Word become flesh, Jesus Christ. The fullness of this communication is achieved in Christ's resurrection; thus any further revelation occurs through contact with the risen Christ as he shares with us the fullness of his Father's communication, which he himself received.

But Christ reveals himself and his Father to us primarily by sending the Holy Spirit. The Spirit is sent to each individual man; but it is sent in a privileged way to the community of believers, especially the Church and its leaders. The Spirit is also sent to men outside the Church, because the influence of Christ cannot be narrowed to include only those of us in visible communication with him. Consequently, if we remember the full range of ways in which we must discern the Spirit—as he touches each of us personally, as he reaches us through both the hierarchical and charismatic Church, as he is at work in the whole world of men—then the ultimate norm of any tradition in the Church is the self-revelation of God in Christ, given through the Spirit, as we can discern it at any given moment.

Basically, this norm is the Gospel—God's own Word to us. But here we must distinguish between revelation as the primordial utterance of God and the tradition which hands on that revelation (and in the process necessarily interprets it). If we use the word *Gospel* as we usually do, to mean the written word of the New Testament, then the Gospel is indeed a privileged norm: it is the result of Christ's first communion with his Church; and since God does not deceive, any further revelation of the Spirit must be consistent with its beginning. The Gospel thus understood, however, is not revelation properly so called, but tradition—the attempt to capture and interpret the original revelation which God made in Jesus of Nazareth. And since Scripture is not itself revelation, it neither could be written nor can be read without the guidance of the Spirit. The action of the Spirit is thus the source of whatever continuity exists between the development of tradition and God's original revelation.[37] In this sense, the Gospel always stands in second place to the recognition of the Spirit's action in the world at any given point in time.

Now if this is true of the interpretation of Scripture, which is necessarily part of the Church, it is all the more true of the interpretation of any tradition in spirituality inherited from the past. To return for a moment to our case study, the tradition of the Society of Jesus is thus a contingent thing which must necessarily prove itself by its consonance with the Spirit-directed experience of Jesuits at any given time in the Church's life, by its consonance with their understanding of Scripture, and by its consonance with the originating vision of Ignatius.

But tradition is, or should be, also a living thing. It is dynamic because it does not exist without antecedents which it in turn interprets for a particular culture and ethos. Tradition is also a vital process, since it exists in a world created by man and is itself created by man in his world which has been modified by divine initiative. Because tradition inevitably grows, it tends to become sophisticated and complex. Consequently, it needs perpetual examination and constant rethinking—a task which is made more difficult since we ourselves are part of tradition and hence we ourselves are questioned.

The tradition of spirituality thus changes as it grows. The norm of its change should be our growing awareness of what the Spirit is effecting in our world and our growing appreciation of the Gospel. If we find something in the tradition of spirituality that is contrary to either of these two more fundamental criteria, it should go. If a specific religious order were to discover that it was changing so much that it would no longer be what it traditionally had been understood to be, this would be a sign that such a group should disappear. Usually, however, the traditions of the larger religious orders present their own special problems in that their development has not been unambiguous. In terms of our preceding discussion, we can readily concede that the Borgia-to-Aquaviva tradition differs in important respects from that of Ignatius; the same conclusion can be drawn just as easily for the Benedictines and Franciscans. But these particular problems are not insoluble. It is, after all, the Ignatian tradition, as well as the tradition of Benedict and Francis, that is the object of the Church's praise and approval—not subsequent "traditions."

Any group, especially any large group, has incumbent upon it the constant re-examination of its own traditions; the first task, of course, is to establish the genuine tradition of the founder. But having found this original spirit we must test it against the action of the Spirit in today's world and against the Gospel. Certainly there can be no debate as to which criterion of authenticity has priority. What must be debated—and debated vigorously—is where we are in spirituality, where our ideas and values come from, and where we are going. To the extent that we do this, we move into areas in which we do not know the answers, where we disentangle ourselves from a multitude of "traditions," and where we open ourselves, in trusting faith and love, to the living action of the Spirit.

Chapter X

POST-REFORMATION SPIRITUALITY

AFTER TAKING a rather detailed look at the spirituality of one school, that inaugurated by Ignatius Loyola and modified by his immediate successors in the Jesuit order, we must shift gears now and try to capture the spirit of an entire age, the Post-Reformation era. Some four centuries long, this era witnessed such enormous political, social, cultural, and intellectual changes that one might despair of attempting to synthesize its spirit. Yet from the point of view of the Church's spirituality, the entire period exhibits remarkably constant characteristics. Our purpose here will be to delineate some of these characteristics and to trace them through a number of important movements both within and outside the Church.

Post-Reformation spirituality is aptly termed Roman Catholic rather than Christian, taking direction more from its fight against the supposed and real heresies of Protestants than from the sources of the entire Christian tradition. Through the middle of the sixteenth century, Catholic ecclesiastics and theologians like Cardinal Gaspar Contarini (1485-1542) continued to talk with their Protestant counterparts. But with the 1555 election to the papacy of Cardinal Gian Pietro Carafa (1476-1559), first director of the Holy Office of the Inquisition, the tide turned against the proponents of Catholic reform and reconciliation. The doors were closed and the tone set for an era. Opposition to innovation became the test of orthodoxy. Carafa (Paul IV) forced a monastic way of life on Ignatius Loyola and his Society for a time. And, despite appeal to the contrary, Carafa and his successors promoted the Latin Vulgate rather than a vernacular Bible, the rigid Latin "Mass of the rubrics" rather than a vernacular liturgy, and the old Latin breviary rather than a simplified, more scriptural one such as that introduced by Clement VII a few decades earlier.[1]

In such a context of reaction and defensiveness, the spiritual writers of the Post-Reformation period expressed themselves more than ever in the battle and combat imagery which the desert fathers had first popularized. In fact, it is not the meekness and openness of Francis de Sales' *Treatise on the Love of God* but the martial tactics of Lawrence Scupoli's *Spiritual Combat* (1589) that typify the period.[2] So successfully did the Church instill this spirit of self-defense that it was able to remain relatively untouched by the outside world until the present century. It would be wrong, of course, to view Post-Reformation Catholic spirituality in simple negative terms. Actually, it exhibits considerable complexity and exuberance—what might be called the spirit of the Baroque. The term "Baroque" is ordinarily used to describe the art and thought of the period from 1550 to 1775. Yet because the defensive posture of the Post-Reformation Church effectively isolated it from the currents of philosophy and literature circulating elsewhere during the later eighteenth century, the entire four centuries of Post-Reformation spirituality may be called Baroque.

A fine illustration of this Baroque spirit is the Escorial, "that enigmatic combination of military power as a foundation, material expense, extremely severe simplicity and glittering pomp, spiritual ideas, the inspiration of artistic genius, deep religious fervor and the 'mystery of the king.' "[3] Built around 1560 by Philip II as a tribute to the heroic struggle which finally liberated Spain after centuries of domination by the Moors, the Escorial is no mere monument of victory, no mere triumphal arch, but a confession of Catholicity born of the Spanish soul. In it one discerns the longing for unity of his "Catholic Majesty," who did not want to "rule over heretics."[4] The architecture tries to express spiritual things—God is the intended goal. In the church, for example, eight hours a day are devoted to the Eucharistic liturgy and the divine office. The Blessed Sacrament is continually adored by a group of one hundred monks. Because the king knows "the power of scholarship for the divine service, the preservation and spread of his holy Catholic faith, and the profit deriving from it for the Christian people,"[5] the Escorial also contains a seminary and a great library; God must be worshipped not only in prayer but through the battle of scholarship against his enemies. Finally, in the midst of all the earthly and heroic splendor of hall and courtyard, living in the simplest apartment as an austere monk, we find the king himself, Philip II.

The Escorial therefore illustrates the glory of the Baroque religious spirit. In it, all earthly things express the grand exuberance of creation and redemption; they ascend to God and find their realization in him.[6] But in the Escorial we can also discern the major problematic tendency of the Baroque, whether in art, theology, or spirituality: its preoccupation with and loving elaboration of the detail, without reference to the structure of the whole. While it can achieve individual effects with great force and power, it is often incapable of achieving over-all patterns. Not in principle but only by accident does it manifest organic unity.

Thus in art the great triumphs of Baroque and its rococo monstrosities exist side by side. It can ruin the effect of a great dome by setting next to it a great tower, either one splendid enough by itself. It can express soaring emotion on one page and descend to sentimental melodrama on the next—and by the application of the same rule. In dogmatic theology it tends to divide the faith into a dozen discrete treatises and as a result talks about grace, for instance, with no more than incidental reference to the Trinity or Incarnation. In Church law it operates with a hodgepodge code which merely lumps together all the canons of previous ages. In piety it elaborates devotions to the point where the Trinity itself becomes just another "devotion." In moral theology and spirituality it concentrates on the quality of individual acts with little attention to the total direction of a person's life.

In this last instance, the Baroque mind tends to regard the religious value of an individual act as residing, not in the act itself as a concrete whole, but in its having been commanded by God or by some other authority. Consequently, the Christian life becomes a stringing together of discrete "obediences," a pattern imposed on one's life experience rather than a pattern discerned within it. Order becomes external to that which is ordered. All acts done in obedience are then elevated (or reduced) to the same level. Writing a book is no more valuable than reciting a thousand ejaculations, provided indeed that both activities are commanded by authority. This is an exaggeration, of course; what one does, and in particular the difficulty one experiences in doing it, remain secondary determinants of an act's merit in the sight of God. But for some reason the content and the command enter into no organic relationship. Grace is a pure superstructure resting on top of, but hardly touching, the order of nature.[7]

Another tendency of Baroque spirituality is its attempt to create a complete inner world, mirroring the outer world except that all disharmony is suppressed. The Baroque thus emphasizes discontinuity with the surrounding world; it stresses the difference and separation of the spiritual, its superior rationality and elegance. Perhaps it is this Cartesian longing for an oversimplified world which pushed the Spanish imagination toward mysticism; no fewer than three thousand "mystical" writings can be counted during the sixteenth and seventeenth centuries.[8] In effect, this mystical movement entailed an unconscious flight from the exterior world of change and disintegration to a still manageable interior world. In such an inner world the mystics saved the old cosmology and spatial imagery that could no longer survive in the real world of the new science. If man could no longer ascend to God on the ladder of an ordered, hierarchical universe, he could still reach him by passing through the many mansions of his interior castle.[9]

Of course such unconscious motivation was not the only factor contributing to the Spanish enthusiasm for myticism at this time. What more powerful incentive could one find than the living example of a Teresa of Avila and a John of the Cross? The herculean labors they carried on for so many years grew out of their prolonged mystical union with God and led them to transform a lax group of Carmelite mendicants into fervent contemplatives. But the call to contemplation was heard far beyond the walls of Carmel. We have already alluded to the Spanish Jesuits who wanted to withdraw from the world of apostolic labor and devote themselves to continual contemplation. Actually we can discern among most devout people in this period a pervasive feeling that a life of contemplation was the only path to Christian perfection.[10]

If for many the contemplative life did offer an environment for heeding a genuine call of the Spirit, it also provided a pretext for "mystical" heresy. The Spanish Inquisition, then at the height of its power, was continually hunting suspected adherents of a doctrine known as Illuminism. The Illuminati (or Alumbrados) propagated views similar to those of the Brethren of the Free Spirit: the impeccability of the person who has left behind the evil things of earth and achieved mystical union, and his independence of all authority except that which comes through his own private illumination by God.

The extent of the Illuminist heresy was probably exaggerated, not least of all by the Inquisitors themselves. In the end, their investigations and condemnations led less to the discovery and punishment of large numbers of heretics than to the creation of a general attitude among ecclesiastics of suspicion toward mysticism—and this despite the clear orthodoxy and obvious sanctity of mystics like Teresa and John.[11] A still greater threat to the Baroque Church, however, was posed by the two great heresies of the seventeenth century—Jansenism and Quietism.

The two show remarkable external resemblances. Both had legitimate, though not infallible, antecedents: Jansenism in the Berullian reaction against Jesuit "humanism," and Quietism in the Carmelite opposition to the rigid, anti-mystical approach to prayer associated with the Jesuits but prevalent in the Church at large.[12] Both seem like partial reincarnations of questionable or heretical doctrines of previous ages: Jansenism of Calvinism, and Quietism of the teachings of Pseudo-Dionysius, Eckhart, the Brethren of the Free Spirit, and the Alumbrados. But more than earlier heresies, Jansenism and Quietism illustrate the Baroque tendency to lavish all one's energy and skill on one element without seeming to care about the whole. Further, there was an actual blood relationship between leading figures in the two parties, the Arnaulds on the one hand and Madame Guyon and Fénelon on the other. Finally, one can even find a certain superficial congruence between the Jansenist emphasis on grace and denigration of human freedom and the Quietist abandonment of self in contemplation. After this, the similarity ceases; for it is a well-known fact that the two groups were bitter enemies.

We must now consider each of these sects separately and in greater detail. Jansenism, in its more orthodox antecedents, arose partly as a reaction to the Pelagian tendencies of Renaissance humanism.[13] To the French Oratorian Peter de Bérulle (1575-1629), for instance, the teaching of Jesuit theologians and moralists issued in a general moral laxity throughout the Church. The Jesuits, he claimed, granted entirely too much of the work of salvation to man, leaving practically nothing to God. What the Church needed was to abandon this neo-pagan adulation of man and return to the more rigorous doctrine of fallen man as expounded by Thomas Aquinas and especially by Augustine. The spirituality of Bérulle and his followers thus accentuated the results of original sin and pushed man's dependence on divine help as far as possible. Whatever the justification for this group's suspicion of the Jesuits, we can discern with the objectifying distance of history that the Jesuits (as well as Francis de Sales who was censured along with them), while exhibiting a radically different temperament and viewpoint from the Bérullians, were no less orthodox.

Such, however, was not the conviction of the authors of Jansenism itself, the Dutch theologian Cornelius Jansen (1585-1638) and John Duvergier de Haurrane (1581-1643), called St. Cyran after the abbey of which he was titular head. For many years these two men planned a program of reform for the universal Church—referred to enigmatically in their correspondence as "Pilmot"—and although they both died without implementing it, their spiritual teaching maintained a tenacious hold on segments of the French Church for many years.

Soon after Jansen's death, his *Augustinus* was published. Although it purported to be a presentation of Augustine's teaching, it concentrated only on the darker aspects and, in Calvinistic fashion, exaggerated them beyond the bounds of orthodoxy. According to Jansen, God was a hard taskmaster, not a father. Since fallen man was unable to resist any temptations, all his actions were sinful. Christ had redeemed only the elect; only to this tiny minority did he give the grace that would enable them to be saved. Consequently, all the Christian could do was to practice penance and in this way try to assure himself of his predestination.

How much of this doctrine was Jansen's own and how much of it he owed to St. Cyran is difficult to determine. Perhaps it is more accurate to say that Jansen wrote the bible of this heresy while St. Cyran was its apostle. In 1634 St. Cyran became director of the aristocratic convent of Port Royal and of its abbess, Angélique Arnauld (1591-1661). Such great influence did he exert over this community that, when his friend Jansen's *Augustinus* was condemned by Church authorities, Port Royal rallied to the defense.

Anthony Arnauld (1612-1694), Angélique's younger brother, became the great defender of Jansen. Earlier he had displayed his Jansenist zeal in excoriating the Jesuit practice of allowing frequent Communion and the general Church practice of giving absolution right after confession. What Arnauld wanted was to reintroduce the early Church practice of deferring absolution until after a long period of penance. Now, arguing that the condemned propositions were not to be found in the *Augustinus*, he convinced the Port Royalists that they could subscribe to the words of the Church's condemnation without ceasing to hold and practice the teachings of both Jansen and St. Cyran. Thus for a time Port Royal escaped suppression.

In defense of the Port Royalists, it must be said that since many of them were not theologians, they were probably unaware of the full implications of Jansen and St. Cyran's doctrine. Disturbed by the moral laxity of the times, they merely took the step of many Christians before them; with great sincerity they entered a fervent and strict religious community to devote themselves to a life of penance and prayer. Nevertheless the over-all temper of their lives tends to destroy any sympathy one might feel for them. For instance, the tender love for Christ which they sometimes expressed is too often overshadowed by their feelings of anxious fear and scrupulosity. Their pessimistic view of human nature is all the more disturbing because it seems based, not on an acquaintance with the heinous crimes committed by individuals or nations in the course of human history, but on a suspiciousness over things relatively insignificant and, in fact, good and virtuous. Thus did the famous Pascal (1623-1662) reproach his sister for caressing her children. When St. Cyran first visited Port Royal after four years in Cardinal Richelieu's prison, the community was overjoyed to see him. St. Cyran considered this reaction so inconsistent with the penitential spirit proper to the group that he postponed the celebration of his return for a week and retired to the chapel to weep and pray. At this, an "unexpressed fear" came over the community which "made each one search the depths of his own heart."[14] Similarly, when the last rites were to be given to Anthony Arnauld's mother (a Port Royal nun during the last years of her life), Arnauld asked the chaplain, St. Cyran's successor, whether he could attend. But the chaplain demurred; he already had a server and to allow a third person to be present would be "conceding too much to nature."[15]

In addition to this suspiciousness of human nature, one senses in the Port Royalists a self-consciousness that amounts to a preoccupation. Mother Angélique, ever conscious of her role as reforming abbess, observes that she would prefer to live in a convent with poor religious discipline because "there will be more merit in it, I shall meet with strong opposition and have few good examples."[16] Speaking in admiration of her director's great discretion, she declares that she would rather be canonized by him than by the pope. The canonization, we observe, she takes for granted. The Port Royal spirit, however, is not merely self-conscious; it is positively self-centered. No note can be struck in conversation or correspondence, it seems, which does not bring St. Cyran back to the engrossing topic of himself. A peasant approaches him lamenting that his wife has just given birth to a stillborn baby. After offering some pious considerations about how the baby is in hell since it died without baptism, St. Cyran proceeds to explain how devoted he himself has always been to the education of children. Such a developed sense of self-importance extended beyond individuals to the community as a whole, for it was well drilled in the doctrine that Port Royal was the only real convent in Christendom. And the more it found itself cut off from all other Christians by its views, the more its tears flowed in pity for them.

Although the absolute number of the Jansenist group was never great, its influence increased through the seventeen fifties and sixties. Eventually Port Royal included not merely a convent of nuns, but a corps of chaplains as well as a house for religious men and an exclusive boarding school for the training of future devotees. After all, its notion of religious conversion consisted in entering Port Royal or at least becoming an associate of the group. Moreover, the friends of Port Royal occupied such high places in the French Church (bishops Arnauld, Colbert, Noailles), at Court (the Duchess de Longueville), and in literary circles (Pascal and Racine) that, when in the last decades of the century the Church moved more vigorously against it, Jansenism hardly became extinct. Even after Port Royal was razed to the ground in 1709, its spirit remained alive in many quarters. By now Jansenist tendencies were so diversified and widespread that Church authorities found it exceedingly difficult to take any effective action against them. The papal bull of 1719, condemning 101 propositions from the *Moral Reflections* of the Oratorian Quesnel, was a last attempt to cure this illness.[17] In the long run a more powerful antidote was the message of God's love brought to the French Church as an eventual result of the revelations of Margaret Mary Alacoque.

For the most part, however, eighteenth-century French religion was overlaid with a joyless moralism. A sharp dichotomy between nature and grace disheartened the libertine, the sinner, and the conscientious Christian alike. Such was the heritage left by Jansenism—a movement that set out with so much fervor to reform the universal Church, yet ended up cold, rigid, and isolated from the mainstream of Christian life and doctrine. "Overlooked in its cradle by the mournful faces of St. Cyran and Mother Angélique, Jansenism never learned to smile. Its adherents forget, after all, to believe in grace, so hag-ridden are they by their sense of the need for it."[18]

We turn now to Quietism, a no less extravagant, but equally abortive, product of the uncontrolled Baroque mind. The first act in this story features the teaching of a number of French spiritual directors of whom Francis Malaval (1627-1719) was perhaps the most representative. It was the practice of many of them, with little discrimination, to urge everyone to a life of exalted contemplation—a contemplation which Malaval defines in his famous *Pratique facile* as "nothing but an unalterable loving gaze upon God present."[19] To perceive the presence of God, another Quietist teaches, the soul has to be "purged," its depth has to become like a "well polished glass" that will reflect the "face of God."[20] After purgation comes the stripping of the mind to make it naked, a theme by now quite familiar. Thus Malaval explains how the senses must be closed against every image and the mind emptied of all concepts. Even the humanity of Christ is an obstacle, because the contemplative seeks union not with the persons of the Trinity, but with the absolutely pure and simple Godhead. In short, Malaval adopts the same *tabula rasa* method in prayer which his contemporary, Descartes, used in philosophy,[21] and with similar unhappy results.

The way in which Malaval pushed people toward mysticism was questionable enough without his claim to have a method for reaching it infallibly. In France, his teaching was severely criticized by Bossuet and Bourdaloue, and in Italy by Segneri. The Italian translation of the *Pratique facile* was condemned by the Inquisition in 1688. Although embroiled in almost constant, though not always just, criticism and condemnation during the last twenty years of his life, Malaval remained a patient, obedient, and even saintly member of the Church.

The same cannot be said of Michael Molinos (1628-1696), a Spanish priest and doctor of theology who came to Rome in 1663 and soon became the most influential spiritual director in the city. His *Spiritual Guide,* a brief handbook on the contemplative life, caused an immediate sensation at its publication in 1675. Those who appeared to attack it had their works put on the *Index of Forbidden Books,* for were not his teachings identical with those of Dionysius the Areopagite and the mystic saints? Those who defended the *Guide,* on the other hand, received ecclesiastical advancement. Then suddenly, in July of 1685, when his reputation with the people was at its height and his favor in ecclesiastical circles—even with the pope himself—was most marked, Molinos was arrested by the pontifical police, put on trial, and sentenced to life imprisonment for heresy.[22]

The condemned teaching is to be found, not in Molinos' *Guide,* but in the conclusions he drew from it and taught in private. The "interior way" of the *Guide,* it now became clear, involved a complete annihilation of the soul's faculties. They must be not only inactive, but inert; the soul is mystically dead. The activity of God thus takes the place of the soul's activity, so that it can will only what God wills. By this stripping away of activity, the soul makes itself nothing and returns to its principle, the divine essence. Here it is so transformed and divinized that it becomes one with the divine essence. Moreover, the soul can persist in this single unrepeated act of unitive repose for the rest of its life—undisturbed by any new acts, any reflection on itself, any consolations or austerities. Although the thought of God himself seems to disappear, God is actually the agent of anything that the soul may seem to do. Now that the soul is so completely purified, no passions or temptations can disturb it; it has become incapable even of venial sin.[23]

During the trial the precise character of this doctrine of impeccability became evident. Molinos' sudden arrest, it seems, had resulted from the discovery of his own personal immorality. Toward the end of his trial he attempted to defend his own sexual aberrations and those of his followers as sinless purifying acts which, brought about by the devil and passively endured by the "interior" Christian, providentially deepen his quiet repose in God.[24]

Finally, at the conclusion of his trial, Molinos admitted his judges' accusations of heresy and immorality and made a solemn retractation before a vast audience in the Church of Santa Maria sopra Minerva. Witnesses describe his demeanor at the time as utterly impassive. To this day, historians are hard put to decide whether he actually repudiated his system in his heart or whether in the strange depths of his mind he looked upon his sentence as another part of the "spiritual martyrdom" God was allowing him to undergo.[25]

Despite the melodramatic character of his career, Molinos cannot be called the central figure of the Quietist movement; this distinction surely belongs to Jeanne Marie Bouvières de la Mothe Guyon (1646-1717). After the death of her husband in 1676, Madame Guyon was converted to the interior life, that is, she put aside meditation in favor of the prayer of simple regard. Soon after this she felt the call to propagate her new discovery. Hence she left Paris and journeyed for several years incessantly through southern France, Switzerland, and northern Italy. By day she taught the way of repose to the multitudes who flocked to her for counsel; at night she turned out her voluminous writings. Bishops welcomed her influence, she tells us; religious gratefully assured her that they never knew what prayer was before she taught them. But always she was forced to move on under pressure of enemies who, she says, poisoned the minds of authority against her. Yet she confesses that her biggest cross during these years was her director, Francis Lacombe, who was slow to understand her and do what she told him. Despite these and innumerable other trials, she kept her soul in utter peace and resignation.[26]

During this period, Madame Guyon published her *Brief Method of Prayer* for the general public; the *Spiritual Torrents* she reserved for her initiates and circulated only in manuscript.

In doctrine she clearly resembles Molinos. She talks about privileged souls reaching a "divine state" in which they are like an

unshakable and invulnerable rock before all kinds of trials. . . . They
are raised so high above all things by the loss of all things that
nothing in heaven or on earth less than God himself can confine and
hold them. God having given them perfect innocence, the holiness of
the holiest actions is not holy for them. God alone is holy. The poison
of the most wicked deeds cannot contaminate these souls when they
are obliged to do them, since for them there is no longer harmfulness
in anything because of their essential unity with God. . . . The soul
shares in God's purity, or rather, having been annihilated, God's own
essential purity subsists in this void; but in so real a way that the soul
is quite unaware of evil and is powerless to do it. . . . Who has ceased
to be, cannot sin.[27]

In July, 1686, Madame Guyon and Lacombe returned to Paris.
The time was inopportune. Molinos' trial had already begun and
he and his Quietism would soon be condemned. Within a year
Lacombe was arrested and went mad through the last twelve
years of his life in prison. He repeatedly but unsuccessfully im-
plored the Madame to visit him, but she had other concerns. At
first confined to a convent by order of the Archbishop of Paris,
she was released through the influence of the uncrowned queen,
Madame de Maintenon. At court, she met the cultured absentee
bishop Fénelon (1651-1715), for whom she discovered a "spiritual
filiation"; perhaps he would make a more tractable subject than
Lacombe. On his part, the bishop was probably helped by her.
He was certainly taken by her personality and her knowledge of
the mystics; and although he prudently avoided looking into her
Spiritual Torrents or *Autobiography*,[28] he set to work restating
her ideas in chastened form. Although Fénelon did not realize it,
this was the beginning of the Olympian battle he was to wage
(and lose) with Bossuet in defense of Quietism.[29]

From this point on Madame Guyon herself recedes into the
background of the struggle; yet it remains her controversy. Just
as Lacombe went to prison as the creature of the Madame, so
Fénelon sacrificed his career, not for himself, but as her cham-

pion. She was indeed the high priestess of Quietism. This is how she presents herself in her *Autobiography*. She has ceased to exist, she keeps telling us; it is God who speaks and acts in her. Unconsciously, we are supposed to believe, she echoes the speech of the Incarnate. It is not enough for her to identify herself with the star-crowned woman of the book of Revelation; to give up praying to the saints because, after all, she belongs to the family; to bind and loose (scruples, she later explains, not sins) like the apostles. She works miracles and feels that power has gone out of her. She refers to Lacombe as her beloved son in whom she is well pleased (even though she usually gives the impression that he is a cross to drag her through the mud and crucify her). She invited a friend to come and visit her in prison and, if imprisonment leads to execution, enjoins her to "do as Mary Magdalen did."[30] Was Madame Guyon a mad woman, a self-deceiver, a charlatan, or a combination of all three? One wonders whether Fénelon would ever have gone to battle in her behalf if he had read the *Autobiography*.

Like Jansenism, Quietism could not hold half-resolved antinomies in organic balance. When the antinomy was between dependence on God and self-activity, the Quietist, with an ultra-supernaturalist exuberance, seized upon the first half and, by completely ignoring the second, was able to draw the first half to any conclusion that logic would permit. Thus the Quietist tries to do away with all human effort; God alone must do everything. Man cannot even cooperate with God, but merely allow God to act in him. Ultimately, as Ronald Knox has observed, the Quietist is an "ostrich, burying his head in the sands of spiritual aridity and pretending he is not there."[31]

Quietists are at bottom much more enamored of their own activity than their theories might lead one to suspect. They try very hard not to try. They are always engaged in allowing God to act and suppressing themselves. In their external lives, too, they are incessantly active in promoting repose. When they feel thwarted in this pursuit, they retaliate with a kind of hysterical humility. Every setback has to be dramatized and exclaimed over. They resign themselves, not with a pious shrug of the shoulders as one might expect, but in a "roaring ecstasy of self-abandonment."[32]

Anyone who wants to study Jansenism or Quietism can start with a whole library of primary sources, before even touching the myriad volumes that have been written about these movements by others. The partisans of both sects, as well as their opponents, seem to have had unlimited time and energy to write about themselves and justify their lives. But there were many other great men and women of the Post-Reformation Church to whom the challenges of the time did not allow the luxuries of self-revelation and justification. They exemplify the Baroque spirit at its finest—with its exuberance directed by the real needs of the Church and the world. For them, the changing and expanding world was not a threat but an opportunity. Many new lands were being discovered; they would bring whole new peoples the Good News. Within Europe itself, population had expanded many times and cities became congested and diseased; these men and women would educate the children, care for the poor, the sick, the homeless. It is therefore inevitable but unfortunate that relatively little material is available to the biographer of these exemplary Christians—the missionaries and the founders of new religious congregations and societies.

While we might like to know much more about the inner lives of the great missionaries than an occasional diary can tell us, perhaps the bold and brilliant hearts of these men are best revealed in their fearless and creative deeds. Think of the unbounded zeal and labor which the North American Martyrs (d. 1642-1649)—highly cultured and sensitive men—expended on behalf of the crude and savage Indians of New France.[33]

Think of the immense patience and creativity exercised by Matthew Ricci (1552-1610) and his successors in mastering the intricacies of Chinese learning and culture—in making themselves Chinese to the Chinese—so that they might bring to China the fulness of wisdom. Think of the culture, education, and stability that the Franciscans brought to the natives of California (c. 1600-1800) and the Jesuits to those of Paraguay (c. 1600-1750). The list could easily be extended, for not a continent was left untouched by the missionary labors of the Baroque Church.

It is possible, of course, from the vantage point of today to say that this missionary effort often brought mixed blessings even when it succeeded. Baroque Christianity was too exclusively encased in European culture. Just as its missionary "successes" usually involved the displacement or destruction of legitimate customs among the evangelized peoples and the imposition of foreign, European ways, so were its failures often due to the rejection of a European (rather than Christian) gospel. One wonders how much farther the missionary enterprise might have gone if Rome had approved the native customs under debate in the Chinese and Malabar Rites controversies, or even if she had reversed her decision and officially encouraged adaptation before the twentieth century.[34] Even taking all this into consideration, however, the missionary achievement of the Post-Reformation Church remains a wonder to behold.

Back home, the activity of the Spirit is likewise discernible in the emergence of numerous new religious societies and congregations, as well as of a burgeoning lay apostolate. Moved by the terrible plight of the peasant masses, that great minister of Christ to the poor, Vincent de Paul (1581-1660), founded the Congregation of the Mission (Vincentians) and, together with Louise de Marillac, the Daughters of Charity. Another Frenchman, John Baptist de la Salle (1651-1719), discerning a call from God in the need of poor boys for free schooling, relinquished his cathedral canonry, gave away his fortune, and devoted himself tirelessly to founding schools and training teachers in new educational methods. He not only founded the Christian Brothers but, to a significant extent, modern education. In Italy in the next century, the new work of preaching missions was given great impetus when Paul Danei (1694-1775) founded the Passionists and Alphonsus Liguori (1696-1787), the Redemptorists.[35]

It is often said that the charismatic element in the Church—that aspect of the life of the Church which, as a balance to the institutional, most clearly evidences the action of the Spirit in renewing the face of the earth—is most often manifested in the founders and founding of new religious societies. This is certainly verified in the Post-Reformation Church by de Paul, La Salle, and the many other religious founders. Not only did these men and women address themselves to new needs that had gone unheeded by the Church and by society at large, but they created new forms of religious life with which to meet these needs. The Vincentians, like Philip Neri's Oratorians, were not religious in the technical sense, but secular priests living a community life and working together in their apostolate. Though living under rule and private vows, they were tied neither to one church nor to monastic observances. Similarly, La Salle had no canonical precedent for the life style of his Christian Brothers. For all its innovation in the form of clerical religious life, the Society of Jesus still looked upon its lay brothers as physical laborers, workmen to take care of menial tasks while the priests carried on their intellectual apostolate. The religious brother, then, in keeping with his gradual emergence from serfdom in the eleventh century, had always been the lesser half of orders dominantly clerical. To us these distinctions may seem rather academic, but they had real consequences for the early Vincentians and Christian Brothers. As with Ignatius and the early Jesuits, there were powerful prelates bent on forcing them into the mold of the older religious institutes.[36]

Even greater opposition was often thrown up against the women religious innovators of the era. The case of Mary Ward (1585-1645) may be taken as typical. Although originally living under modified Poor Clare rule, she and her companions found the contemplative, monastic form incompatible with their intense apostolic work. They wanted to be uncloistered nuns, without distinctive habit, bound together only by vows and rule, and under a superior who could send them wherever need arose. Such dangerously novel ideas as well as their adoption of the Jesuit rule aroused hostility especially in anti-Jesuit ecclesiastical circles. Despite the favorable reception (without formal approbation) of Mary's "Scheme of the Institute" by Paul V in 1616, opposition continued to mount until in 1629 the Roman Congregation of the Propaganda suppressed these "Jesuitesses." Mary's attempts to bolster the confidence of her companions was interpreted as rebellion; she was imprisoned for a while until a personal appeal to the pope secured her release. Although final and definitive suppression came a few years later, Mary managed to obtain permission for some of the sisters to continue their communal apostolate while living under private vows. Not until 1877 did Mary Ward's Institute of the Blessed Virgin Mary (Ladies of Loretto) receive final approbation from the Holy See. Meanwhile, many modern congregations of women patterned their rule upon hers.[37]

Something of the same spirit which fostered the birth of these new forms of religious life was at work in laying the foundation for a viable lay spirituality and lay apostolate. The popular aspirations for a meaningful lay Christian life, poorly directed in the later Middle Ages, found new guidance in the sixteenth and seventeenth centuries. Thomas More (1477-1535) was a living demonstration of the possibility of such a life. His friend Desiderius Erasmus (1466-1536) taught it in his *Enchiridion Militis Christiani*. Francis de Sales (1567-1622) counseled it in his *Introduction to the Devout Life*. And it was fostered by the religious art and architecture of the age.

We can see this spirit of the lay apostolate coming to full flower toward the end of the Post-Reformation era in Frederic Ozanam (1813-1853), a nineteenth-century "Man for All Seasons." Lawyer, doctor of literature, historiographer, and all-round scholar, he still found time to serve the poor, both through his writing and teaching and in person. He denounced economic liberalism on one side and socialism on the other; in their place he offered a Christian social doctrine that clearly foreshadowed Leo XIII's *Rerum Novarum*. Inspired by the great apostle of the poor, he founded the Society of St. Vincent de Paul, which became a model for many lay apostolic groups that were to follow.

The nineteenth century offered other hints of the possibilities for Christian life and spirituality that would be developed in the future. New congregations of apostolic religious (e.g., the Sisters of Mercy and the Salesians) sprang up everywhere. With John Henry Newman (1801-1890) in England and Matthias Scheeben (1835-1888) in Germany, theology was beginning to rise above the level of seminary textbook and sterile academic debate. Another nineteenth-century figure, Prosper Guéranger (1805-1875), Benedictine abbot of Solesmes, is usually considered the father of the liturgical movement. The Dominican Marie-Joseph Lagrange (1855-1938) resurrected Catholic biblical scholarship from near extinction.

Still the time was not ripe. The old defensiveness of the Counter-Reformation remained just below the surface ready to erupt at any moment. However justified the 1907 condemnation of Modernism may have been, it resulted in a climate of fear. Only with a basically protective and closed attitude could the predominant style of Catholic spirituality have remained so stagnant from the late Middle Ages through the beginning of the twentieth century. In the light of our previous discussion of late medieval and Baroque piety, consider the following representative picture of a devout and fervent young man at the turn of the twentieth century:

Sunday was dedicated to the mystery of the Holy Trinity, Monday to the Holy Ghost, Tuesday to the Guardian Angels, Wednesday to Saint Joseph, Thursday to the Most Blessed Sacrament of the Altar, Friday to the Suffering Jesus, Saturday to the Blessed Virgin Mary.

Every morning he hallowed himself anew in the presence of some holy image or mystery. His day began with an heroic offering of its every moment of thought or action for the intentions of the sovereign pontiff and with an early mass. The raw morning air whetted his resolute piety; and often as he knelt among the few worshippers at the side-altar, following with his interleaved prayerbook the murmur of the priest, he glanced up for an instant towards the vested figure standing in the gloom between the two candles which were the old and the new testaments and imagined that he was kneeling at mass in the catacombs.

His daily life was laid out in devotional areas. By means of ejaculations and prayers he stored up ungrudgingly for the souls in purgatory centuries of days and quarantines and years; yet the spiritual triumph which he felt in achieving with ease so many fabulous ages of canonical penances did not wholly reward his zeal of prayer since he could never know how much temporal punishment he had remitted by way of suffrage for the agonising souls: and, fearful lest in the midst of the purgatorial fire, which differed from the infernal only in that it was not everlasting, his penance might avail no more than a drop of moisture, he drove his soul daily through an increasing circle of works of supererogation.

Every part of his day, divided by what he regarded now as the duties of his station in life, circled about its own centre of spiritual energy. His life seemed to have drawn near to eternity; every thought, word and deed, every instance of consciousness could be made to revibrate radiantly in heaven: and at times his sense of such immediate repercussion was so lively that he seemed to feel his soul in devotion pressing like fingers the keyboard of a great cash register and to see the amount of his purchase start forth immediately in heaven, not as a number but as a frail column of incense or as a slender flower.

The rosaries too which he said constantly—for he carried his beads loose in his trousers' pockets that he might tell them as he walked the streets—transformed themselves into coronals of flowers of such vague unearthly texture that they seemed to him as hueless and odourless as they were nameless. He offered up each of his three daily chaplets that his soul might grow strong in each of the three theological virtues, in faith in the Father Who had created him, in hope in the Son Who had redeemed him, and in love of the Holy Ghost Who had sanctified him; and this thrice triple prayer he offered to the Three Persons through Mary in the name of her joyful and sorrowful and glorious mysteries.

On each of the seven days of the week he further prayed that one of the seven gifts of the Holy Ghost might descend upon his soul and drive out of it day by day the seven deadly sins which had defiled it in the past; and he prayed for each gift on its appointed day, confident that it would descend upon him. . . .[38]

The passage, as many will recognize, is from James Joyce's *Portrait of the Artist as a Young Man*. For our purposes, however, its significance lies in the fact that the ideas and even the phrasing (except for the ironic mockery of the cash register image) are taken from the *Sodality Manual* which Joyce and his fellow students at Belvedere were given by their Jesuit mentors.[39]

In sum, the Post-Reformation era was the age of the Baroque, in spirituality as in art. To call it this is to say at once that it had glories and pitfalls and that both issued from the same temper and source. At its best, which is usually its simplest, Baroque has great power to impose its vision; it elevates and does not confine. But it is intrinsically limited by its method. The more it achieves itself by tending to its own natural form, following out its inner logic, the more artificial, overelaborate, and absurd it becomes, like a gigantic frosted cake. From within, on its own terms, it is plausible, complete, a symbol of supernatural power over nature. But in full sunlight its elegance can seem oppressive, artificially elegant and peculiar, like Louis XIV's wigs and perfume. Like rationalism, it is a one-angle vision, hyperconscious and voluntaristic; it disregards the given structure of things; it smells of confinement. In the end, Baroque succeeds only when it refuses to follow out these immanent tendencies and instead moderates itself by opening its doors to the world, to experience, to "reality."

Chapter XI

SECULARIZATION, PERSONALISM, RELATIVISM

IT IS ALMOST COMMONPLACE to observe that new forms of spirituality are emerging in today's Church. The rapid evolution in our society has wrought profound changes in the consciousness each of us has of our own history, of our destiny, and of the role we must play in the contemporary world.

Obviously there have been many previous changes from the earliest ages of man up to our own time. But throughout the whole of recorded history such changes seem to have occurred within fairly narrow limits. They appear mainly as movements of ebb and flow: Civilization alternates with barbarism; empires grow and decay. Civilization left man still close to nature, pulsating to her rhythm, resigned in advance to failures as inevitable as the march of the seasons. Man has always been, since the time of his first awakening, an impatient animal, discontented with his lot, ready to rise in revolt. But in the past his rebellions were merely local and sporadic, hardly more than outbreaks of fever, never the successive stages of conscious, planned activity.

But our age has produced a new ambition and with it a new society. Little by little man has raised his head against the oppressive weight of his destiny. He wants to escape those fatalities which, from time immemorial, he has believed inescapable. To achieve this ambition he has developed a society full of promise which signifies the possibility of life and education on a truly democratic basis. The chaos of massive, conflicting urbanization has given birth to a metropolis which offers the possibility of a unified human society where children may find a climate conducive to growth, where education may enrich life as well as capacities, where men and women may have opportunity to participate as members and receive their rewards, and where advantages may be distributed with equity.[1]

Yet, the hope of this new society is clouded by the threat of worldwide holocaust; the promise of its productive power is darkened by alienation between social classes and racial groups. Not only is the "new city" failing to realize its promise as a land of freedom and fulfillment, but it has also become a breeding ground of disorganization and conflict that threatens to subvert the very ideals it seeks to promote. Contemporary man is quickly losing both his ability to experience and have faith in himself as a worthy, unique human being and the capacity for meaningful communication with other men. Nowadays men everywhere seek to know where they stand, where they may be going, and what—if anything—they can do about the present as challenge and the future as responsibility.[2] Such questions no one can answer once and for all. Looking back in history, we can see that each period provides its own answers. But just now, for us, there is a difficulty. We are at the ending of an epoch, and we have to work out our own solutions.

The ending of one epoch and the beginning of another is, to be sure, a matter of definition. But definitions, like everything social, are historically determined. At the present time our basic definitions of society and of self are being overtaken by new realities. This is not to say that never before within the limits of a single generation have men been so fully exposed at so fast a rate to such earthquakes of change. Nor does this merely mean that we feel we live in an epochal kind of transition in which we struggle to grasp the outline of the new age we suppose ourselves to be entering. Rather, the problem is that when we try to orient ourselves—if we do try—we find that too many of our standard categories of thought and feeling disorient us as often as they help to explain what is happening around us; that too many of our explanations are derived from the great historical transition from the medieval to the modern age; and that when they are generalized for use today, they become unwieldy, irrelevant, unconvincing.

Such changes in man's fundamental consciousness call forth profound changes in his spirituality. There is in the Church today a growing awareness, especially among the young, that a large segment of what has generally been called Christian spirituality is no longer adequate. This criticism concerns much more than practical matters—the amount of time given to private prayer, the method of conducting liturgical worship, or even the contemporary emphasis on individual freedom and initiative. The charge of inadequacy refers rather to a mental outlook, a vision of God, man, and the world, which is the ultimate factor in anyone's style of approaching God. Modifications in the particular forms of spirituality, or the manner in which faith penetrates and transforms the human situation, depend on the particular awareness that Christians have of the Gospel preached to them, as well as on a definite understanding of the world in which they are to live and must bear witness. Over the centuries these modifications have taken place within a certain fixed framework of thought, and it is precisely this fundamental Christian image of life which is now undergoing reappraisal. Any re-evaluation is a difficult and subtle task. It is one thing to reject old styles and attitudes but quite another to get along without them or to put new ones in their place. There is also the danger that the new image we create may filter out completely certain balancing elements in the old view against which we are reacting, so that our new vision of life may in the end produce just as many difficulties as the old.

The drive toward reappraisal is all the more evident because new members of the faithful are showing such a strong desire for an authentic spirituality.[3] It is noticeable among people of all classes who, as serious witnesses of their faith, find themselves drawn toward spiritual challenges they never expected. It is also noticeable among those who feel they have rediscovered the Gospel in all its original strength. The fact is more remarkable when we notice that Christians who began by rediscovering the apostolate—the Christian meaning of work, the metropolis as God's new creation among men—also began by rejecting virtually all that resembled the spirituality and piety they had previously been taught. But these same people, as they develop and are enriched by their attempts to interpret the Gospel for a world come of age, increasingly realize that they need a spirituality— what Paul called "the wisdom of God"—and that they need spiritual guides to teach them. For these people, spirituality no longer means the glorious ornament of clerical or monastic families who have practiced it until now because of ancient or more recent traditions. Rather, their desire for spirituality seems to spring directly from the Gospels and not from schools or centers of spirituality.

But if we are correct in sensing the beginnings of a new spirituality, it is quite another thing to trace its distinctive shape. For one thing, it is difficult to discern among the current trends those elements which are ephemeral and those which are deep enough to serve as a solid basis for an authentic new spirituality. In spirituality as in other things there are styles, passing fads that turn into catchwords; after a few years they are cast aside just as vigorously as they were previously accepted. Another reason for uncertainty is that spirituality itself refers to a living synthesis of human and scriptural elements, a structuring of an adult personality in faith according to its own genius and limitations, as well as the laws of the universal Christian mystery. Each of these elements is so rich and varied that one can scarcely foresee the single result of such a synthesis; actually, several syntheses are possible.

In order to shed some light on this situation, therefore, we intend in the present chapter to propose a few simple observations that may serve as points of departure for the reader's own more detailed consideration. For the sake of simplicity, one may list the major trends that characterize contemporary spirituality under three headings:[4] We are today evolving a spirituality which emphasizes the importance of the world in man's relation to God and takes as its starting point life lived in the world we know; this is a spirituality which aspires to genuine personal experience and self-fulfillment in one's relation to God; it is also a spirituality that repudiates all absolute, changeless formulas and emphasizes the present historical experience of rapid change at all levels of human life. In considering each of these qualities we will often refer to one of the most symbolic figures in current discussions of spirituality, Pierre Teilhard de Chardin. Indeed, Teilhard's whole perspective offers an apt illustration of both the strengths and weaknesses of these three contemporary tendencies.

The spirituality which today's Christian seeks is, above all, a spirituality that is to be lived in the world. A spiritual doctrine interests him, in other words, only if it offers a better opportunity to give himself to God and to more effectively organize the substance of his daily life in the name of God. Thus, people will speak of the need for a spirituality of marriage, of work, of human relations, of leisure, not in the sense of coloring their actions with a spiritual purpose or sprinkling them with pious blessings, but of penetrating the real meaning of their actions from beginning to end. Christians today seem acutely aware that spiritualizing life does not mean vaguely adverting to God in the intervals between their professional duties or vital concerns, nor injecting some spiritual refreshment into their spare time. This is the spirituality they have rejected most vigorously. Rather, the very stuff of their existence must acquire a new quality in its very depths, a quality that enables it to be the deepest expression of their contribution to the kingdom of God.

What this means, in more theological terms, is that the traditional dualities of natural-supernatural, matter-spirit, immanent-transcendent, sacred-secular, are becoming increasingly irrelevant to the modern Christian. Not that he cannot recognize these distinctions when they are explained to him, but they no longer have any significance for his spiritual development; in reality, such terms create nothing but confusion for him. Actually the reasons for this confusion have their roots in the current theological discussions of "secularization." In order to understand better the significance of these discussions for contemporary spirituality, it will be helpful to trace some of their broader outlines.[5]

The vague, common-sense meaning of secularization refers to the decline of conventional religiosity as well as to the loss of respect for the powers of deity and tradition. From this viewpoint, secularization is a threat to the religious community whenever the community begins to take on the coloring of its surroundings in an effort to Christianize the world. It was Harnack who popularized this use of the term when he spoke of the Church's involvement with Greek thought as a "secularization."[6] Kierkegaard, although he did not use the word, attacked the same phenomenon with his attack on a Christendom that was indistinguishable from the "present age"; and in the twenties Protestant theologians Karl Barth, Emil Brunner, and Friedrich Gogarten thundered at secularization of the Church in a culture-bound Protestantism.[7] On the American scene, Will Herberg has led the way in probing the "widespread secularism of American religion, in which religion is made to provide the sanctification of dynamic goals and values otherwise established."[8]

More relevant to the problem of spirituality is the historical understanding of secularization which applies the term to any aspect of life that has been withdrawn from the control of the Church or interpreted apart from the Christian world view. The essential characteristic of this process is the transformation of institutions, ideas, and experiences that were once considered the work of divine providence into the product of purely human thought and action. Maritain, for example, writing about the secularization of the Christian image of man, says it is "bringing back to the realm of man himself" what had been "consecrated, elevated above nature by God, called to a divine perfection."[9] Extending the same idea to the totality of Western culture since the waning of the Middle Ages, we may accept Roger Mehl's definition of secularization as society's disengagement from the "religious beliefs and institutions that have previously commanded its existence in order to constitute itself as an autonomous reality, to find in itself the principle of its own organization."[10]

The story of this secularization of the West can be told primarily in terms of the rise of the "secular" state and the decline of ecclesiastical influence in political matters. But the broader social dimensions of the process are nearly all bound up with the impact of technology in the forms of industrialization, urbanization, and mass communication. There is the classic theory that the move from the rural-village environment to the cities dissolved the force of convention. Sensitivity to the sacredness of the created world tended to be lost when industrialization siphoned the peasant off the land into this man-made domain where the "rationalization" of production and distribution took the place of providential rain and growth.[11] Historically, at any rate, it would seem that the middle class of the towns became secularized chiefly because of its absorption in transforming the world through capital, technology, and the adventure of discovery. For Mehl, technology itself is the purest form of secularization, since it pretends to deal only in "facts" and proposes no goal except "results." "Not only does society refuse all recourse to the divine . . . but it denies even the distinction of the sacred and profane; it recognizes only a single domain over which technology rules."[12]

These institutional and social factors of secularization necessarily rest on certain intellectual and affective underpinnings. A world governed by divine providence has given way to a world of human power and plans where man guides his own destiny. As Bonhoeffer taught, man has become mature in relation to himself, since he no longer needs God as a hypothesis or helper, and mature in relation to the world, since the sacred no longer appears to bless or terrify him.[13] The affective counterpart of this intellectual maturity has been the sense of breaking off the shackles of a real or imagined ecclesiastical-supernatural tyranny. Even today, when nearly all agree that the process has reached its fulfillment (the "death of God"), general histories of the period since the Renaissance are written as a "story of liberty."

Theologians further concur that the prime instrument of this intellectual secularization has been the evolution of science. Science has produced the "miracles" that validate the new faith; it has allowed itself to be used as a new kind of magisterium whose results are not only fearlessly expendable but infinitely expandable. Although the Church tried to limit the freedom of science in the name of an Aristotelian-Biblical hodgepodge of pseudo-science, the defenders of science fought back in the name of autonomy by propounding science as the final and sufficient justification for life. The importance of this intellectual defense of secularization lies not only in its construction of a new set of ideas or values, but in a new mode of existence, a new relationship between man and his world. The peculiar relation of modern man to the world has become "the conquest of the world as a picture."[14] We cannot let things be but must grasp and represent them in an effort to certify their reality. As the one who represents beings to himself, modern man has thus thrown himself down as the ultimate foundation upon which all existence and truth is grounded: he has become the self-grounded subject who is responsible for the world only to himself.[15]

Religious writers from Maritain to Bultmann are willing to affirm and even accept this secularity and autonomy, finding its roots in the Judeo-Christian tradition itself. In the Old Testament the radical transcendence of God the creator means that the world as such is profane, and that the personal character of God as creator and man as creature leads to a concept of the world as given over to the dominion of man (Gen. 1:24). Yet, the Old Testament still involved a unity of the political and religious community which was not broken until the Christian proclamation called men out from every nation and tongue. Paul argues, for example, that the Christian man is an heir come of age, a mature son whose inheritance is the world. Such independence and responsibility was to be achieved by maturing Christian man through a long process of historicization. Man exists historically only when he is responsible for his destiny, and this responsibility becomes the full possession of man through the mystery of Christ.

Anathemas against secular history and culture did occur later in the literature of Christianity in certain isolated mouths, and these found little echo among the truly great patristic writers. When Augustine described the two cities of God and man, for example, he took every precaution not to make the city of God an imaginary and separate city, but to underline its incorporation into the earthly city. "It is indifferent to the city of God what attire the citizens wear, or what rules they observe, as long as they contradict not God's holy precepts, but each one keeps the faith, the true path to salvation. And therefore when a philosopher becomes Christian, they never make him alter his manners, which are no hindrance to his religion, but his false opinions."[16] What Augustine speaks of is a sort of Christian *indifference* to the world—not an indifference of abstention but of relation; to be exact, it is an indifference of projection. Men of the stature of Origen, Cyprian, Ambrose, or Augustine did not say, "Avoid the affairs of the world for they are insignificant," but on the contrary, "Because they are insignificant do not withdraw from them. Take them as they come." And when they added, "Penetrate the works of others with the Christian spirit," they started the Christian on an endless road of supplementary tests and travails. The Christian was thus bound to the world with ever stronger ties until he had to seek with difficulty the secret ways to answer the call of grace.[17]

Still, Christian responsibility for the world is a *received* responsibility. In it man is aware of a responsibility *to* God from which he has received the world. In a son's autonomy he makes every decision on his own, but as an heir he cares for the world as one who knows he has been cared for.[18] The chief characteristic of much of modern "maturity," however, is a negative independence. This kind of autonomy is referred to by contemporary theology as "secularism," in contrast to secularization, since it functions as a substitute for religion. In the end, secularism constitutes a profanized sacrality. Such elimination of the Jewish-Christian God as the ground and goal of culture removes the transcendent limit that keeps secular society secular.

If there is general agreement among contemporary theologians that faith is compatible with secularization but not secularism, there still remains considerable disagreement over just how far faith can go toward a strict secularity without surrendering its own nature. In a rough way we might separate the position along H. Richard Niebuhr's pattern of "Christ transforming culture" and "Christ and culture in paradox."[19] The writers who would fit under the first category are willing to accept secularity, but insist that the role of Christian faith is to permeate all facets of society with the leaven of the sacred. In M.-D. Chenu's view, for example, the modern attitude provides an "opportunity to do away with a false conception of God, a conception which sees him as a kind of jack-of-all-trades trouble-shooter, waiting on the side lines to jump in and bolster our ineptitudes. . . . A sacred society tended to see God as intervening wherever and whenever man proved impotent. This was a species of inferior religion."[20] Chenu, therefore, welcomes the present movement of secularization insofar as it compels us through the force of circumstances "to get out of a mental and institutional complex of Christianity."[21] In other words, the question today is not one of sociologically christianizing the masses, but of allowing the Gospel to witness more purely, respecting the autonomous process proper to the world, while still maintaining the primacy of God's Word through the Church. The point is not that the Church "should build for itself a Christian world alongside of the 'world,' but that it should Christianize the world as it grows, as it is in the process of growing in this extraordinary twentieth century."[22]

While writers like Chenu are willing to consider secularization a "normal process," their final intention is not to preserve the integrity of secularity but, in Maritain's words, to bring about a "sanctification of the temporal order." For Niebuhr, on the other hand, the counterpart of secularization is the "sanctification of all things," the transformation of both the secular and the sacred. Thus everything is secular insofar as the sacred ceases to be localized; yet everything is sacred insofar as it is related to the transcendent God. What is common to Chenu, Maritain, and Niebuhr is their positive appraisal of the sacred and their concern that the secular not be left to its own devices but "transformed" or "vivified" by faith.[23]

Another approach to secularization follows Niebuhr's second type—the Christ-and-culture paradox. Unquestionably the writers who have developed this position are considerably more radical in their outlook. Whereas the views we have already discussed emphasize transforming the secular, other theologians see the main problem as one of keeping the secular genuinely secular. As Gogarten has observed, the man who has become responsible *for* the world is always in danger of becoming responsible *to* the world, of falling into servitude under new forms of spiritual power. The task of faith is not primarily to transform society but to keep man's responsibility for the world limited to partial goals.[24] From this point of view, the greatest virtue of science, philosophy, or the state is precisely their "godlessness"—that they remain critical, proximate, and entirely secular. A "sanctified" or "transformed" science or political structure would be a hybrid in which neither Christian faith nor secular responsibility could preserve their integrity. In the words of Carl Michalson, "Christianity tells us nothing we cannot find out for ourselves except that in Christ God has turned the world over to man."[25]

It is not altogether clear that the new radical theologians are intending to get along without the sacred, although they are certainly reappraising and relocating it. And one of them, Paul Van Buren, does seem willing to jettison the sacred completely. Perhaps the revealing point of Van Buren's discussion of the secular meaning of the Gospel is his decision not to use the word "God" at all in his theological writing and, instead, to replace "God the Father" by the assertion that faith consists of a single "orientation to the whole world."[26] Certainly Van Buren is aware that many will be troubled by his reduction of Christian faith to its secular dimensions, but he asks what "more" we could speak about in a secular age that demands an empirical anchorage for all thought and language. The issue between other radical theologians and Van Buren—the most radical of them all—is not whether the Christian is autonomous and can live in a world ruled by technology and social planning, but whether the dimension of mystery or depth is essential to Christian faith.

Our purpose in reviewing this admittedly complex topic of

secularization has been to sketch the background of a first characteristic of contemporary spirituality. Today people are striving for a spirituality in which the world is accepted in such a way that the dualism between living in the world and being a Christian is overcome. Spirituality thus appears as a way of coping with one's human situation and as a way of living in this world. By way of summing up this first tendency, let us turn to the writings of Teilhard de Chardin. Indeed, Teilhard's whole evolutionary system puts such strong emphasis on the continuity of matter and spirit and his theological speculation places such importance on the physical relationship between Christ and the material world that, when he applied this perspective to Christian living, what resulted was a call to experience God in the secular world in a way that was impossible for Christians of a former age.[27]

As Teilhard conceived it, the great need in spirituality was "to discover what there could be that is divine and predestined within the matter itself of our cosmos, our humanity and our progress."[28] To him the supernatural was a ferment, not a finished organism. Its role was to transform nature, but it could not do so apart from the matter which nature provided it with. Again he wrote: "God reveals himself everywhere, beneath our groping efforts as a universal milieu, only because he is the ultimate point upon which all realities converge. . . . It is precisely because he is so infinitely profound that God is infinitely near, and dispersed everywhere. It is precisely because he is the center that he fills the whole sphere."[29]

Nevertheless, Teilhard well recognized that an emphasis on the importance of the material (secular) world is not without its dangers. What he wanted, above all, was actually to find God, to be aware of his presence in people and things, to possess him and be possessed by him. "The veneer of color and scene bores me to tears," he once wrote from China. "What I love is hidden. . . . Even when I am most absorbed in geology, my interest has already wandered elsewhere. It is the Other that I seek."[30] Such an attitude toward matter explains why Teilhard could look upon the world as a crystal lamp illumined by the light of Christ.[31]

Teilhard's penetrating desire was to see through people and things and find God; it is for this reason that he struggles with such intensity to show that material evolution is ultimately oriented toward growth in the spiritual. "The whole movement of material growth in the universe is ultimately directed toward spirit, and the whole movement of spiritual growth is ultimately directed toward Christ."[32] Thus he could pray: "By virtue of your suffering Incarnation, disclose to us the spiritual power of matter, and then teach us to harness it jealously for you."[33]

Not everyone who has written about secularization would share Teilhard's concern to possess God in an intimate, personal, non-utilitarian relationship. Harvey Cox explains, for example, that the Gospel is merely "a call to imaginative urbanity and mature secularity. . . . Like his relationship to his work partner, man's relationship to God derives from the work they do together. . . . God manifests himself to us in and through secular events."[34] For Teilhard, God indeed manifests himself in the material world and in the events of our own lives, but we shall never find him there unless we have first found him within ourselves. The sanctification of all things depends "upon the initial and fundamental role of one's intention, which is indeed . . . the golden key which unlocks our interior world to the presence of God. . . . It is God and God alone whom [the Christian] pursues through the reality of created things. His interest lies truly in things, but in absolute dependence upon God's presence in them."[35]

Our preceding discussion of Teilhard's view of God and the world should be sufficient to underline the significance of the first trend of contemporary spirituality and put the question in proper perspective. Modern man is earnestly seeking an approach to God which emphasizes the importance of the secular world and uses his life in this world as a starting point for spirituality. The question is, of course, whether the irreversible process of secularization really does offer a new opportunity for the sanctification of man. Certainly secularization is something tragic when it creates a void in man's consciousness of God. But insofar as it coincides with a radical exposure of the illusions of an inadequate "religious" consciousness, it may paradoxically serve the sacred element of authentic spirituality. In this sense, the conquest of the universe, and the consequent decline of the sacred, fall in line with the process of desacralization that lies at the heart of Christianity. If this process develops in the direction of the truth of man, i.e., of autonomy, responsibility for one's life and solidarity with other men, then it can help the growth of spirituality enlivened by faith. For building the earth can have no Christian significance unless individual men give it that significance; and they do this by their personal union with Christ and their steadfast desire to seek and to find him in every earthly task to which they commit themselves. Only then will they have the right to say with Teilhard that nothing here below is profane for those who know how to see.[36] But this kind of vision is a gift of God; it is given only to those who desire it.

A second tendency emerging today in Christian spirituality is the concern for genuine personal religious experience and self-fulfillment in one's relation to God.[37] Here again, what is represented is a reaction against a certain antihumanist, implicitly mechanistic approach in previous spiritual teaching—an emphasis on specific ascetical practices, the performance of fixed penances, and a distrust of any purely spontaneous natural inclination.

Few will doubt that a stress on personal experience and self-fulfillment is a good thing, or that it is a needed reaction to a false kind of objectivism inside and outside the Church. In secular culture, the experimental sciences were thought to provide such exclusive access to reality that anything beyond their reach became tinged with unreality. The whole realm of personal and moral values was thus separated from its unity in human experience. Within the Church, on the other hand, excessive preoccupation with external structure and overemphasis on sheer conformity to regulations conspired to stifle selfhood and render it suspect. The reaction that occurred took the form of a reinstatement of the initiating, personal subject as that without which there would be no science and as that for which Church structures exist in the first place.

This current emphasis on the personal dimension of spirituality should come as no surprise. We are living in the era of the person; failure to grasp the significance of this development underlies much of the confusion that presently besets us. And if Christians today want a spirituality that is truly personal and personally experienced, they do not romantically seek experience for the sake of experience. Rather, today's Christian seeks to live by Christ in a universe that subjects him to very real tensions and contradictory allurements. Perhaps, we must admit, he is simply seeking to survive as a Christian.

Man has, to be sure, always been personal. But in the past, who an individual was and what he was supposed to do were defined by the place he occupied in objective human society. If it was recognized that an individual man somehow transcended mankind and was of absolute worth in himself, still this worth could not be realized in any other way than by sheer submission and conformity to the determinate patterns of collective human living. It was freely assumed that one's place in the larger whole of concrete humanity was what enabled the individual's life to make sense.

Today, however, this approach no longer seems adequate. For one thing, the prodigious increase in communications confronts the individual in his formative years with such a range of competing world-views and traditions that automatic acceptance of only one of them is no longer possible. Right from the start, the individual experiences a need to decide for himself the meaning and scope of his life. Moreover, this heightened sense of self is further exacerbated by the dominance of the organizational aspects of modern living.

Large-scale organizations, of course, are nothing new.[38] Since the time of the early empires, military machines have exhibited rational planning of structures on the basis of centralized command, complex division of labor, and a growing body of coordinating personnel. Mammoth construction projects like the great pyramids, the Roman aqueducts, or the civil administration of empires and large commercial ventures have required rational organization of considerable complexity. But these structures, impressive as they were, only remotely touched the lives of the vast majority of people. Goods and services for the satisfaction of man's daily needs were produced and distributed almost entirely at the level of personal interaction. Until two hundred years ago some ninety-five per cent of the population even of "advanced" states lived in self-supporting communities—so self-supporting, in fact, that local crop failures meant local famine although relative abundance prevailed only a few miles away.

Now a rapidly enlarging stream of goods and services flows into the hands of large organizations to be processed and distributed through organizational channels. Few needs remain which are not satisfied in this way: food from the regional chain of supermarkets, clothing from nationwide distributors, housing from development contracting firms and the giants of finance, plus federal loans. Education is dispensed at the multiversity; medical service is distributed by Blue Cross; religion is filtered through a hierarchical Church or a member of the World Council of Churches, and defense comes from the Pentagon. The terms on which we work are decided by big business and organized labor, our old-age pensions are provided by nation- and state-wide systems and, as if that were not enough, we draw our entertainment from CBS or Hollywood and go abroad on tours planned for us by travel bureaus. Even when the most personal of institutions fails to function, it is serviced by a caseworker from the welfare department or a member of the national association of professional marriage counselors.

Although this picture has been somewhat overdrawn, there is no escaping the fact that contemporary society is dominated by organizational structure to an extent unheard of in the past. Its growth coincided with the growth and perfection of the machine. And there is reason to suspect that the same logical processes were at work in the development of both: consistent and rational (efficient) application of the principle of division of labor, the coordination of specialized parts in the pursuit of a predetermined goal. Social critics talk of "mass society," blame technology, or believe that society is becoming too instrumentalized, functionalistic, or conformist. Even though we may not wish to join the chorus of romantic anti-intellectuals who long for a supposedly more "natural" order and ascribe satanic properties to organizations, we must also acknowledge that an increasing number of people, especially among the young, are in a mood of rebellion against something that is vaguely sensed but little understood.

The emergence of the person as an original value transcending the whole order of the factual has also been strongly underscored by the Second Vatican Council. The tone of its *Pastoral Constitution on the Church in the Modern World,* for example, is a sharp departure from earlier Church pronouncements on the same question. Christ is he who "fully reveals man to man himself" and "whoever follows after Christ, the perfect man, becomes himself more of a man." It is Christ who "animates, purifies, and strengthens those noble longings by which the human family strives to make its life more human and to render the whole earth submissive to this goal." Indeed, it is precisely the plan of God that the Church "contribute greatly toward making the family of man and its history more human."[39]

While we welcome a more humanistic approach to Christian living, we must also know that a desire for the more personal dimension of spirituality is a dangerous venture. It is one thing to make room for personal initiative and freedom; it is quite another to isolate the individual subject and make him the supreme value. When the latter happens, subjectivism takes over; an individual can begin to consider his own desires as the only ones that deserve consideration and fulfillment. Because I am ultimately answerable for everything I do, I alone have the right to determine what I shall do. I may cooperate with authorities when I happen to agree with their decisions, but I will not when I don't; to act otherwise is to betray my dignity and responsibility as a person. So, at least, runs an argument that is often heard.

The consequences of such solipsism are widespread. As can easily be imagined, it plays havoc with any kind of authentic spiritual life. In the name of subjectivity, there are no more "subjects"; everyone is his own superior. The chaos in civic life is

just as disastrous. What can fairly be labeled as "uncivil diso-
bedience" is being justified on moral and spiritual grounds.[40]
Inequalities in the system—Church or state—become not challenges for correction, but reasons for destruction.

The problem in all this, then, is how to promote subjects and
avoid subjectivism. It cannot be done so long as personal responsibility is thought to preclude genuine obedience, or reasonable-
ness is identified exclusively with "what I think." If spirituality
(or morality) means anything, it means not presuming to decide
on my own about the justice and goodness of actions that affect
others; it means giving an evangelical direction to one's life and
participating in the world without ceasing to participate in God
through Jesus Christ. The determination of the good is, therefore, a double task. It requires a willingness on the part of all to
submit both to the requirements of community and to the Word
of God.

Certainly one of the exciting developments of contemporary
thought is its new insistence on the social character of man. This
means that human nature is not the possession of an individual
taken by himself. Mankind is not merely a collection of separate
units that come together in various accidental groupings in order
to satisfy their common needs. Man is essentially a community, a
community of persons in relation, and he exists only insofar as
genuine community is not a dread but a reality.[41] To be a man,
therefore, is to be a person; but to be a person is to exist only as
an appeal and a response to other persons. Without the other—
an other who takes account of me and for whom my free response
means something—I do not exist. But if I need you in order to be
myself, you likewise need me. Each of us holds his "personhood"
as a gift from the other, so that to betray the other is always to
betray oneself.

To define mankind as a community of persons, then, is not to
define a matter of fact, i.e., something that exists in a settled and
determined way independently of the intentions of those who
share in it. The reality of man is not a matter of fact but a matter
of freedom. Therefore, mankind exists only as a conspiracy of
individual liberties, each continually turning itself toward the

others and spending itself to provide the environment in which all can flourish. It is in this reality of human persons in community that the Christian bears witness to the Word of God. It is here that he searches always for a greater justice, a deeper truth, a richer love.

An emphasis on the personal dimension in spirituality, therefore, is never an absolute value. It is essentially correlative to community and to the Gospel. When it commits itself to the requirements of social process, its innovating capacity is a force for social reconstruction and reform. When personalism cuts loose from these requirements, however, it sinks into subjectivism; unfortunately the harm it then does is far more than subjective.

Yet within certain sectors of the personalist movement itself, perhaps one can find an antidote for some of the dangers we have been discussing. Here we refer to the revival of the communitarian values in Christianity.[42] Indeed the liturgical renewal has become inseparable from this communitarian, or social, discovery. The whole Church, in fact, is finding again a keen sensibility toward what is its very essence: a communion in Christ and the Spirit on all levels where the mystery of "assembly" is present. The fact that the Council has preferred the term "People of God" to that of "Mystical Body" and that the collegial structure of the hierarchy has been brought to public notice are examples of this tendency which begin to give an accepted status in the Church to the idea and actual working of a small community group.

These groups fulfill several functions for the contemporary Christian. First of all, one notices their search to carry out evangelical aspirations, to satisfy the need of a community where they will be able to realize certain values of the Gospel. They want, as they say, to "incarnate" these values, to render them tangible. They are no longer satisfied to talk about justice and freedom and love; they want to live them. And they instinctively understand that a community is the Gospel made visible, that the Holy Spirit can use everyone in the Church to work out God's plans, that all can be bearers of charisms.

It would be quite unfair to associate this concern for fostering the prophetic element in the Church with the rise of religious anarchy, unless such a concern would imply that no one in the Church possessed any more authority than anyone else. It is more correct to understand this new emphasis on charisms as a reaction to an overconcern about the right of the Church to provide true discipline and to command. Out of anxiety that something false might be preached or practiced, the right of preaching was restricted to clerics and to the ecclesiastical magisterium. Out of fear that theology might fall into the wrong hands, it was confined to the intellectual pursuits of a few consecrated souls, as if the oils of consecration conferred the ability to think. The responsibility for the mediation of salvation, which according to the will of Christ devolves on the whole Church, was thus restricted to a small circle—mainly to the ordinary and extraordinary magisterium. Others were freed from responsibility, and no one took them seriously. It is to the credit of those concerned with reviving the communitarian values in Christianity that both clergy and laity are beginning to understand that, by their membership in the Church and by its sacramental character, they have received something which makes them apt and able to share in Church authority and in the mission of Christ to the whole world.

Another function of these groups concerns the apostolic life. If the community is the Gospel made visible, it is also a witness for a world which has mistaken ideas, or knows nothing, of this Gospel. Solitude and mission, it would seem, are seen today as mutually exclusive. The missionary pioneers deliberately choose to put themselves in teams or brotherly associations; there are also many laymen who seek a communal witness to their faith in their own milieu. In such groups certain circumstances readily communicate spiritual values: diverse and complementary charisms, faith by dialogue among members of the team, and mutual correction and encouragement.

Certainly there are potential difficulties in this group approach to personal spirituality. It is only too easy for it to turn into a kind of sect, a spiritual fraternity that would cease to be a faithful and true manifestation of the Church. Further, the hierarchy will often fear that the multiplicity of groups scatters energies to the detriment of the Church's central mission in the world.

There is also the danger that the faithful might go off to seek in these new communities what they should have found in existing structural communities in churches or parishes. Despite these dangers, we cannot fail to recognize that the modern phenomenon of the smaller association reveals an authentic seeking of the common good. And while this movement sometimes involves a decidedly defensive attitude with regard to society which is considered too all-encompassing and too anonymous, it would be a mistake to undervalue the real needs answered and objectives achieved.

In the end, however, the most obvious shortcoming of the personalist dimension in spirituality is that, by emphasizing self-fulfillment, one might lose sight of the corresponding need for detachment and purification in his Christian life. As Teilhard reminds us: "To create or organize material energy or truth or beauty brings with it inner torment which prevents those who face its hazards from sinking into the quiet and closed-in life wherein grows the vice of self-regard and attachment. . . . Over and over again he must go beyond himself, tear himself away from himself, leaving behind him his most cherished beginnings."[43] Such detachment means purification, and there is no purification without pain. How is self-fulfillment to be integrated into the feelings of futility which come with sickness, human misunderstandings, or the inevitable failures which must somehow be part of every effort to take part in the creative activity of God? To the Christian the real world is not merely a set of problems to be solved, but an unfathomable mystery; it is the world where Christ was crucified. If the Cross means anything, it must mean that all men, even those who labor to improve the world and to fulfill themselves as men, must expect and accept suffering before achievement, self-renunciation before self-fulfillment, death before life. To return to Teilhard: "What we have to learn is to preserve a real appetite for life and action while at the same time renouncing once and for all any desire to be happy just for ourselves. There is the secret—and not the illusion—of living in the divine milieu."[44]

A third trend which characterizes the Christian's relationship with God today may be described quite simply as relativism. Its origin is the thoroughly modern experience of rapid change at all levels of human life, an ever growing sense of time and history as well as an increased acceptance of the idea that all determinate patterns and structures, man's own human nature included, are contingent products of evolutionary development. What was once taken as fixed by eternal decree and thus able to afford the individual a stable framework is now seen as radically involved in process—a process, moreover, in which man himself is increasingly to have a hand. On the cognitional level the problem is whether one can be absolutely certain any more about anything. In a world of religious pluralism, it is no longer easy to accept the Church as something unique, its official pronouncements as more than directives, its authority in matters other than revelation as more than provisional. In terms of spirituality this means that the Church is conceived of more as a society in process than as a finished community, that universal and fixed patterns are no longer important to the spiritual life.

An essential quality of the relativism we have just described is contemporary man's orientation toward the future.[45] Man today, situated at a particular point in time, can only look toward the future to find his meaning. Either he plunges into the stream of history and is swept along with those who are striving for a dream or he stands aside with his eyes fixed on the horizon and waits for the coming of the kingdom of God (or man). Today is thus a fragment whose meaning depends upon tomorrow. The present lacks ultimate depth. Not where we are but where we are going, not what is but what is to be—this is our basic orientation of expectancy. Clearly such an attitude leaves little room for absolutes.

While this approach is capable of stimulating great enthusiasm, a desire to build a world that will be better for all men, there is danger that modern man has lost his "feel" for the present, and with it his capacity for leisure. He is forever in a state of tension. Divided between what is and what will be, he lacks a sense of wholeness. Life for him means simply being farther down the road of tomorrow than today, and the consequence has been to chain him to the wheel of progress. Living always in expectation, he lives without fulfillment. Distracted from the present, he misses the reality about him and his life becomes a kind of anxious vigil.

To some extent this orientation of expectancy is inevitable, as well as the relativistic attitude toward past and present values which it breeds. Actually, it is nothing more than a psychological translation of the process of "becoming."[46] To the degree, therefore, that man is involved in a movement toward a future term, temporalized consciousness is necessarily wrapped up with his whole set of attitudes and values. Discontent with the present and unceasing restlessness, uncertainty, and relativism are the consequences. Indeed these qualities become inseparable characteristics of his life as well as of his relation to God.

There should be no need to elaborate here the impetus which Teilhard de Chardin's evolutionary system has given to this orientation of modern man toward the future. "The world holds no interest for me, unless I look forward," he told a friend, "but when my eyes are on the future it is full of excitement."[47] Or again: "The past has revealed to me how the future is built, and preoccupation with the future tends to sweep everything else aside."[48] Nor did Teilhard hesitate to rebuke the Christians he knew for failing to integrate their human hope in man into the supernatural hope in God; for in his system the object of the world's development as well as the source of this development was the person of Christ. "O you of little faith, why fear or hold aloof from the onward march of the world? Why foolishly multiply your prophecies of woe? On the contrary, we must try everything for Christ; we must hope everything for Christ. . . . We can never know all that the Incarnation still asks of the world's potentialities. We can never hope for too much from the growing unity of mankind."[49]

If there is genuine virtue in stressing the element of dynamic change in human life and institutions, there is also risk in looking on change as being an end in itself and completely self-justifying. The risk is especially crucial today when in religious matters we so easily tend to absolutize the relative. Teilhard himself, of course, did not have this problem. "As far back as I go into my childhood," he writes, "nothing appears to me more characteristic or familiar in my interior make-up than the taste or irresistible need for something all sufficient and all necessary. To be really satisfied and completely happy meant for me a knowing that something 'essential' exists, of which all else is merely addition and ornament."[50] His evolutionary system was thus an extension of this psychological need, an effort to endow the evolution of the universe with a stability it could not otherwise have had, by demanding for its very existence a real attraction from a supreme personal Being. For this reason Teilhard was convinced that the present is more than a moment in a process; though man and his world are essentially changing, they must somehow transcend change. But many of those who quote Teilhard with enthusiasm give little evidence of a similar conviction.

The only factor which can give human and cosmic evolution such a transcendent ground is the power of love. Through love man unites himself to the terminus of all human progress, even while dedicating himself to the onward movement of the world at any particular moment in time. The union accomplished in loving and being loved by God transcends the whole order of becoming and thus balances expectation with possession and surrounds the relative with an all-embracing absolute. In this light, the whole movement of evolution becomes a means by which the divine presence is mediated to the world; it is precisely by exercising charity that man enters into this presence. To the extent that one's commitment to an endless series of relatives is impregnated with charity, it becomes an element in man's union with God and therefore of absolute significance. It becomes a force for promoting that peace and capacity to rest which so many have lost in the turmoil of our technological age.[51]

Nevertheless, Teilhard's synthesis does not provide all the correctives necessary to avoid the dangers of contemporary relativism. Certainly, with Teilhard, we can be thrilled by the spectacle of human progress. We can be convinced that evolution must succeed, that if the force of love triumphs, the risk of abso-

lutizing the relative and losing sight of the transcendent God
will be overcome, and that only a society united in love will be
capable of receiving Christ in his fullness as he will appear at the
end of time. But at the same time, we have to recognize that God
is utterly free to intervene as he pleases in history or at the end of
history. In the end, God can use or dispense with the service
which we seek to render. As Rahner puts it, our task is to labor
while it is day, for soon the night comes in which no man can
labor. Social evolution of itself will never succeed in stopping the
growth of evil in the world.

To Christianity and the Church her founder promised not only that
they would endure until the end of time but, just as clearly, that his
work would always be a sign of contradiction and persecution, of dire
and (in secular terms) desperate combat; that love would grow cold;
that he, in his disciples, would be persecuted in the name of God; that
the struggle would narrow down to an ever more critical point; that
the victory of Christianity would not be the fruit of immanent development and widening and a steady, progressive leavening of the world
but would come as the act of God coming in judgment to gather up
world history into its wholly unpredictable and unexpected end.[52]

  If our efforts fail, if there are woes and defections, if we are
thwarted in our striving to spread the Gospel of Christ, our
hearts need not be troubled. We neither have nor seek to have a
lasting city here on earth. God is greater than either our success
or our failures. He is the *Deus semper major,* our only lasting
hope.[53] If, then, the active presence of God in the world and the
act of God coming in judgment contain the absolute element
which stabilizes our process of evolution and our orientation
toward the future, it is this absolute of which we are in desperate
need in order to balance our equally pressing need to emphasize
the relative in our spiritual life.

  The purpose of this chapter has been to chart the tendencies
which we feel are most characteristic of Christian spirituality
today—the emphasis on the world, the personal, and the relative.
If it has become obvious in the course of the discussion that these
trends are mutually dependent upon one another, it should also

be clear that the most significant of them is man's attitude toward the world. Perhaps more than anything else Christians today want to feel that they can reach God through the world, through the whole scientific, technological, humanistic enterprise. To treat the world merely as an agglomeration of material goods and objects outside ourselves and to reject these goods and objects in order to seek other things which are "interior" and "spiritual" is, in fact, to miss the whole point of the challenging confrontation between Christ and the world.[54]

Do we really choose between the world and Christ as between two conflicting realities absolutely opposed? Or do we choose Christ by choosing the world as it really is in him—that is to say, created and redeemed by him, and encountered in the ground of our own personal freedom, our own relative understanding, and our love? Do we really renounce ourselves and the world in order to find Christ, or do we actually choose our own deepest truth in choosing both the world and Christ at the same time? If, as Teilhard reminds us, the deepest ground of my being is love, then in that very love itself and nowhere else will I find myself, the world, my brother, and Christ. It is not a question of either/or, but of all-in-one. It is not a matter of exclusivism and "purity," but of wholeness and wholeheartedness.

Thus the world cannot be a problem to anyone who sees that ultimately Christ, the world, his brother, and his own unique personal fulfillment are made one and the same in grace and redemptive love. If all the current talk about the world, personalism, and relativism help people to discover this, then it is fine. But if it produces nothing but a whole new divisive gamut of obligatory positions and "contemporary answers" to past problems, we might as well forget it.

To this extent it always seems of questionable validity to use the expression "new spirituality" to speak of contemporary Christian aspirations, when we really mean only a different light thrown by the same Gospel on the existence of the believing Christian. Nevertheless, because of the social and cultural conditions of Christian existence and the new historical situation created for the Church in the present time, it is beyond doubt that we are going through a period of change, contention, and insecurity in which the traditional spiritualities in the Church are being questioned.

The spiritual movements which we have discussed indicate the unmistakable vitality of the Church; for this reason we can only hope for and favor their development. But they are also the most delicate and vulnerable flowerings of life in the Church; all sorts of maladies can afflict them. It would be a grave error for any of us to be aloof either to today's needs and objectives or to the balances necessary in developing a contemporary spirituality. The advice which Paul gives is always pertinent: "Never try to suppress the Spirit or treat the gift of prophecy with contempt; think before you do anything—hold on to what is good and avoid every form of evil" (I Thess. 5:19-22).

Chapter XII

THE DESERT
AND THE CITY

WE ARE CURRENTLY WITNESSING in Catholic theology a formal and profound renewal whereby the Church wishes not simply to update herself or to make her message relevant, but fundamentally to apprehend her primal consciousness anew, to examine it, to purify it, to see if it is still rooted in the Gospel, and only then to relate it to our modern era. In this sense the Church stands before her normative document, Holy Scripture, and seeks a living interpretation of this document both within her own confines and, hopefully, within the world. It is in the context of this living interpretation that we hope for reform in institutions, reform in ideas, reform in decisions, and reform in spirituality.

As tradition in the Church grows, it inevitably tends to become sophisticated and complex, thus needing perpetual examination and constant rethinking. This process is not always simple because we ourselves are part of tradition: in questioning tradition we question ourselves. As Josiah Royce has observed: "Each contemporary person . . . may be regarded as the heir to the 'education of the human race' insofar as he possesses both the recorded experience and the knowledge of his predecessors as well as that of his own time."[1]

To read about the past, therefore, is always in fact to ask ques-

tions about the present. The patient reader who has labored with
us through the preceding historical discussion of spirituality still
faces the task of trying to live by the Gospel in today's world. In
the light of the tradition of spirituality, where is he to stand?
What is the "truth" about man's spiritual life? What should his
view of this history be in face of the risks which confront him in
the present and the future?

Certainly these are not idle questions. Because they are not
posed abstractly and theoretically, but are part of the lived experience of a concrete, existing human being, they can become
extremely pressing questions about one's own Christian existence
in the world. Is it at all possible to live as a Christian in today's
world—not just to get along somehow, but to really live by the
Gospel? Or, if one genuinely desires to live by the Gospel, does
he not have to forsake the city and retire into the "desert"? It is
to such questions that we must, by way of summary, turn our
attention in this final chapter. Of necessity our reflections here
will be more random than systematic, indicating certain points of
emphasis and discomfort raised by the preceding historical considerations. Our approach will follow the development of spirituality to a certain degree backward, that is, starting at the
point reached in the last chapter, the discussion of the present
problematic.

The world today has become secular, and unless all appearances are deceptive, the end of the process is by no means in
sight. This universal secularization puts the challenge squarely:
what should a spirituality be for a man in the world? Spirituality
can, of course, attempt to curtain itself off from such an uncomfortable question; it can continue to presume from behind closed
doors that the well tried formulas of theology and piety will
continue to operate—as though the day of Pentecost had not yet
dawned, and with it the need to understand and interpret the
action of the Spirit in each successive age. This kind of timeless
faith certainly avoids embarrassment from within—that salutary
embarrassment through which God opens new paths. Such a spirituality, moreover, is never at a loss for words; it can talk about
God and the world with astonishing but complacent fluency. Yet

all too noticeably it lacks the ring of the true answers required, for it has lost the sound of reality.

Today's spirituality asks whether the world must be desacralized to make room for God. Perhaps this is the essential meaning, not only of the new emphases (which we optimistically call "developments") in spirituality in recent years, but of the change in the whole modern era, beginning with the Protestant Reformation. In reaction against this "threat," the basic tendency of Catholic spirituality since the late Middle Ages has been to sacramentalize life in all its details. Religious zeal has tried to infuse an "objective" sacred meaning into each activity of the day. One attained God in discrete, individual acts, rather than through a prolonged activity, a period, a whole life. Thus, morality focused on individual acts while spirituality centered on the atomic moment. From both the theological and the psychological points of view, one almost *had* to believe that in fulfilling formal obligations—attending Mass, making one's private devotions, working in the office, doing housework, and even following a particular vocation in life—one was in immediate union with the will of God, and this not in a generic sense, but in the most specific sense—that God willed precisely this act and no other.

Why did one *have to* believe this? The necessity for this kind of spirituality came from the psychological need to have a way of distinguishing between "doing God's will" and "just living"—in other words, between religious and worldly existence. But why was such a criterion needed? It was required both from the desperate desire to experience life as meaningful, in immediate relation to the Absolute; and from the whole structure of Catholic spiritual and theological thought, which was designed to satisfy this need and, in doing so, confirm it. The whole function of the spiritual life, therefore, was to put one in authoritative and infallible contact with the absolute will of God by giving that will an unambiguous, particularized content—God wills this rather than that. The Catholic understanding of revelation led one to expect such divine guidance in daily life; the Catholic theology of obedience enabled one to satisfy the expectation. Otherwise one was at the mercy of one's freedom, with all the chance calamities that entailed. Catholic piety since the Reformation thus invested concrete particular choices with the force of an absolute, and turned contingency into necessity in a prolonged effort to avoid what Eliade has called "the terror of history," that is, the anxiety of exposure to the chance event, the secular city of impersonal happenings.

Thus the fear that keeps some Catholics worriedly confessing their absence from Sunday Mass—although they were "juridically" excused from this obligation because of sickness or extraordinary circumstances—or keeps some religious continually anxious over cutting short the prescribed time for formal prayer is as much the fear of the void as of God's displeasure. For to allow excuses from absolute obligations is to introduce psychological or even physical factors not immediately of religious significance and set them up on the same level as religious ones. In a way, of course, the need to evade the terror of history, the need to have the absolute in the midst of the relative, is still universal; but it does not have to be experienced as such in an empirically discriminatory way. Such needs are the structural needs of human life, not its daily nourishment.

To some extent, Protestant criticism of Catholic spirituality is correct. Catholics have tended to absolutize the relative—to take individual human acts of feeling or thinking, and to set them up as universal and definitive. But this danger is fast disappearing. Once the spirituality of the past is seen as relative, human, ambiguous in effect, it loses that very absoluteness which gave it much of its value. For the person who is conscious that previous forms of piety—types of medieval devotion like the Nativity or the rosary—represent particular and relative ways of "ordering" Christian belief and experience, is also aware that they are one-sided, partial, potentially misleading. He must adopt toward them a critical attitude, which inhibits his simply dwelling in them, giving himself to them with full confidence as to something independent of himself and wholly trustworthy. Once the tradition of Christian spirituality is seen as relative, human, and subject to error and distortion, it loses that very independence of the individual which gave it its psychological force. The truth is not something simply out there and imposed upon him, but something he himself must measure, judge, and weigh—something-to-be-found. Even one's attitude toward the Scriptures is inescapably critical. The Holy Word itself may be infallible, but any particular understanding of it may not be. This kind of critical consciousness does not make either faith or the spiritual life impossible, of course, but it does seem to increase its risk considerably.

But Protestants are mistaken in regarding the tendency to absolutize the relative as a species of idolatry. It is not the religious value, the divine transcendence, which suffers—that is, God being turned into a clock-watcher or moral bookkeeper. Instead it is human values and relative goods—married love, human emotions, the intellectual life—which are cast out as if they were evil.

One of Luther's central insights was the inefficacy of "works," the powerlessness of human efforts to placate God by asceticism of any kind. In this he seems to have rediscovered a genuinely biblical theme and to have helped create a significant aspect of modern consciousness—including religious consciousness. Today we feel strongly and spontaneously that much of the asceticism of the past labored over a shallow level of the human personality, that emphasis on pure intentions and acts of the will was misguided and left untouched the more basic layers of our moral and spiritual being. We are and remain pretty much the same people that we always were; our conscious efforts at spiritual progress and moral improvement do not seem to effect a great deal. Still, Luther's insight must be reconciled with the no less biblical conviction that what we do with our lives, what we make of ourselves, matters extremely—that God will reward all men according to their works, and that interior purity is a supreme value.

As we reflect on the history of spirituality, it becomes increasingly difficult to understand what the words "spiritual progress" might mean or to think of the spiritual life as any sort of autonomous entity at all. While the traditional understanding seems to have had great meaning and reality for a number of the

saints, today it appears that life is the same, always and everywhere—that if in the course of it some of us are brought to a
more intense realization and more effective service of God, this is
not the effect primarily of a carefully cultivated "interior life." It
can happen only as a function of a person's total life experience
(youth, education, family, work, marriage, success or failure),
and not by some independent process, a self-contained spiritual
life of withdrawal and contemplation. The spiritual life is only
an aspect of the total life, not a separate and parallel life of its
own. All this is no doubt obvious. But the problem then becomes
that of grasping the relationship between one's religious practices
and the rest of life, so that they can be seen as continuous and yet
significantly distinct. For unless they *are* distinct, one's whole life
dissolves into a series of ascetical exercises, loses all of its meaning, and evaporates.

The conviction that God must be already present in ordinary
human life *to begin with*—instead of having to be dragged in by
the aid of morning offerings, pure intentions, and spiritual
thoughts—surely requires a new understanding of the function
of human existence. This, of course, was the problem with
medieval piety. How could the distinction between God and "the
world" be maintained within the context of a necessary effort to
see their connectedness?

As we have pointed out repeatedly in preceding chapters, past
religious (or spiritual) orientation generally tended to be either
indifferent or hostile to the factual, the particular structure of
the contingent-created world. This was necessarily so, since the
religious orientation was thought to move down from the universal, the always-and-everywhere Absolute God; individual
variations in history were at best irrelevant, at worst a temptation to be spurned. This stands out especially in the ascetical-
mystical approach to charity and obedience. What is mystically
relevant is that this is a person loved by God or that this is a
command willed by God; *who* the person, *what* the command,
should be of no account. The particularity is not so much denied
as ignored; knowledge of it is submerged, tacit. Obviously this
"mystical" approach contains a primary truth. But is it not also

true that the more contingent reality—my everyday human life—
is absorbed into transcendent response, the more solid, more
human, more meaningful it becomes? Such absorption of the
secular into the sacred is legitimate, of course, only to the extent
that awareness of the world is not allowed to weaken the vigor of
faith itself. The fact that such weakening of faith is always possible is one of the reasons for monasticism and all forms of world-
rejection. But a proper mixture, the actual interplay of withdrawal and involvement in the life of faith, of prayer and action
in the world can by no means be determined in advance as a
matter of fixed quantities.

In its own way spirituality must posit the secular as distinct
from itself in order to realize its own essence. Yet the Christian
knows that the secular can never be a reality outside him for
which he exists—a firm and absolute objective structure which
has to be accepted merely on its own inexorable terms. The
world has in fact no terms of its own. If anything, the world
exists for us and we exist for ourselves. It is only in assuming full
responsibility for our world, for our lives and for ourselves that
we can be said really to live for God. Thus the way to find the
real world is not merely to measure and observe what is outside
us, but to discover our own inner ground. This "ground," this
"world," where I am mysteriously present at once to my own self
and to the freedoms of all other men, is a living and self-creating
mystery of which I am myself a part and which defines me as the
person that I am.

What place, then, should we give to religious and ascetical
practices in our lives? Religious acts, it would seem, derive their
primary value from their symbolic function. To ratify and personally endorse our pre-existent relationship, our union with
God, we re-bind ourselves to live according to a certain significant pattern in token of our dedication to him. Like an artist,
who in his work achieves a symbolic mastery of experience, we
perform certain symbolic acts to confirm and express a relationship which is beyond us, a ritual consecration. Most of the time
this kind of ritual act is indeed all we can do; it makes us aware
of our dedication and our faith even when life (and through life,

God) is not actually making severe demands on us—thus helping us to respond to the true meaning of those demands when they come.

But such ritual patterns of life are open to a degree of cultural fluctuation. Life, with its own inner structures and finality, changes its demands from age to age. Especially in a period of rapid transition, there is danger that the symbol will be preferred to the thing itself, that the ritual, rather than mediating deeper contact with reality, will be maintained in defiance of that reality. For example, there may be a conflict between making a novena and taking care of the children, or between the Benedictine ideal of rhythmic balance of liturgical prayer, *lectio divina,* and manual labor and the pressing needs of education and apostolic service, or between the "don't-step-on-a-crack" rules of the cloister and the needs of humanity—even one's own humanity. There is also danger of the significant pattern of ascetical practices losing its significance and becoming merely eccentric and arbitrary, if not the sign of an obsession with ritual purity, like the outlandish penances of eastern monasticism. Finally there is the danger of the spiritual life fostering a spirit of Pharisaism quite opposed to real religion—persuading one who has no trouble in keeping his self-constructed, self-imposed "law" that he is not just holy, but extra-holy!

This clinging to isolated and nonfunctional religious practice both grows out of and reinforces an extrinsic view of the spiritual life—one in which religious ideals are seen as something outside of man to which he must conform and bring the rest of his life. Besides, it too often unwittingly promotes an anthropomorphic notion of God: he becomes the heavenly king always on the watch to make sure he receives due service from his none-too-devoted subjects. To this extent Tillich and Robinson are clearly right. Such a God who is simply "out there," a transcendent "Thou" set over against my "I," is a being alongside other beings, a myth, not God at all.

In the same way it is rather easy (often inevitable) to slip into the habit of regarding God as a kind of impersonal background that can be relied upon, like the sun, to provide light and warmth, while at the same time remaining quite remote and unchanging regardless of what I am. Nothing I do or fail to do makes much difference; he is always "there," at the same infinite distance. In this context it becomes very difficult to believe in the possibility of any sort of *personal* "will" of God in one's own regard—to believe, for instance, that he could actually expect something of me that is not already written in my "nature" and personality or already given in the religious practices which I have taken upon myself to please him. The spiritual life thus becomes very much of a monologue; its limitless risk is drastically reduced, and with it any sense of importance or urgency.

Genuine spiritual life is clearly more than this; it springs from the immanent purpose of God in creating man and enabling him to realize his humanity fully—historically, personally, socially. To the degree that this immanent purpose is achieved, creation also realizes its extrinsic purpose, the glory of God. But one of the components of man's humanity-to-be-achieved is precisely the recognition of the transcendent source of his being and personality. This recognition should take place when and as the transcendent manifests itself. A man should pray when he is moved to pray. And his spirituality, his experience of life as meaningful and worthwhile within the dimension of faith, should not depend so directly on a conscious seizure of the Absolute on a moment-to-moment basis as on the over-all orientation of his enduring relationship to God. But because he is a sinner, man must foster the conditions of spontaneous, over-all union with God; hence he adopts a particular pattern of religious practice to insure the expression of this continuing union.

Certainly there is truth in the humanist claim that religion (and spirituality) is for man's sake, since God himself needs nothing—neither the "blood of goats and bulls" nor human praise and service. The content of a religious act cannot even be specified apart from the good of man; that is, the appropriate form of praise and service is determined immediately by its relation to man and its "utility" (in the highest sense), not by a direct relation to some arbitrary "decrees" of God. In a sense, of course, God does need man and man's work to complete his reality in the created world—as the contingent term of a contingent need. God needs man for much the same reason that human love needs externalization and expression. Without such incarnation in matter, love rapidly ceases to exist at the level of spiritual consciousness. God needs the work of man's hands to guarantee his continued presence in the world at the specifically human level—that level at which, precisely, man runs the risk of losing his own being. In short, God needs man as a means of satisfying man's own need for God.

Still, the question arises as it did in the last chapter: Is not God sufficiently glorified in man's self-achievement? And does not such achievement adequately contain whatever spirituality man needs? Is it not artificial and unnecessary, at best, to try to stir up in people an explicit spirituality, since what is not expressed spontaneously had better be left unexpressed? Certainly there is truth in this too. If explicit spirituality is required, it can only be because such express recognition is human, and the want of it discourteous. But man's spiritual response to God is not a fixed tribute, preordained; it is measured by immanent necessity. When all this is said, it still must be added that spirituality only benefits man when it is sought unconditionally—like art.

In the end, then, it is true that much traditional spirituality has been based on a cultural misjudgment as well as a theological fallacy. The effort to create a spiritual ghetto—"spiritual" meaning intellectual *and* religious—was only a microcosmic imitation of the attempt of Catholic culture since the Reformation to be self-sufficient despite the loss of half of that self; to shut its doors firmly against a world that rejected its ideas and ideals. Like counter-reformation Catholicism, monastic and "neomonastic" spirituality tended to create an "unreal" world, geographically as well as intellectually closed against the world at large. Within those walls were pursued the old ideals of recollection, purity of conscience, the exclusion of all that could contaminate. The basic question, however, is whether or not such enclosure can be or even should be maintained. Have not the same forces which conspired to create the Catholic diaspora also shattered the cloister walls?

The spiritual ghetto was still possible in a world which politely stayed outside, which made few demands and offered no challenges to the Christian's life. Even if the missionary-monk could move out into that world, he could operate there without really being *of* it—knowing that before sundown he would return to the safety of monastery walls. But effective action *in* the world (not to mention the need for a halfway contemporary and adult spiritual life within the cloister) demands more permanent intellectual and psychological involvement. As a result, the "spiritual" structure of today's world imposes itself on the mental-moral-affective life of everyone—even in the monastery—to a degree never before imaginable. The demand can be ignored only at the cost of effective exclusion from the world of thought and culture. The ideals of retirement and non-contamination harmonize poorly with those of service to others and involvement in a world of action.

This is not to say that there is no place in today's secular society for a monastic and contemplative spirituality. It does say, however, that there is no place for a view of the world as something to be "escaped" in a monastery or in certain pious ascetical exercises. The world is not just a physical space traversed by jet planes and full of people running in all directions. It is a complex of responsibilities and options made out of the love and hate, the fear and hope, the faith and trust, the kindness and suspicion of us all. It is both an object of choice and something about which there is and can be no choice. Historically, as we have seen, these notions have sometimes got mixed up, so that what is simply "given" appears to have been chosen, and what there is to be chosen, decided for or against, is simply evaded as if no decision were legitimate or even possible.

In relating itself to the world, authentic spirituality, whether monastic or apostolic, is basically admitting that the world can once again become an object of choice.[2] In fact it must be chosen. If one has no choice about the age in which he is to live, still he has a choice about the attitude he takes and about the way and the extent of his participation in its living, ongoing events. To choose the world is not merely a pious admission that the world is acceptable because it comes from the hand of God. It is primarily an acceptance of a task and a vocation in the world, in history, and in time. To choose the world is to choose to do the work I am capable of doing, in collaboration with my brother, to make the world better, more free, more just, more livable, more human. It has now become obvious, in other words, that mere automatic "rejection of the world" or "contempt for the world" is in fact not a choice but the evasion of choice.

True monastic spirituality is an honest and legitimate attempt to allow that dying with Christ which was essentially brought about in Baptism to become a reality throughout a whole life and in its complete significance. The monk is the man who dies into Christ, the man for whom the enjoyment of the world has been submerged by poverty, earthly love by virginity, self-assertion and human autonomy by obedience. The monk, then, does not reject the world as much as he chooses a certain relation to the world. By freely and visibly withdrawing from some of its aspects, he exhibits a kind of artistic respect for them—neither taking advantage of them nor allowing them to take advantage of him; rather, he gives witness to the fact that they are not absolutes, that they come from the gracious and merciful Lord who alone is above all and greater than all, whom alone man can serve without danger of dehumanizing himself.

But just as monastic spirituality runs the risk of slipping into a stereotype of world-escapism which cannot be accepted, so apostolic spirituality, in its legitimate involvement with the secular world, runs the risk of building bridges to a vanishing shore—or at least to a shore where it might find few people waiting to respond. There is danger, in other words, that world-escapism is being replaced by a collection of equally empty stereotypes of world-affirmation which carry just as little meaning. If only we can move worship of God out of the sanctuary and into the street; if only we can be relevant in the inner city and the public universities; if only theology can become desacralized and divested of its historical concerns; if only, in short, we can live "out there" in the secular world with an open sense of engagement—then, so the argument goes, Christianity in general and spirituality in particular will have a new lease on meaning and purpose. The question is whether or not we are in danger of carrying on an over-romanticized relationship with the secular world, one doomed not to be reciprocated.[3]

The secular world does not seem to be standing around waiting to hear what a secularized Christianity has to say. Certainly it is important for the Christian to feel at home in a world come of age, to risk jettisoning those elements of traditional spirituality which are merely the product of a specific time and culture. But the world affirms itself; it does not need much help from Christian theology. And it is certainly not idle to ask whether the world will suddenly turn to Christianity or the Church when these have themselves succeeded in becoming "secularized." .

When members of religious orders say that they might desert community for the family because that is where *real* community lies, one wonders if they have ever taken a second look at modern marriage and family. When a priest says he would like to leave the clergy because he feels trapped in a complex, obsolete, depersonalized institutional structure and that he would like to become involved in the modern university, research center, corporation, or even social service agency because then he could move beyond such entrapment, one wonders whether he has ever taken a real look at these alternatives. Does the secular world automatically offer freedom in the way its life is organized? Are not such reactions actually motivated by a certain romanticization of the secular? Perhaps what has been called "secular theology" must now be seen for what it is: only half—even if a long-neglected half—of the story. It is vitally important to face up to the other side of the coin: how men deal with religion, with the sacred, with prayer and renunciation, with a personal relationship to God and witness to Jesus Christ in such a world that is so obviously secular. The positive lessons of Christian secularity are quickly learned; angelism, docetism, self-obsession with ecclesiastical forms, musty incense, and superstitious practices are not the main threats to Christian life today.

What most profoundly does threaten the Christian believer today is a subtle but pervasive sense of hopelessness. God has exalted man and given him the prospect of a life that is wide and free, but man hangs back and lets himself down. God promises a new creation of all things in justice and peace, but man acts as if everything remained just as before. God honors him with his promises, but man does not believe himself capable of facing what is required of him. Hence we try to remain on the solid ground of "reality," to think clearly and deal with the pressing problems of the present, finding little meaning in faith and less ground for hope.

But, as recent theology is emphasizing, Christian faith is a straining after and an anticipation of the future of Christ which is the future of the world; it is a faith based on hope which revolutionizes and transforms the present.[4] The Christian God is the God of the exodus and of the resurrection. His revelation is not primarily a word of information, of address, nor merely a word expressing personal self-communication; his revelation is a word of promise. His statements are announcements, his preaching is the proclamation of what is to come; and the God who is so revealed is not an eternal presence, but the God of promise, the God in front, the God with future as his essential nature, whom we "await" and "follow" with active hope. Christian faith, however, does not offer man a groundless ideology of the future. Rather, it is anchored in a definite reality which is Jesus Christ. The Christ-event "sets the stage for history, on which there emerges the possibility of the engulfing of all things in nothingness and of the new creation."[5] It does not fulfill all promises, but itself becomes promise. Hence the Christian mission is not a mere repetition of the event, but an expectation of new "fulfillment of the promised righteousness of God in all things, the fulfillment of the resurrection of the dead that is promised in the resurrection, the fulfillment of the lordship of the crucified one over all things that is promised in his exaltation."[6]

Such a fulfillment is more than a projection of man's own possibilities; it is the call to create something new which never before has been—not a utopian romanticism for things that have no place, but a realistic striving for things that have no place as yet. Only with this perspective can the Christian contribute something to the world—not the world as it is but the world *as possible,* as straining after future realization. As Paul reminds us, Christians are simply "those who have hope" (Eph. 2:22; I Thess. 4:13). Thus the Christian is a man who draws his stimulus and inspiration from the future promised by God and who calls into question the "new world" emerging from merely human possibilities. Christianity, therefore, fosters a continual criticism and transformation of the present in the light of the universal future kingdom; the "new world" rather corresponds to the promise expressed in the cross and resurrection of Christ and the hope for its fulfillment which originally sets in motion our search and creative drive toward the future.

How, then, does the Christian realize this mission for the future of the world? It cannot be achieved through pure contemplation, since contemplation by definition is related to what has become and what is now. The future for which the Christian hopes is rather something which is being formed and to-be-formed. The "Kingdom of God," the New Testament symbol for the content of Christian hope, is a double-barrelled word. It denotes both future and present reality—the future coming of God among his people, but also God in our midst (at times identified with Jesus himself, at other times with the concrete community of believers). Christian hope must retain this tension, neither demythologizing the prophetic element in the Christian message to such an extent that new events in salvation history are seen as impossible, nor stressing the future to such an extent that present movements in culture (whether in science, art, or politics) are totally rejected. Christian hope, as an expectation for the future, involves a love that accepts and responds to people as they are now, without sacrificing them for some abstract ideal.[7]

A spirituality built on this kind of creative and militant hope is far from a spirit of naive optimism. It does not canonize the progress we are bringing about. It is and remains the expression of a hope which we set against the self-erected idols of secularized society. It does not attempt to pierce through the future and rob it of mystery, claiming to know more than others about the future. A Christian spirituality of hope values precisely the poverty of its knowledge about the future. It does not attempt to outbid by its optimism all forms of human suffering and limitation, but strives to remain faithful to such experiences and, precisely through them, to realize all the painful breadth and depth of its hope—hope against hope. For a spirituality of hope is aware of the greatest risk of all: it is aware of death before which all the glittering promises are threatened and grow dim.[8]

Within this context, Christian life is seen to have a double movement. It is a life of dying with Christ, a life of the cross, a life beyond the aims and purposes that belong to this world alone. But at the same time Christian life is an incarnation, an acceptance of the world for its transformation by faith, a hopeful witness to the victory of the risen Christ made visible in history by his power of healing, preservation, and redemption—a witness carried on within the world of our brothers, a self-forgetting love for others (for the "least of our brothers"), in selfless commitment to *their* hope.

To speak of spirituality, especially a spirituality for our time, thus involves an option not for the desert *or* the city, but the desert *and* the city—withdrawal and involvement—knowing that ultimately Christ, the world, our brother, and our own inmost selves are united in grace and redemptive love. Yet God must be recognized and chosen above and beyond all things before everything can be accepted not merely for God's sake or its own, but for God's sake *and* its own. For this reason contemporary Christian spirituality must be seen as a continuity between the traditions of the past which it incorporates and transcends and the transcending events of the future. Only with such a perspective can man enter into sacred history and remain open to the renewing action of God in every historical event in the world. The recurring danger is that a theology of the spiritual life will turn into an ideology of religious idealism which so absolutizes a past or future idea that it denies the continual possibility of newness and the continual creative activity of God in the movements of history. Spirituality must affirm past, future, and present; memory, expectation, and activity; faith, hope, and love—to overcome the faithless rebellion and hopeless servitude of a loveless world.

As for me brothers, when I came to you, it was not with any show of oratory or philosophy, but simply to tell you what God had guaranteed. During my stay with you, the only knowledge I claimed to have was about Jesus, and only about him as the crucified Christ. Far from relying on any power of my own, I came among you in great "fear and trembling" and in my speeches and sermons that I gave, there were none of the arguments that belong to philosophy; only a demonstration of the power of the Spirit. And I did this so that your faith should not depend on human philosophy but on the power of God.

But still we have a wisdom to offer those who have reached maturity; not a philosophy of our age, it is true, still less of the masters of our age, which are coming to their end. The hidden wisdom of God which we teach in our mysteries is the wisdom that God predestined to be for our glory before the ages began. It is a wisdom that none of the masters of this age has ever known, or they would not have crucified the Lord of Glory; we teach what scripture calls: "the things that no eye has seen and no ear has heard; things beyond the mind of man, all that God has prepared for those who love him."

These are the very things that God has revealed to us through the Spirit, for the Spirit reaches the very depths of everything, even the depths of God. . . . Therefore we teach, not in the way in which philosophy is taught, but in the way that the Spirit teaches us: we teach spiritual things spiritually. An unspiritual person is one who does not accept anything of the Spirit of God: he sees it all as nonsense; it is beyond his understanding because it can only be understood by means of the Spirit. A spiritual man, on the other hand, is able to judge the value of everything, and his own value is not to be judged by other men. As scripture says: "Who can know the mind of the Lord, so who can teach him?" But we are those who have the mind of Christ.

(I Cor. 2)

Notes

1. For example, in discussing Evagrius and the Evagrian tradition, we would now give more attention to the positive value of "apophatic" (wordless) prayer—especially as re-interpreted by someone like Basil Pennington (*Centering Prayer* [Garden City, N.Y.: Doubleday, 1980])—while continuing to caution against the world-denying, body-denying "anthropology" that produced it and has accompanied it so closely. In our technological age, we have come to know more clearly that the enemy is not the body, but the controlling rationalist mind (see Charles Davis, *Body as Spirit* [New York: Seabury, 1976], chs. ii and iii), to which "centering prayer" can be an effective antidote.

CHAPTER I: A SPIRITUALITY FOR OUR TIME

1. The definition is Christian Duquoc's ("Theology and Spirituality," *Spirituality in the Secular City*, ed. Christian Duquoc, O.P. [Glen Rock, N.J.: Paulist, 1966], p. 89).

2. Among their writings, cf. Adrian Van Kaam, C.S.Sp., *Religion and Personality* (Englewood Cliffs, N.J.: Prentice-Hall, 1964), and *Personality Fulfillment in the Religious Life* (New York: Dimension, 1966); John J. Evoy, S.J., and Van H. Christoph, S.J., *Personality Development in the Religious Life* (New York: Sheed and Ward, 1963), and *Maturity in the Religious Life* (New York: Sheed and Ward, 1965); Eugene C. Kennedy, M.M., " 'The Answer Is Not in the Stars': Some Thoughts on the Vocation Crisis," *Bulletin of the National Catholic Educational Association*, LX (1963), 509-512, "Differentiated Discipline in the Seminary," *BNCEA*, LXI (1964), 79-85, "Aggiornamento, Anxiety and the Seminary," *The Critic*, XXIII (1965), 33-35, and, together with Paul F. Darcy, *The Genius of the Apostolate* (New York: Sheed and Ward, 1965).

3. John Powell, S.J., "The Retreat Master Comes to the Convent," *The Retreat Master Faces the Nun in the Modern World*, ed. John Powell, Eugene Grollmes, and Lammert Otten (St. Mary's, Kansas: St. Mary's College, 1965), pp. 42-43.

4. Adolph Tanquerey, S.S., *The Spiritual Life: A Treatise on Ascetical and Mystical Theology* (Baltimore: St. Mary's Seminary, 1930; original French edition 1923); Joseph de Guibert, S.J., *The Theology of the Spiritual Life* (New York: Sheed and Ward, 1953; original Latin edition 1937); published about the same time as de

Guibert was *The Three Ages of the Interior Life* by Reginald Garrigou-Lagrange, O.P.

5. Tanquerey, *op. cit.,* p. 182.

6. Louis Bouyer, *Introduction to Spirituality* (New York: Desclee, 1961).

7. A similar lack of discrimination, it seems, is to be found in Louis Bouyer's *The Spirituality of the New Testament and the Fathers* (New York: Desclee, 1963), the first volume of a new four-volume history to be translated: "[Bouyer] covers so much ground that he has to sacrifice reflection to the mere amassing of material. The eight pages of general conclusion at the end of the book are woefully inadequate . . ." (*The Way,* IV [1964], 159).

8. Columba Marmion, *Christ, the Life of the Soul* (St. Louis: B. Herder, 1922), and *Christ in His Mysteries* (St. Louis: B. Herder, 1924); Anscar Vonier, *The Collected Works* (Westminster, Md.: Newman, 1952), 3 vols. For some of the information and judgments in this and the following paragraph, the authors are indebted to Elmer O'Brien's essay, "English Culture and Spirituality," *Spirituality in the Secular City,* pp. 142-153.

9. Alban Goodier, *The Public Life of Our Lord* (New York: Kenedy, 1930), 2 vols., and *The Passion and Death of Our Lord* (New York: Kenedy, 1933); Goodier's little pamphlet, *A More Excellent Way* (Bombay, no date) was, however, ahead of its time in teaching dedication to Christ in place of the innumerable methods and devotions inculcated by his contemporaries.

10. Edward Leen, *Progress through Mental Prayer* (New York: Sheed and Ward, 1935); Boylan, *Difficulties in Mental Prayer* (Westminster, Md.: Newman, 1943).

11. Ronald Knox, *Occasional Sermons* (New York: Sheed and Ward, 1960), *The Gospel in Slow Motion* (New York: Sheed and Ward, 1950), *The Window in the Wall: Reflections on the Holy Eucharist* (New York: Sheed and Ward, 1956), *Bridegroom and Bride* (New York: Sheed and Ward, 1957), *Pastoral Sermons* (New York: Sheed and Ward, 1960), *University and Anglican Sermons* (New York: Sheed and Ward, 1963).

12. Gerald Vann, *The Heart of Man* (New York: Longmans, Green, 1945); *The Divine Pity* (New York: Sheed and Ward, 1946).

13. Francis LeBuffe, *My Changeless Friend* (27 vols.; New York: Apostleship of Prayer, 1915-1943); Martin Scott, *God and Myself: An Inquiry into the True Religion* (New York: Kenedy, 1917),

You and Yours: Practical Talks on Home Life (New York: Kenedy, 1921), *Religion and Common Sense* (New York: Kenedy, 1926), *Happiness* (New York: Kenedy, 1931), *Answer Wisely* (Chicago: Loyola University Press, 1938).

14. Fulton Sheen, *Peace of Soul* (New York: McGraw-Hill, 1949), *Life Is Worth Living* (New York: McGraw-Hill, 1953-1957).

15. Thomas Merton, *The Seven Storey Mountain* (New York: Harcourt Brace, 1948), *The Sign of Jonas* (New York: Harcourt Brace, 1953).

16. O'Brien, *op. cit.,* pp. 152-153. Cf. Robert Gleason's *Christ and the Christian* (New York: Sheed and Ward, 1959), and *To Live Is Christ* (New York: Sheed and Ward, 1961); the work of Charles Davis ought also to be mentioned here (e.g., *Liturgy and Doctrine* [New York: Sheed and Ward, 1960], and *The Making of a Christian* [New York: Sheed and Ward, 1964]).

17. The emergence of promising new American theologians like Avery Dulles and Gabriel Moran gives hope that our theological balance of payments problem is starting to be solved. In Scripture studies, of course, American Catholic scholars have long been holding their own, as the names Ahern, Brown, McKenzie, W. Moran, Stanley, and Vawter attest.

18. Teilhard de Chardin, *The Future of Man* (New York: Harper and Row, 1964), p. 12.

19. In its classical statement, this is the heresy of the age of the spirit, "the third age," as Gabriel Moran calls it ("The God of Revelation," *Commonweal,* LXXXV [February 10, 1967], 499), where institutional forms will fade away and each individual will be immersed in the spirit. Modernism, of course, did not have the tools to carry out its ambitious project. But few would deny that—stripped of excesses—the Modernist quest was a legitimate one—to experience God, or, at least, to search for a God who would speak in one's own life.

20. Avery Dulles, S.J., "The Ignatian Experience as Reflected in the Spiritual Theology of Karl Rahner," *Philippine Studies,* XIII (1965), 472-474. We are indebted to Dulles' precis of Rahner in developing our own formulations in these paragraphs.

21. Quoted by Christopher F. Mooney, S.J., "Ignatian Spirituality and Modern Theology," *Downside Review,* LXXX (1962), 334. The original distinctions in spirituality in the following pages, especially in

the distinction between vision and technique, are Mooney's; see pp. 333-335.

22. Cf. David Knowles, *From Pachomius to Ignatius* (Oxford: Clarendon Press, 1966), pp. 21-22.

23. For further development of this point, see Peter L. Berger and Thomas Luckman, *The Social Construction of Reality* (Garden City: Doubleday, 1966), pp. 74-85.

24. Evagrius, *On Prayer,* No. 61 (Migne, *Patrologia Graeca,* LXXIX, 1180; translated in Elmer O'Brien, *Varieties of Mystic Experience* [New York: Holt, Rinehart and Winston, 1964], p. 62).

25. For a fuller elaboration of this discussion of the sources of contemporary heresy in the Church, see Karl Rahner, *On Heresy* (New York: Herder and Herder, 1964), pp. 58-67.

26. "Decree on the Appropriate Renewal of the Religious Life," *The Documents of Vatican II,* ed. Walter M. Abbott, S.J. (New York: Guild Press, 1966), No. 2.

27. Karl Rahner, *The Christian Commitment* (New York: Sheed and Ward, 1963), p. 140; see also Dulles, *op. cit.,* p. 474.

28. Cf. Berger and Luckman, *op. cit.,* p. 145.

29. Cf. Moran, *op. cit.,* p. 500.

30. Karl Rahner, *The Christian Commitment,* p. 104.

CHAPTER II: IDEALS OF THE DESERT

1. Jerome, *Epistolae,* XIV, 10 (Migne, *Patrologia Latina,* XXII, 353-354).

2. Owen Chadwick, *John Cassian* (Cambridge: University Press, 1950), p. 3.

3. A. D. Knock, *Conversion* (London: Oxford University Press, 1961).

4. Adolph Harnack, *Monasticism: Its Ideals and History* (London: Williams and Norgate, 1901), p. 28; see also his *History of Dogma* (London: Williams and Norgate, 1897), III, 131 n.

5. Herbert Workman, *The Evolution of the Monastic Ideal* (Boston: Beacon Press, 1962), p. 7. Our discussion of the content and patterns of the eastern monastic ideal in the first half of this chapter largely follows Workman's provocative analysis.

6. Basil, *Epistolae,* XC; also LXX and XCII, 2 (Migne, *PG,* XXXII, 473; 433-436, 480).

7. Workman, *op. cit.,* p. 10.

8. Bouyer, *Introduction to Spirituality*, pp. 187-188.

9. A. V. G. Allen, *Christian Institutions* (New York: Scribner's, 1897), p. 139.

10. Cf. L. Duchesne, *Early History of the Christian Church* (New York: Longmans, Green, 1910), II, 390; Palladius, *Heraclidis Paradisus*, ii (Migne, *PL*, LXXIV, 258).

11. Workman, *op. cit.*, p. 14.

12. Dom Cuthbert Butler, *The Lausiac History of Palladius* (Cambridge: University Press, 1898), I, 237.

13. Cf. Workman, *op. cit.*, pp. 23-24.

14. Harnack, *History of Dogma*, III, 127.

15. Bouyer, *Introduction to Spirituality*, p. 186.

16. Jerome, *Epistolae*, LVIII, 5 (Migne, *PL*, XXII, 582-583).

17. Cf. Thomas Merton, *Disputed Questions* (New York: Farrar, Straus and Cudahy, 1960), pp. 177-207.

18. Pelagius the Deacon, *Verba Seniorum*, xvii, 5; cf. Paschasius the Deacon, *Verba Seniorum*, xxxiv, 1 (Migne, *PL*, LXXIII, 973-974; 1052).

19. Merton, *Disputed Questions*, p. 182.

20. Palladius, *Historia Lausiaca*, ii, 1 (Migne, *PL*, LXXIII, 1093).

21. Quoted by Workman, *op. cit.*, p. 42; see also Migne, *PL*, LXXIII, 325-334, and LXXIV, 98-108.

22. Jerome, *Vita Pauli*, 6; Cassian, *De Institutis*, V, xxxvi (Migne, *PL*, XXIII, 22; XLIX, 255-256).

23. Theodoret, *Philotheus*, xxx (Migne, *PL*, LXXIV, 114).

24. Helen Waddell, Introduction to *The Desert Fathers* (New York: Holt, 1936), p. 18; *Sententiae Patrum* (Wilmart, "Le recueil latin des Apophtegmes," *Revue Benedictine*, XXXIV [1922], 196); Pelagius the Deacon, *Verba Seniorum*, xi, 5 (Migne, *PL*, LXXIII, 934).

25. Cf. Norman J. Bull, *The Rise of the Church* (London: Heinemann, 1967), p. 278.

26. H. Bacht, "Pakhôme et ses disciples," *Théologie de la vie monastique* (Paris: Aubier, 1961), p. 67.

27. Workman, *op. cit.*, p. 28.

28. Derwas J. Chitty, *The Desert a City: An Introduction to the Study of Egyptian and Palestinian Monasticism under the Christian Empire* (Oxford: Basil Blackwell, 1966), ch. iii.

29. Chadwick (*op. cit.*, pp. 19-20) refers his reader to the Coptic

Life of Schnoudi (early fifth century) and to sources behind the *Historia Monachorum.*

30. An Alexandrian philosopher, born about 20 B.C., who worked to reconcile Judaism with Hellenism.

31. Cf. Pierre Pourrat, *Christian Spirituality* (Westminster, Md.: Newman, 1953), I, 63-68; and Jean Daniélou and Henri Marrou, *The First Six Hundred Years* (New York: McGraw-Hill, 1963), ch. x.

32. For instance, Clement identifies Christian perfection with the *"knowledge* of the good" (*Stromata,* ii, 22). Cf. Jules Lebreton and Jacques Zeiller, *The History of the Primitive Church* (New York: Macmillan, 1949), II, ch. xxiii. G. Bardy has questioned just how real an entity the school of Alexandria was and how real a connection Clement and Origen had with it and with each other ("Aux origines de l'Ecole d'Alexandrie," *Recherches de science religieuse,* XXVII [1937], 65-90).

33. In the third century, as events in Origen's own life indicate, such witness unto death for Christ was still a very real possibility. Though tortured fiercely, Origen himself was not directly put to death; we may think of him less as a martyr in the strict sense than as the pivotal figure who prepared the way for a conception of the whole Christian life as a martyrdom (cf. Edward E. Malone, *The Monk and the Martyr* [Washington, D. C.: Catholic University Press, 1950], ch. i, especially pp. 14-18).

34. The complexity of Origen's thought and the volume of his work, a good deal of which is not extant, make most judgments of him rather problematic; his importance, however, is unquestioned. Cf. Daniélou and Marrou, *op. cit.,* pp. 181-186; and Elmer O'Brien, *Varieties of Mystic Experience,* pp. 27-43.

35. Cf. J. N. D. Kelly, *Early Christian Doctrines* (2nd ed.; New York: Harper and Row, 1960), pp. 346-347.

36. See Henri Crouzel, "Origène, précurseur du monachisme," *Théologie de la vie monastique,* pp. 15-38.

37. Cf. Chitty, *op. cit.,* pp. 49-50 *et passim;* and O'Brien, *Varieties of Mystic Experience,* pp. 56-60.

38. Chadwick, *op. cit.,* p. 82.

39. Cf. A. Guillaumont, *Les "Kephalaia gnostica" d'Evagre le Pontique et l'historie de l'origénisme chez les Grecs et chez les Syriens* (Paris: Editions du Seuil, 1962), p. 336.

40. Irenée Hausherr, "Le traité de l'oraison d'Evagre le Pontique," *Revue d'ascétique et de mystique,* LXV (1934), 117; Hans Urs von

Balthasar feels that the doctrine of Evagrius "comes closer to Buddhism than to Christianity" ("Metaphysik und Mystik des Evagrius Ponticus," *Zeitschrift für Aszese und Mystik*, XIV [1939], 39).

41. O'Brien, *Varieties of Mystic Experience*, p. 56.

42. Chadwick, *op. cit.*, p. 83.

43. Evagrius, *Capita Practica ad Anatolium*, 50 and 51 (Migne, *PG*, XL, 1233).

44. *First Century*, 86 (Frankenberg, *Nachrichten von der Gesellschaft der Wissenschaften zu Göttingen, Phil-hist. Klasse*, N.F. XIII [1912], 123).

45. In his work *On Prayer*. Although this work is listed in Migne under Nilus of Ancyra, Hausherr's attribution of it to Evagrius has been virtually unchallenged (*Revue d'ascétique et de mystique*, LXV [1934], 34-94 and 113-170).

46. Evagrius, *On Prayer*, 3, 52, 61, 57, 70, 117, 142, and 17, in the translation of O'Brien, pp. 60-63.

47. For a more favorable interpretation of Evagrius than that found here or among most Evagrian scholars, see Bouyer, *The Spirituality of the New Testament and the Fathers*, pp. 380-394.

48. In this account of the Origenist controversy of 399, we have followed the reconstruction of Chadwick, *op. cit.*, pp. 33-36.

49. It is under these names that they still appear in Migne, *PG*.

50. See Chadwick, *op. cit.*, also S. Marsili, *Giovanni Cassiano ed Evagrio Pontico* (Rome: Herder, 1936).

51. The work is supposedly addressed to the Timothy of the Pauline epistles.

52. Translation by O'Brien, *op. cit.*, pp. 78-79.

53. For a short account of the work of Pseudo-Dionysius together with some fine translations, see O'Brien, *op. cit.*, pp. 73-91.

54. See Karl Rahner, *Theological Investigations* (Baltimore: Helicon, 1966), V, 112-114.

55. Workman, *op. cit.*, pp. 323-324.

56. *Ibid.*, pp. 331-332.

CHAPTER III: THE EVOLUTION OF WESTERN MONASTICISM

1. Augustine, *Confessions*, VIII, vi.

2. If the candidate had married prior to ordination, he was required to leave his wife before taking orders; cf. Pierre Pourrat, *Christian Spirituality*, I, 153-154.

3. Cf. J.-R. Palanque *et al., The Church in the Christian Roman Empire* (New York: Macmillan, 1953), pp. 500-503; and Pourrat, I, 150-155.

4. See Palladius, *Historia Lausiaca,* cxix; Socrates, *Historia Ecclesiastica,* IV, xxiii; John Chrysostom, *De Virginitate,* xiv; Augustine, *City of God,* XIV, xvi; *Soliloquia,* I, x and xiv; *Confessions,* X, xxx (Migne, *PL,* LXXIII, 1202; *PG,* LXVII, 509-512; XLVIII, 543-544; *PL,* XLI, 424-425; XXXII, 878-879, 882-883, 796-797).

5. C. S. Lewis, *The Allegory of Love* (London: Oxford University Press, 1938), p. 13.

6. Augustine, *De quantitate animae,* xxxiii (Migne, *PL,* XXXII, 1073-1077).

7. The original letter is number CCXI in the collection of Augustine's letters. In addition to this, the Rule draws on his sermons CCLV and CCCLVI, in which he describes his common life with the clergy of Hippo.

8. The complete account of Martin's life written by a contemporary admirer, Sulpicius Severus, may be consulted for further details. If this biography is generally trustworthy—and the point is debatable —its account of Martin's miracles must be taken with reserve.

9. Constantius, *Vita Germani,* I, xxviii, cited in Herbert Workman, *The Evolution of the Monastic Ideal,* p. 187; cf. Bede, *Historia Ecclesiastica,* I, xvii-xxi (Migne, *PL,* XCV, 45-52). Whatever truth there may be in Germanus' reputed success with the invaders, the native Britons had such a hatred for them that they made no attempt at all to Christianize them (Workman, p. 187). Of the origin of British monasticism and Christianity, little is known; see Workman, p. 184, nn. 1 and 2.

10. J. W. Willis-Bund, *The Celtic Church of Wales* (London: Nutt, 1897), p. 39; the claim may be exaggerated.

11. Columban, *Regula Coenobialis,* i-iii and x; cf. John Ryan, S.J., *Irish Monasticism: Origins and Early Development* (Dublin: Talbot, 1931), pp. 278-284. Any just evaluation of this predilection for physical punishment must be made within the context of the Irish culture of the times: "The punishment of the body was always a strongly marked feature of the Celtic Church" (Workman, *op. cit.,* p. 214; cf. also *The Irish Penitentials,* ed. and trans. Ludwig Bieler [Dublin: Dublin Institute for Advanced Studies, 1963]). Ryan (*ibid.*) finds no difference in principle, only in degree of harshness, between the Irish penal code and the disciplinary measures of other branches of monasticism (e.g. Pachomius, Cassian).

12. The *Navigation of St. Brendan*, quoted by Workman, p. 196.

13. *Adamnan's Vita Sancti Columbae*, ed. William Reeves (Dublin: Irish Archaeological and Celtic Society, 1857), p. 9. Here we have followed the interpretation of Jean Leclercq (*Aux sources de la spiritualité occidentale: étapes et constantes* [Paris: Cerf, 1964], ch. ii, especially pp. 54-58). It would be interesting to speculate how much Dom Leclercq's background as a Cistercian may have influenced his emphasis on the renunciatory over the apostolic aspects of monastic peregrination.

14. Gregory, *Dialogi*, II, xxxvi (Migne, *PL*, LXVI, 199-200). The preceding account of Benedict's life is based on this work of Gregory. Although its historical accuracy has often been challenged, it seems likely that, apart from the many miracle stories, the work is basically accurate (cf. Louis Bouyer, *The Spirituality of the New Testament and the Fathers*, p. 513).

15. Here and elsewhere the Rule is quoted in the translation of Justin McCann (*The Rule of Saint Benedict in Latin and English* [London: Burns, Oates, 1952]). We have felt it unnecessary to enter into the question of the authenticity of the Rule or of the accuracy of the text. The interested reader is referred to a summary of recent controversy on these and other points by David Knowles: "Some Recent Work on Early Benedictine History," *Studies in Church History*, ed. C. W. Dugmore and Charles Duggan (London: Nelson, 1964), I, 35-46.

16. David Knowles, *From Pachomius to Ignatius*, p. 6. Benedict did establish at least one other community, at Terracina.

17. See chs. xxxv, xxxviii, lix, and lx.

18. See chs. lx and lxii.

19. Cassian, *Collationes*, I, xiii (Migne, *PL*, XLIX, 497).

20. There is a long-standing dispute as to the precise kind of work Benedict had in mind; see the account of this controversy in T. F. Lindsay, *Saint Benedict* (London: Burns, Oates, 1949), pp. 128-132.

21. Workman, *op. cit.*, pp. 154-155.

22. Lowrie J. Daly, S.J., *Benedictine Monasticism: Its Formation and Development through the Twelfth Century* (New York: Sheed and Ward, 1965), pp. 88-89.

23. Montalembert, *Monks of the West* (Boston: Noonan, no date), I, 343. Cf. John Henry Newman, *Historical Sketches* (London: Longmans, 1917), II, 365-430; and Hubert Van Zeller, *The Benedictine Idea* (London: Burns, 1959), pp. 1-2.

24. Among them, Cassian, Basil, Pachomius, and Augustine stand

out. See the fine treatment of Benedictine sources in Cuthbert Butler's edition of the Rule: *Sancti Benedicti Regula Monachorum* (Freiburg im Breisgau: Herder, 1912). Regarding Benedict's probable dependence on the anonymous contemporary (?) author of the *Regula Magistri*, see David Knowles, "The *Regula Magistri* and the *Rule* of St. Benedict," *Great Historical Enterprises* (London: Nelson, 1963), pp. 135-195.

25. See his best-known work, *An Introduction to Divine and Human Readings*, trans. and with an introd. and notes by L. W. Jones (New York: Columbia University Press, 1946).

26. The story was chronicled a century later by Bede in his *Historia Ecclesiastica*. See also Christopher Dawson, *The Making of Europe* (London: Sheed and Ward, 1932); S. J. Crawford, *Anglo-Saxon Influence on Western Christendom, 600-800* (Oxford: University Press, 1933); and E. Emerton, *Letters of St. Boniface* (New York: Columbia University Press, 1940).

27. Cf. Richard E. Sullivan, "The Carolingian Missionary and the Pagan," *Speculum*, XXIX (1953), 738-739, 721-726.

28. This influence, however, was not as pervasive and constant as has sometimes been claimed; cf. Sullivan, "The Papacy and Missionary Activity in the Early Middle Ages," *Medieval Studies*, XVII (1955), 46-106.

29. Leclerq, *op. cit.*, ch. ii, especially pp. 58-64.

30. Among the many who interpret the data this way, see Van Zeller, *op. cit.*, pp. 55-63. In keeping with their apostolic interests, these monks developed an ideal of study as the suitable kind of work, for they were to be priests, not laymen.

31. David Knowles, *From Pachomius to Ignatius*, pp. 6-7.

32. S. Brechter, "Monte Cassino's erste Zerstörung," *Studien und Mitteilungen zu Geschichte des Benediktinerordens*, LVI (1938), 109-150; K. Hallinger, "Papst Gregor der Grosse und der Hl. Benedikt," *Studia Anselmiana*, XLII (1957), 231-319. Hallinger seems to overstate the case, however, when he claims that Gregory was hardly familiar with the Rule.

33. Quotations in Workman, *op. cit.*, pp. 231-234; cf. Philip Hughes, *A History of the Church* (London: Sheed and Ward, 1939), II, 222-234.

34. Quoted from *A Source Book of Mediaeval History*, ed. Frederic Austin Ogg (New York: American Book Co., 1907), p. 249.

35. *From Pachomius to Ignatius*, pp. 12-13. Much of our treatment of Cluny is based on this work of Knowles.

36. Workman, *op. cit.*, p. 229.

37. Knowles, *From Pachomius to Ignatius*, p. 18.

38. There were six hundred *conversi* at Rievaulx in England; many continental houses had more. The virtual monopoly on the wool trade which the English Cistercians enjoyed was due to the industry of their *conversi*. But the converse system did not always have happy results. When Gilbert of Sempringham gave his *conversi* complete control of administration, thus making his canons and nuns their pensioners, they responded by embezzling funds and blackmailing Gilbert into giving them an easy regime (*ibid.*, pp. 33-34).

39. *Ibid.*, p. 23.

40. Quoted by Workman, *op. cit.*, pp. 148-149. Cf. Christopher Butler's comparison of monasticism with the British Constitution and the Society of Jesus with the American Constitution ("An Interview with Christopher Butler," *Theologians at Work*, ed. Patrick Granfield [New York: Macmillan, 1967], pp. 212-213).

41. Van Zeller, *op. cit.*, p. 185.

42. "The monastic life is a form of religious life which has no secondary goal [beyond the love of God himself]"—Leclercq, *op. cit.*, p. 306; cf. "An Interview with Christopher Butler," *loc. cit.*, p. 213.

43. Cf. Workman, *op. cit.*, pp. 220-224.

44. Newman, *op. cit.*, II, 409-411 and 426-428.

CHAPTER IV: THE CITY, THE FRIARS, AND THE PEOPLE

1. Gustav Schnürer, *Kirche und Kultur im Mittelalter* (Paderborn: Schöningh, 1926), II, 441.

2. Cf. A. S. Turberville, *Medieval Heresy and the Inquisition* (London: Crosby, Lockwood, 1920), p. 32.

3. Josef Pieper, *Guide to Thomas Aquinas* (New York: Pantheon, 1962), p. 23.

4. Ronald A. Knox, *Enthusiasm: A Chapter in the History of Religion* (Oxford: Clarendon Press, 1950), p. 76.

5. Cf. *ibid.*, pp. 71-89. We prescind here from the question whether the rosary actually originated with Dominic or whether early Dominicans merely popularized a practice already existing in one form or another among the laity and clergy of the time.

6. Quoted in Herbert Workman, *The Evolution of the Monastic Ideal*, p. 272.

7. *Little Flowers of St. Francis*, ch. xvi.

8. See Mark Stier, O.F.M.Cap., *Franciscan Life in Christ* (Paterson, New Jersey: St. Anthony Guild Press, 1953); Raphael M. Huber, O.F.M. Conv., *History of the Franciscan Order, 1182-1517* (Milwaukee: Nowiny Publishing Apostolate, 1944).

9. There are two schools of interpretation regarding Franciscan spirituality—the Italian and the German. Although the two are actually quite complementary, there are certain distinctive differences in emphasis. Following the writings of Scotus and Bonaventure, the Italian school has stressed the *theological* Christocentricism of Francis (until recently this has been the approach adopted by American Franciscans). The German school, on the other hand, has been deeply influenced by "kerygmatic theology" and generally takes as its starting point Francis' sensitivity to the whole history of salvation and his role in communicating and participating in the gospel of salvation. Since it is not our task, nor strictly within our competence, to pass final judgment on the validity of these schools, we have attempted to highlight their complementarity in our treatment.

10. Cajetan Esser, *Repair My House* (Chicago: Franciscan Herald Press, 1963), p. 16.

11. Theodosius Foley, O.F.M.Cap., *Spiritual Conferences for Religious Based on the Franciscan Ideal* (Milwaukee: Bruce, 1951), pp. 36-37.

12. Cf. Philbert Ramstetter, "Introduction to a Franciscan Spirituality," *Franciscan Studies*, II (1942), 366, 350-352, 356.

13. Cf. A. Lemonnyer, *La Vie Romaine, ses formes, ses états*, p. 522, as cited by Aidan Carr, O.F.M. Conv., "Poverty in Perfection according to St. Bonaventure," *Franciscan Studies*, VII (1947), 421.

14. Bonaventure, *Expositio super Regulam Fratrum Minorum*, i (*Opera Omnia*, ed. Peltier [Paris: Vives, 1868], XIV, 560); see also Carr, *op. cit.*, pp. 421 ff.

15. Christopher Dawson, *Medieval Religion* (New York: Sheed and Ward, 1934), p. 49.

16. *Legend of St. Francis, by Three Companions*, trans. E. G. Salter (New York: Dutton, 1902), pp. 36-37; cf. Workman, *op. cit.*, p. 286.

17. "The Rule of 1223," *The Writings of St. Francis of Assisi*, trans. Benen Fahy (Chicago: Franciscan Herald Press, 1964), p. 60.

18. In this connection, see Ignatius M. Brady, "The History of Mental Prayer in the Order of Friars Minor," *Franciscan Studies*, XI (1951), 328-329, 334.

19. H. C. Scheeben, *Der heilige Dominikus* (Freiburg im Breisgau: Herder, 1937), p. 57; Pieper, *op. cit.*, pp. 25-30; M.-H. Vicaire, O.P., *St. Dominic and His Times* (New York: McGraw-Hill, 1962), ch. vii.

20. *Q.D. de Veritate*, q. 11, a. 1, c and ad 6.

21. John-Baptist Reeves, O.P., *The Dominicans* (New York: Macmillan, 1930), pp. 65-88.

22. Cf. Workman, *op. cit.*, pp. 258-268.

23. Cf. G. R. Galbraith, *The Constitutions of the Dominican Order, 1216-1360* (New York: Longmans, Green, 1925), pp. 8-36, 175-192.

24. See M.-D. Chenu, O.P., *Toward Understanding Saint Thomas* (Chicago: Regnery, 1964), pp. 44-50.

25. See A. Savine, *English Monasteries on the Eve of the Dissolution* (Oxford Studies in Legal and Social History, no. 1 [1909]), pp. 265-267; Workman, *op. cit.*, pp. 293-298.

26. See Alfons Auer, *Open to the World* (Baltimore: Helicon, 1966), chs. i and ii.

27. The Peckham Constitutions (*Concilia Magnae Brittaniae et Hiberniae*, ed. David Wilkins [London, 1737], II, 51-61).

28. See Homer G. Pfander, *The Popular Sermon of the Medieval Friar in England* (New York: New York University, 1937), pp. 1-19; also A. Lecoy de la Marche, *La Chaire Française au Moyen Age*, 2ième ed. (Paris: Renouard, H. Laurens, successeur, 1886).

29. Denzinger, *Enchiridion Symbolorum*, no. 437 (812).

30. Karl Rahner, *Theological Investigations*, III, 191; cf. Bernhard Poschmann, *Penance and the Anointing of the Sick* (New York: Herder and Herder, 1964), chs. i and ii.

31. Rossel Hope Robbins, "Popular Prayers in Middle English Verse," *Modern Philology*, XXXVI (1939), 337; spelling slightly modernized.

32. British Museum MS. Egerton 1821, f. 8v, reproduced in J. W. Robinson, "The Late Medieval Cult of Jesus and the Mystery Plays," *PMLA*, LXXX (1965), opposite 513; spelling somewhat modernized and abbreviations filled out. The fantastic size of the indulgence was probably not typical, but seems incontrovertible in this MS.

33. The fact that Jesus appears with the cross and bloody even in the Resurrection plays gives us an insight into the medieval theology of redemption.

34. Cf. Robinson, *op. cit.*, pp. 508-514.

35. Joseph A. Jungmann, S.J., *The Mass of the Roman Rite: Its Origins and Development* (*Missarum Sollemnia*) (New York: Benziger, 1959), pp. 90-92.

36. *Ibid.,* pp. 63-70, 77-83, 88-90.

37. *Ibid.,* pp. 97-100.

38. *Religious Lyrics of the XIVth Century,* ed. Carleton Brown (Oxford: Clarendon, 1924), p. 7.

39. "An Orison of the Passion," lines 105-106 (*Meditations on the Life and Passion of Christ,* ed. Charlotte d'Evelyn [London: Early English Text Society, 1921]) ; spelling slightly modernized.

40. Huizinga, *The Waning of the Middle Ages* (London: Edward Arnold, 1924), p. 1.

41. *Ibid.,* pp. 136-137; see Suso's *Life,* ch. vii.

42. Huizinga, *op. cit.,* pp. 150-151, 156.

43. *Ibid.,* pp. 167-168. Here, as in presenting details about other individuals, groups, or the populace at large, the authors have no intention of judging interior disposition or imputing bad will. No one would want to deny the possibility of God's grace triumphing even in the life of a Pierre de Luxembourg. The issue is whether someone like this ought to be held up as a model by and for the whole Church. The fact that Pierre's cause was introduced and that he was beatified tells us something about the age's conception of sanctity.

44. There was, for instance, a proposal before the Council of Trent that Latin be abandoned in the liturgy in favor of the vernacular; but the bishops were afraid to follow the path of the Reformers and no action was taken except to reassert the *status quo.* Cf. Denzinger, *op. cit.,* no. 946 (1749).

CHAPTER V: THE MYSTICISM OF THE LATE MIDDLE AGES

1. Elmer O'Brien, *Varieties of Mystic Experience,* p. 176.

2. O'Brien makes the following observation on Rolle's mysticism: "As many another before his time and since, [he] seems desperately to have wished to be a mystic. And he thought he was. And he said he was. But no one believes him" (*op. cit.,* p. 158). Even if one accepted this criticism, he would have to admit that Rolle, especially in his later, less self-conscious works, is a spiritual writer of importance and charm.

3. See Denzinger, *Enchiridion Symbolorum,* nos. 471-478 and 484-490 (891-897 and 910-916).

4. Cf. Heinrich R. Schlette, *Die Nichtigkeit der Welt: Der philosophische Horizont des Hugo von St. Viktor* (Munich: Kösel, 1961).

5. *The Cloud of Unknowing*, ch. v; *The Epistle of Privy Counsel*, ch. i (*The Cloud of Unknowing and Other Treatises*, ed. Justin Mc-Cann [6th ed.; Westminster, Md.: Newman, 1952], pp. 13, 103).

6. Meister Eckhart, sermon "Expedit vobis" (translation in O'Brien, *op. cit.*, p. 154).

7. "Of the most powerful Prayer of all," Meister Eckhart, *The Talks of Instruction*, 2 (our translation).

8. Quoted in Huizinga, *The Waning of the Middle Ages*, p. 203.

9. Quoted in O'Brien, *op. cit.*, p. 151.

10. One is more inclined to grant this indulgence when he is convinced that the writer is a genuine mystic attempting to articulate his own experience.

11. Otto Karrer, *Meister Eckhart Speaks* (New York: Philosophical Library, 1956), p. 7; sermons "Expedit vobis" and "Intravit Jesus in templum"; "Why God often allows people who are really good to be hindered in doing pious works," *The Talks of Instruction*, 19 (*Meister Eckhart: A Modern Translation*, by Raymond B. Blakney [New York: Harper Torchbooks, 1957], pp. 156-160, 197-202, 26-27).

12. See sermon "Et cum factus esset Jesus" (Blakney, pp. 118-124).

13. This tendency is still common enough among contemporary theologians (cf. Karl Rahner, *Theological Investigations*, IV, 77-102).

14. We are not suggesting a lack of apostolic zeal in Eckhart's life—history proves the opposite—or even in parts of his teaching. He is actually much more favorable toward the active life than, say, Rolle and the author of *The Cloud;* at times he can speak eloquently of the obligation of service toward the neighbor (see "How the will is capable of anything . . . ," *The Talks of Instruction*, 10 [Blakney, *op. cit.*, pp. 12-15]), but such sections are in conflict with his overall system.

15. Oddly enough, some mystics, like Suso and Ruysbroek, seem to have combined elements from these two apparently opposite styles.

16. Huizinga, *op. cit.*, pp. 178, 175.

17. Karl Rahner, *Visions and Prophecies* (New York: Herder and Herder, 1963), pp. 66-68; Huizinga, *op. cit.*, p. 180.

18. Ray C. Petry, *Late Medieval Mysticism* (Philadelphia: Westminster, no date), p. 265.

19. This work exists in two different versions, a shorter one which she probably wrote soon after her great visions of May, 1373 (*A Showing of God's Love*, ed. Anna Maria Reynolds, C.P. [London: Longmans, 1958]), and a longer one, on which she probably continued to work till her death (*Revelations of Divine Love*, ed. Grace Warrack [13th ed.; London: Methuen, 1950]).

20. She limits her treatment of prayer to three of her eighty-six chapters, and here her doctrine is the opposite of the "cult of contemplation": "I [God, not you, man] am Ground of thy beseeching" (ch. xli [Warrack, p. 84]).

21. Ch. viii (*ibid.*, p. 19).

22. Ch. v (*ibid.*, p. 10).

23. Chs. xxvii, xxix, xxxii (*ibid.*, pp. 55-56, 60, 66-67). In connection with Julian's "It behoved that there should be sin," see Karl Rahner's presentation of the theological concept of "must": *The Christian Commitment*, pp. 14-17.

24. E. I. Watkin, "Dame Julian of Norwich," *Poets and Mystics* (New York: Sheed and Ward, 1953), p. 79; though brief, this is probably the finest interpretation of Julian's *Revelations* available to date.

25. *Ibid.*, p. 98.

26. Cf. Joseph de Guibert, S.J., *The Theology of the Spiritual Life* (New York: Sheed and Ward, 1953), pp. 306, 305.

27. If it seems wise to begin a discussion of mysticism by stressing its discontinuity with ordinary human knowledge, still one should proceed to see mysticism within the context of the life of grace—as the culmination in this world of God's possible communication of himself to man. Thus in the long-standing controversy between those who assert discontinuity at the expense of continuity and vice versa, we hope to assume a mid-position (cf. M. D. Knowles, *The Nature of Mysticism* [New York: Hawthorn, 1966], chs. i and ii; de Guibert, pp. 312-324).

28. A. Poulain, S.J., *The Graces of Interior Prayer* (St. Louis: B. Herder, 1950), pp. 7-20. It is a sad fact that many who were initially committed by desire and/or profession to a life of prayer after some time give up in *ennui* or despair. One wonders how often a person's distaste for prayer is the result of trying to stay with the prayer methods he learned as a beginner, when all the laws of psychology

and spirituality suggest that after some years of experience he should be moving from meditation toward affective prayer and perhaps even toward the prayer of simplicity.

29. The term is meant to stress the exclusive activity of God and the total passivity of the mystic; in this usage it is opposed to "acquired contemplation," which is still ordinary prayer and therefore can be spoken of as being at least in part the result of human effort. The terms are the heritage of a long-standing debate over the propriety and possibility of striving for mystical prayer, and according to David Knowles are now best abandoned (*The Nature of Mysticism,* ch. iii).

30. De Guibert, *op. cit.,* pp. 305-307; cf. Poulain, *op. cit.,* ch. v, and the introduction, pp. l-li.

31. This is the opinion, for instance, of philosophers as far apart as Aristotle, Aquinas, Cassirer, and (the later) Wittgenstein.

32. The pairs are not necessarily equivalent to one another. The tradition of "Ignatian mysticism" includes figures from Ignatius of Antioch through Basil, Augustine, and Benedict in the early Middle Ages and Catherine and Bernardine of Siena in late medieval times, to Ignatius of Loyola (cf. Hugo Rahner, *The Spirituality of St. Ignatius Loyola* [Westminster, Md.: Newman, 1953], pp. 58-88).

33. Evelyn Underhill, *The Mystics of the Church* (London: Clarke, 1926), p. 15.

34. Karl Rahner, *Visions and Prophecies,* p. 65.

35. *Ibid.,* p. 61.

36. We shall not treat these other "concomitant phenomena," although the reader will recognize that something of what is said about visions is applicable also to these. For a fuller treatment, see Herbert Thurston, S.J., *The Physical Phenomena of Mysticism* (London: Burns, Oates, 1952).

37. Karl Rahner, *Visions and Prophecies,* p. 32; Poulain, *op. cit.,* ch. xx.

38. While some writers talk about a kind of intellectual vision that does not make use of any concepts, actually such a "vision" would not be a vision at all, but rather mysticism itself, unmediated knowledge of God.

39. To be discussed in ch. vii.

40. Karl Rahner, *Visions and Prophecies,* pp. 31-41. We may thus presume that the visions discussed earlier in this chapter are imaginative ones.

41. *Ibid.,* pp. 61-63. To conclude from this fact that Margaret

Mary's visions were not authentic, of course, would be as invalid as to conclude, without the aid of the other convincing evidence, that they were.

42. *Ibid.,* pp. 55-58.

43. Poulain, *op. cit.,* p. 322; Karl Rahner, *Visions and Prophecies,* pp. 73-74, 81.

44. Karl Rahner, *Visions and Prophecies,* pp. 17, 27.

45. *Ibid.,* p. 26.

46. Because a prophetic vision is meant for a particular age, the relevance of its message for succeeding ages is open to question. The visions of Margaret Mary were God's word for a French Church frozen by Jansenism. If we ask about his word for our times, we may have to seek the answer in sources other than visions (Vatican II perhaps), especially since the events at Fatima and the way they have been reported by both the principals and others raise so many disturbing questions for the historian (cf. the footnotes throughout Rahner's *Visions and Prophecies*).

47. Rahner, *Visions and Prophecies,* pp. 89-106.

48. Cf. Klaus Riesenhuber, S.J., "The Anonymous Christian according to Karl Rahner," translated as an afterword in Anita Röper, *The Anonymous Christian* (New York: Sheed and Ward, 1966), pp. 145-179.

49. Following Rahner, we are here speaking not of "natural" man, man as he might have been in some other world order, but of man as he is in the actual world order, man who thanks to God's gratuitous love possesses the "supernatural existential."

50. "Man accepts revelation when he fully accepts himself, since revelation is deposited in himself. . . . 'One who fully accepts the fact of being man . . . has accepted the Son of man,' because 'the center of man is God himself and his form is the form of God incarnate himself'" (Riesenhuber, *op. cit.,* p. 168, in part quoting from Rahner).

51. Because of the difficulty of correctly verbalizing inner revelation without the aid of public revelation (witness the aberrations of belief and practice in non-Christian religions whether primitive or even "highly cultured"), the reader should not expect to find confirmation of this argument in an identical verbal articulation of mystical experience by Christians and non-Christians.

52. Cf. Karl Rahner, *Visions and Prophecies,* p. 14, n. 12; the questionable tendencies of this negative mysticism can be all the more

dangerous because, as we noted earlier in discussing Evagrius, they are covered over by verbally orthodox references to Christ and the Trinity.

CHAPTER VI: THE COST OF ENGAGEMENT

1. Yves Congar, *Lay People in the Church* (London: Geoffrey Chapman, 1959), p. 384.

2. Alfons Auer, "The Changing Character of the Christian Understanding of the World," *The Christian and the World: Readings in Theology Compiled at the Canisianum, Innsbruck* (New York: Kenedy, 1965), p. 4.

3. Alfons Auer, *Open to the World*, pp. 41-50.

4. Karl Rahner, *The Christian Commitment*, p. 52.

5. George Eliot, *Mill on the Floss* (New York: Dutton, 1952), p. 272 (bk. IV, ch. iii).

6. Thomas a Kempis, *The Imitation of Christ*, I, xxiii; II, v, ix; III, xxvii.

7. *Ibid.*, I, xix.

8. *Ibid.*, I, viii, x, xx; III, i.

9. According to M. Mourret, the four books of the *Imitation* are "only the collection of a man of genius" (*A History of the Catholic Church* [London: Herder, 1955], V, 135). This view is accepted today as the most likely one, for in their early days the Canons Regular of Windesheim did not write books. As Pourrat has remarked, they simply delivered conferences to their brethren with the sole object of edifying them. These conferences were kept and compiled, and other monks added to them from their own knowledge. From these efforts, we have the collections of anonymous phrases which formed the basic data from which Thomas a Kempis constructed the *Imitation* (see Pierre Pourrat, *Christian Spirituality*, II, 255). As to the problem of the authorship of the *Imitation*, see Pourrat, II, 262-264.

10. A Kempis, *op. cit.*, I, iii, i.

11. St. Thomas Aquinas, *Summa Theologiae*, II-II, q. 184, a. 1.

12. *Ibid.*, qq. 179, 188.

13. The following discussion of Thomas' theory of contemplation is heavily indebted to the seminal analysis of Emerich Coreth, "In Actione Contemplativus," *Zeitschrift für Katholische Theologie*, LXXVI (1954), 55-82. See also Reginald Garrigou-Lagrange, O.P.,

Reality: A Synthesis of Thomistic Thought (St. Louis: B. Herder, 1950), pp. 318-346; M.-D. Chenu, O.P., *Toward Understanding St. Thomas*, pp. 50-68.

14. *ST*, II-II, q. 179, a. 2 ad 3.
15. *Ibid.*, q. 180, a. 2.
16. *Ibid.*, q. 182, a. 1.
17. *Ibid.*, q. 180, a. 4.
18. *Ibid.*, q. 182, a. 1.
19. *Ibid.*, q. 180, a. 7.
20. *Ibid.*, q. 181, a. 1.
21. *Ibid.*, q. 188, a. 2.
22. *Ibid.*, q. 188, a. 6.
23. For a fuller documentation of the varying usage of the concepts of contemplative and active life, see Sister M. Elizabeth Mason, O.S.B., *"Active Life" and "Contemplative Life": A Study of the Concepts from Plato to the Present*, ed. George E. Ganss, S.J. (Milwaukee: Marquette University Press, 1961), or a shortened version of the same study by Ganss, " 'Active Life' or 'Contemplative Life,' " *Review for Religious*, XXII (1963), 53-66.
24. *A Catholic Commentary on Holy Scripture*, ed. Bernard Orchard, *et al.* (London: Nelson, 1953), p. 954.
25. R. A. Gauthier, *Magnanimité. L'idéal de la grandeur dans la philosophie païenne et dans la théologie chrétienne* (Paris: Vrin, 1951), p. 493; see also pp. 295-371, 489-497.
26. Congar, *op. cit.*, pp. 391 ff.
27. Auer, *Open to the World*, p. 57.

CHAPTER VII: FINDING GOD IN ALL THINGS

1. Juan Polanco, quoted by James Broderick, S.J., *Saint Ignatius Loyola* (New York: Farrar, Straus, and Cudahy, 1956), p. 45.
2. *Saint Ignatius' Own Story, As Told to Luis Gonzales da Camara*, trans. William J. Young, S.J. (Chicago: Regnery, 1956), pp. 22-24.
3. Joseph de Guibert, S.J., *The Jesuits: Their Spiritual Doctrine and Practice* (Chicago: Loyola University Press, 1964), pp. 29-30; Hugo Rahner, *The Spirituality of St. Ignatius Loyola*, pp. 50-58.
4. *Saint Ignatius' Own Story*, pp. 66-67.
5. See Elmer O'Brien, *Varieties of Mystic Experience*, pp. 244-245.

6. A. Poulain, S.J., *The Graces of Interior Prayer*, pp. 37-40.

7. Pierre Pourrat, *Christian Spirituality*, III, ch. i, especially pp. 4-12; Poulain, *Graces of Interior Prayer*, p. 40.

8. Pourrat, *Christian Spirituality*, III, 23-29.

9. *Saint Ignatius' Own Story*, p. 22; Jean Daniélou, S.J., "The Ignatian Vision of the Universe and of Man," *Cross Currents*, IV (1954), 357-366; for the most part the following description is based on Daniélou's essay.

10. *The Spiritual Exercises of St. Ignatius*, trans. Louis J. Puhl, S.J. (Westminster, Md.: Newman, 1953), no. 236.

11. *Ibid.*, nos. 92-98.

12. *Ibid.*, nos. 137-147, 314-336.

13. Cf. the concepts "tantum-quantum" and "indifference," *ibid.*, no. 23.

14. Quoted by Daniélou, *op. cit.*, p. 362.

15. *S. Ignatii Epistolae*, ed. M. Lecina *et al.* (Madrid: Lopez del Horno, 1906), IV, 127.

16. *Epistolae P. Hieronymi Nadal*, ed. F. Cervos (Madrid: Lopez del Horno, 1905), IV, 651-652.

17. Maurice Giulani, "Finding God in All Things," *Finding God in All Things*, ed. William J. Young, S.J. (Chicago: Regnery, 1958), p. 11.

18. *Constitutions of the Society of Jesus*, Pt. III, ch. i, 26 (*Constitutiones et Regulae* [Rome: Institutum Historicum Societatis Jesu, 1938], III, 91-92).

19. For a closer investigation of this topic than is possible here, see Emerich Coreth, "In actione contemplativus," *Christus: Cahiers spirituels*, III (April, 1955); Louis Verny, S.J., "In actione contemplativus," *Revue d'ascétique et de mystique*, XXVI (1950), 60-78. The general position on Ignatian prayer and his over-all spirituality follows the lines developed by these authors, rather than the excessively "mystical" approach of writers like K. Truhlar, S.J., "La découverte de Dieu chez S. Ignace pendant les dernières années de sa vie," *Revue d'ascétique et de mystique*, XXIV (1948), 313-337, or Joseph F. Conwell, *Contemplation in Action* (Spokane, Wash.: Gonzaga University Press, 1957).

20. Coreth, *op. cit.*, p. 75.

21. Francois Charmot, S.J., "Some Thoughts on 'Prayer and Action,'" in *Finding God in All Things*, pp. 143-144.

22. Daniélou, *op. cit.*, pp. 364-366.

23. See especially Ignatius' *Constitutions,* Pt. IX.

24. Daniélou, *op. cit.,* p. 366.

25. The following discussion rests heavily on Karl Rahner's penetrating essay, "The Ignatian Mysticism of Joy in the World," *Theological Investigations,* III, 281-293; see also pp. 47-85.

26. *Primum ac Generale Examen,* iv, 44 (*Const. et Reg.,* III, 28-29).

27. Karl Rahner, *Theological Investigations,* III, 281.

28. This and the following paragraphs are derived from Dulles, "The Ignatian Experience as Reflected in the Spirituality of Karl Rahner," pp. 486-487.

29. Karl Rahner, *Theological Investigations,* III, 284-290.

30. *Ibid.,* p. 287.

31. Karl Rahner, "De termino aliquo in theologia Clementis Alexandrini, *Gregorianum,* XVIII (1937), 426-431.

CHAPTER VIII: THE LOGIC OF CHRISTIAN DISCERNMENT

1. To those familiar with contemporary scholarship on Ignatian spirituality, it will be clear that we have opted here for one of two possible interpretations of the purpose of the Exercises; namely, that the Exercises are principally a decision-making process. Others hold that the Exercises are much more a school of prayer. Regardless of the position one takes, however, the place of discernment in the spirituality of the Exercises remains central. It is only this aspect of the Exercises that we are focusing on in the present discussion. Cf. de Guibert, *The Jesuits: Their Spirituality and Practice,* pp. 122-126; also William Peters, S.J., *The Spiritual Exercises of St. Ignatius: Exposition and Interpretation* (Jersey City: Program to Promote the Spiritual Exercises, 1968).

2. *St. Ignatius' Own Story, As Told to Luis Gonzales da Camara,* trans. William J. Young, pp. 8-9, 69.

3. *Ibid.,* pp. 19-20.

4. These personal observations, interwoven as they are throughout the present chapter, necessarily involve certain departures from a strict descriptive analysis of Ignatian discernment.

5. See John L. McKenzie, *Dictionary of the Bible,* p. 819.

6. Heinrich Bacht, "Good and Evil Spirits," *The Way,* II (1962), 194.

7. For a fuller discussion on Paul's teaching on discernment, see

David M. Stanley, S.J., *A Modern Scriptural Approach to the Spiritual Exercises* (Chicago: Loyola University Press, 1967), pp. 312-313.

8. Jean Daniélou, S.J., *Origen* (New York: Sheed and Ward, 1955), pp. 240-241.

9. Cassian, *Collationes*, II (Migne, *PL, XLIX*, 523-558).

10. See Avery Dulles, "Finding God's Will," *Woodstock Letters*, XCIV (1964), 139-152.

11. See Hugo Rahner, "Discernment des esprits," *Dictionnaire de spiritualité*, III, 1222-1291.

12. *The Spiritual Exercises of St. Ignatius*, trans. Louis J. Puhl, S.J., no. 4.

13. *Ibid.*, no. 6.

14. The term is Bacht's, *op. cit.*, p. 189.

15. *Spiritual Exercises*, no. 7.

16. *Ibid.*, no. 17.

17. *Ibid.*, no. 32.

18. The distinctions involved here are found in Scripture, which uses the contrast between the spiritual and the unspiritual man: "An unspiritual person is one who does not accept anything of the Spirit of God: he sees it all as nonsense; it is beyond his understanding because it can only be understood by means of the Spirit. A spiritual man, on the other hand, is able to judge the value of everything and his own value is not to be judged by other men" (I Cor. 2:14-15).

19. *Spiritual Exercises*, nos. 313-337.

20. *Ibid.*, no. 315.

21. *Ibid.*, no. 329.

22. *Ibid.*, no. 316.

23. *Ibid.*, no. 333.

24. *Ibid.*, nos. 136-148.

25. *Ibid.*, no. 325.

26. In this connection, and in the illustration of several other points in this chapter, we are indebted to Francois Roustang's discussion of discernment. See his *Growth in the Spirit* (New York: Sheed and Ward, 1966), pp. 105-110.

27. *Directoria Exercitiorum Spiritualium*, ed. Ignatius Iparriguirre, S.J. (Rome: Institutum Historicum Societatis Jesu, 1955), p. 76.

28. The following discussion of Ignatius' notion of consolation is heavily dependent on Karl Rahner's brilliant study of discernment, "The Logic of Concrete Individual Knowledge in Ignatius Loyola,"

The Dynamic Element in the Church (New York: Herder and Herder, 1964), pp. 84-170.

29. *Spiritual Exercises*, no. 331.

30. *Ibid.*, no. 331.

31. *Ibid.*, no. 333.

32. *Ibid.*, no. 330.

33. *Ibid.*, no. 330.

34. Cf. W. W. Meissner, S.J., "Psychological Notes on the Spiritual Exercises: III," *Woodstock Letters*, XCIII (1964), 180; Dulles, *op. cit.*, pp. 143-147.

35. *Letters of St. Ignatius Loyola*, trans. William J. Young, S.J. (Chicago: Loyola University Press, 1959), p. 22.

36. *Spiritual Exercises*, no. 316.

37. Karl Rahner, *Theological Investigations*, III, pp. 281-282.

38. *The Spiritual Journal of St. Ignatius Loyola*, trans. William J. Young, S.J. (Woodstock: Woodstock College Press, 1958), p. 1.

39. *Ibid.*, p. 34.

40. *Ibid.*, pp. 34-36.

41. *Ibid.*, p. 39.

42. *Ibid.*, p. 41.

43. *Spiritual Exercises*, nos. 186-189.

44. *Ibid.*, no. 333 (italics added); see also Roustang, *op. cit.*, pp. 100-112.

45. *Spiritual Exercises*, no. 174.

46. *Ibid.*, no. 169 (italics added).

47. *Ibid.*, no. 175.

48. *Ibid.*, no. 176.

49. *Ibid.*, no. 177.

50. Translated in *Existentialism from Dostoevsky to Sartre*, ed. Walter Kaufmann (New York: Meridian Books, 1963), pp. 287-311. We are indebted to Avery Dulles for this example; see his "Finding God's Will," pp. 139-140.

51. Kaufmann, *op. cit.*, p. 297 f.

52. *Spiritual Exercises*, no. 33.

53. This and the following paragraphs derive from Roustang, *op. cit.*, pp. 106-108.

54. *Spiritual Exercises*, no. 353.

55. *Ibid.*, no. 89.

56. *Ibid.*, no. 213.

57. Karl Rahner, "The Logic of Concrete Individual Knowledge in

Ignatius Loyola," *The Dynamic Element in the Church,* p. 166. For a
further elaboration of the theology of the will of God underlying
these observations, see John H. Wright, S.J., "The Eternal Plan of
Divine Providence," *Theological Studies,* XXVII (1966), 27-58; M.
John Farrelly, *Predestination, Grace and Free Will* (Westminster:
Newman, 1964), pp. 102-106, 145.

58. This is the wish which Ignatius places at the end of his letters
to the greater number of his correspondents.

59. *Spiritual Exercises,* no. 62.

60. *Directoria Exercitium Spiritualium,* p. 781.

61. Cf. "Dogmatic Constitution of the Church," *The Documents
of Vatican II,* nos. 21, 23, 32.

62. *Spiritual Exercises,* no. 89.

63. *Ibid.,* nos. 77, 333-336, 342.

64. Because this is a sensitive topic and one which has concerned
spiritual writers since the days of eastern monasticism, it should be
emphasized that our own remarks are not intended as a defense or
extension of any specific approach to religious obedience. In particular, the fact that we cite obedience as an area where discernment can
be employed does not imply that we are sketching Ignatius' own
teaching on obedience. Such an undertaking, worthwhile as it might
be, would require subsequent and more detailed discussion than the
limits of this book allow.

65. This position is developed more at length in Heinrich Oster-
mann, S.J., "Mitbestimmung in der Kirche und in den Geistlicheor-
den," *Orientierung,* XVIII (September 30, 1966), 194-198.

66. Charmot, *Finding God in All Things,* p. 194.

67. Teilhard de Chardin, *The Divine Milieu* (New York: Harper
and Row, 1960), p. 46.

CHAPTER IX: SPIRIT VERSUS TRADITION

1. The following analysis is not presented as an original contribution to historical research. It rests on the excellent scholarship which
has been made possible over the past years by the publication of
various parts of the *Monumenta Historica Societatis Jesu,* as well as
several important secondary analyses of these sources. On the basis of
this material, historians can now be better acquainted with the genetic
development of both Jesuit history and spirituality and thus make
valid value judgments on certain aspects of the history of spirituality

which have been obscure. The works which provide the basic data for the following presentation include: J. Aicardo, S.J., *Comentario a las Constituciones de la Compañia de Jesus* (Madrid: Blass, 1920), II, 386-409; A. Astrain, S.J., *Historia de la Compañia de Jesus en la Asistencia de España* (Madrid: Blass, 1920), II; P. Bouvier, S.J., *Les origines de l'oraison mentale en usage dans la Compagnie* (Wetteren: J. De Meester, 1923); H. Fouqueray, S.J., *Histoire de la Companie de Jésus en France* (Paris: Alphonse Picard, 1910), I, 435-436; Joseph de Guibert, S.J., *The Jesuits: Their Spiritual Doctrine and Practice* (Chicago: Loyola University Press, 1964), pp. 185-280; Otto Karrer, *Der heilige Franz von Borja* (Freiburg im Breisgau: Herder, 1921), pp. 249-274; Robert E. McNally, S.J., "St. Ignatius: Prayer and the Early Society of Jesus," *Woodstock Letters*, XCIV (1965), 109-134; P. Leturia, S.J., "La hora matutina de meditacion en la Compania naciente," *Archivum Historicum Societatis Jesu*, III (1934), 47-86.

2. De Guibert, *The Jesuits*, p. 127.

3. "Formula Instituti Societatis Jesu," *Const. et. Reg.*, I, 16.

4. "Regimini militantis ecclesiae," *ibid.*, I, 25.

5. Astrain, *op. cit.*, II, 73 ff.

6. McNally, *op. cit.*, p. 113.

7. The following comments follow closely those of McNally, *op. cit.*, p. 114.

8. *Epistolae P. Hieronymi Nadal*, ed. F. Cervos, IV, 645.

9. *Ibid.*, p. 652.

10. Cf. Aicardo, *op. cit.*, II, 389.

11. *Constitutions*, Pt. VI, ch. iii, 1 (*Const. et. Reg.*, III, 187-188).

12. *Ibid.*

13. *Epist. Nadal*, IV, 671.

14. *Scripta de Sancto Ignatio* (Madrid: Lopez del Horno, 1904), I, 515.

15. *S. Ignatii Epistolae*, ed. M. Lecina *et al.*, XII, 650 ff.

16. *Constitutions*, Pt. IV, ch. iv, 3 (*Const. et. Reg.*, III, 113).

17. *Ibid.*; see also *S. Ign. Epist.*, XII, 126.

18. *Epist. Nadal*, IV, 572; *Scripta S. Ign.*, I, 307; *S. Ign. Epist.*, VI, 90; VIII, 95.

19. *S. Ign. Epist.*, III, 510.

20. Karrer, *op. cit.*, pp. 260 ff.

21. *Scripta*, I, 250.

22. *Epist. Nadal*, II, 32.

23. *Scripta*, I, 278 f.
24. *Ibid.*, p. 250 f.
25. See Astrain, *op. cit.*, II, 482-500.
26. General Congregation I, decree 97 (*Institutum Societatis Jesu* [Rome: Civilta Catholica, 1869], I, 163).
27. Karrer, *op. cit.*, p. 261.
28. General Congregation II, decree 29, *loc. cit.*
29. *Epistolae Mixtae*, ed. V. Agusti (Madrid: R. Fortanet, 1901), V, 48 ff., 118 ff.; Astrain, *op. cit.*, II, 135, 267, 447.
30. Fouqueray, *op. cit.*, pp. 1, 479.
31. *Epist. Nadal*, III, 487, 514.
32. Leturia, "De oratione matutina in Societate Jesu documenta selecta," *Archivum Historicum Societatis Jesu*, III (1934), 97-98.
33. This discussion of the historian's difficulty with "providentialism" is based on the remarks of John W. O'Malley, S.J., "De Guibert and Jesuit Authenticity," *Woodstock Letters*, XCIV (1965), 103-110.
34. Henri de Lubac, "The New Man," *Cross Currents*, I (1950), 72-73.
35. See McNally, *op. cit.*, pp. 130-131.
36. The following paragraphs are a paraphrase of the discussion of tradition and the discernment of spirits by Joseph Wall, S.J., in the *Proceedings of the Conference on the Total Development of the Jesuit Priest* (University of Santa Clara, August 1967), Vol. III, Part 2, pp. 155-158. See also Karl Rahner and Joseph Ratzinger, *Revelation and Tradition* (New York, Herder and Herder, 1966).
37. Of course the degree of continuity will necessarily correspond to the ability of the Church in a given age to discern the action of the Spirit. In this task the Church enjoys the negative guarantee of indefectability; as the Church it will never teach positive error. But anyone possessing even a slight acquaintance with the history of theology will admit the weakness of the Church—even in some of its so-called glorious ages—in presenting adequately the ineffable Mystery of God in all its fullness.

CHAPTER X: POST-REFORMATION SPIRITUALITY

1. Hans Küng, *The Council, Reform and Reunion* (New York: Sheed and Ward, 1961), pp. 81-83.
2. "Since . . . you seek the highest degree of perfection, you must

wage continual warfare against yourself and employ your entire strength in demolishing each vicious inclination, however trivial" (Lawrence Scupoli, *Spiritual Combat,* i [trans. William Lester and Robert Mohan (Westminster, Md.: Newman, 1947), p. 6]).

3. Hermann Tüchle, "Baroque Christianity: Root of Triumphalism?" *Historical Problems of Church Renewal,* ed. Roger Aubert (Glen Rock, N.J.: Paulist, 1965), p. 138.

4. *El Escorial, 1563-1963* (Madrid: Ediciones Patrimonio Nacional, 1963), cited in Tüchle, *op. cit.,* p. 139.

5. *Ibid.*

6. See H. Lützeler, "Grosse und Grenze der Barockfrömmigkeit," *Magazin für religiöse Bildung,* CII (1939), 309-317; L. A. Veit-L. Lenhart, *Kirche and Volksfrömmigkeit im Zeitalter des Barock* (Freiburg: Herder, 1956).

7. For a critique of this conception of the relation between nature and grace, see Karl Rahner, *Theological Investigations,* IV, 165-188.

8. Marcelino Menéndez y Pelayo, cited by E. Allison Peers, *The Mystics of Spain* (London: Allen and Unwin, 1951), p. 15.

9. See Michel de Certeau, "Culture and Spiritual Experience," *Spirituality in the Secular City,* pp. 10-17.

10. Teresa and John, among others, escaped this pitfall, aided no doubt by the experience of the apostolic activity they carried on constantly but wrote about with little of the attention or eloquence used to describe their inner lives.

11. Ronald A. Knox, *Enthusiasm: A Chapter in the History of Religion,* pp. 241-242.

12. As indicated in the previous chapter, the Jesuits' insistence on methodical prayer as *the* Ignatian method represented a fundamental misunderstanding of their founder's notion of prayer.

13. What follows is based on Knox, *op. cit.,* chs. ix and x, and on Pierre Pourrat, *Christian Spirituality,* IV, ch. i.

14. C.-A. Sainte-Beuve, *Port-Royal* (Paris: Hachette, 1888), II, 33, quoted from Fontaine, *Mémoires pour servir à l'histoire de Port-Royal.*

15. *Ibid.,* II, 24, quoted from Lancelot, *Mémoires pour servir à la vie de Saint-Cyran.*

16. Quoted in Knox, *op. cit.,* p. 190.

17. See Denzinger, *Enchiridion Symbolorum,* nos. 1351-1451 (2400-2502).

18. Knox, *op. cit.*, pp. 212-213.

19. *Pratique facile pour élever l'âme à la contemplation*, quoted in Pourrat, *op. cit.*, IV, 133.

20. John de Bernières, *Chrétien Interieur*, quoted *ibid.*

21. *Pratique facile . . .*, pp. 277, 364-365, 333-334, quoted *ibid.*, pp. 139, 136, 134.

22. Knox, *op. cit.*, pp. 301-311.

23. Denzinger, *op. cit.*, nos. 1221-1288 (2201-2269).

24. "God allows and wills the devil to violate the bodies of some perfect souls (quite apart from the case of possession) and makes them do wicked things, knowingly and without any scruple" (*ibid.*, no. 1261 [2241]; see Elmer O'Brien, *Varieties of Mystic Experience*, p. 304).

25. See Knox, *op. cit.*, pp. 310-311.

26. *Ibid.*, pp. 319-322.

27. Guyon, *Spiritual Torrents* (text and translation based on Pourrat, *op. cit.*, IV, 181).

28. Knox, *op. cit.*, pp. 334-339.

29. In the decision that came from Rome, Fénelon himself was not condemned, only some of the doctrines he espoused, e.g., relinquishing all desire to be saved. Although Bossuet was completely (and pompously) orthodox, it is at times easier to sympathize with Fénelon in view of the character assassination Bossuet practiced on him during the controversy. Who is more to be condemned—Fénelon, who eliminated hope, or Bossuet, who eliminated charity?

30. Knox, *op. cit.*, pp. 333-334, 330.

31. *Ibid.*, p. 350.

32. *Ibid.*, p. 298.

33. It is interesting to note that these French Jesuit missionaries came under the influence of the great spiritual director and mystical teacher, Louis Lallement; the mystical graces which some of them certainly received were probably an important source of their herculean labors and endurance under torture.

34. The censures issued by Rome forbade only a certain few practices, and it remains difficult to this day to say that the Church was simply wrong in condemning these. Unfortunately, however, the condemnation had a negative effect on the movement for missionary adaptation, which never had too many exponents in the baroque Church (see Henri Bernard-Maître, "The Chinese and Malabar Rites,"

Progress and Decline in the History of Church Renewal, ed. Roger Aubert [New York: Paulist, 1967]), pp. 73-89.

35. The achievements of these men extend, of course, beyond preaching missions and founding their congregations; Paul was a great visionary and mystic of the Cross and Alphonsus a writer of spiritual and moral theology and a crusader against Italian Jansenism.

36. See Pierre Coste, *The Life and Labours of St. Vincent de Paul* (3 vols.; London: Burns, Oates, 1934-1935); W. J. Battersby, *De La Salle: A Pioneer of Modern Education* (London: Longmans, Green, 1949).

37. See M. C. E. Chambers, *The Life of Mary Ward* (2 vols.; London: 1882-1885). In this context of problems with ecclesiastical approval for new forms of religious life, the holy subterfuge of Vincent de Paul is instructive. When confronted with the fact that canon law did not allow women to carry on work outside the cloister as his Daughters of Charity were doing, Vincent simply decided—since he had no intention of having them discontinue their apostolate—that *his* sisters would not be "religious women." "It cannot be maintained," he writes, "that the Daughters of Charity are 'religious,' because they could not be Daughters of Charity if they were" (*Saint Vincent de Paul, Correspondance, Entretiens, Documents,* ed. Pierre Coste [Paris: Gabalda, 1920-1925], IX, 662).

38. James Joyce, *A Portrait of the Artist as a Young Man* (New York: Viking Compass Books, 1964), pp. 147-148.

39. Kevin Sullivan, *Joyce among the Jesuits* (New York: Columbia University Press, 1958), pp. 134-143.

CHAPTER XI: SECULARIZATION, PERSONALISM, RELATIVISM

1. For a fuller discussion of the nature of this new society and the new man emerging within it, see Gibson Winter, *The New Creation as Metropolis* (New York: Macmillan, 1963); Harvey Cox, *The Secular City* (New York: Macmillan, 1965).

2. C. Wright Mills, *The Sociological Imagination* (New York: Oxford University Press, 1959), pp. 165-176; see also Rollo May, *The Meaning of Anxiety* (New York: Ronald Press, 1950), pp. 3-15. The problem of man's search for meaning has been provocatively described by W. H. Auden in *The Age of Anxiety* (New York: Random House, 1947), p. 42.

3. This is a noteworthy fact that might have been predicted once Christian people found again the true source and meaning of their faith. See Albert-Marie Besnard, O.P., "Tendencies of Contemporary Spirituality," *Spirituality in Church and World* (New York: Paulist Press, 1965), pp. 27-28.

4. For a similar division of topics, see *ibid.*, p. 29; Christopher Mooney, "Teilhard de Chardin and Christian Spirituality," *Thought,* XLII (1967), 383-402.

5. Our discussion of secularization is heavily dependent on several excellent studies which have appeared recently, especially Larry Shiner, "Toward a Theology of Secularization," *The Journal of Religion,* XLV (1965), 279-295; Johannes B. Metz, "A Believer's Look at the World," *The Christian and the World: Readings in Theology* Compiled at the Canisianum, Innsbruck, pp. 68-92; Robert L. Richard, S.J., *Secularization Theology* (New York: Herder and Herder, 1967).

6. According to Harnack, the early Church faced the dilemma of either "effectively entering the Roman social system" or of keeping the original forms of life. "Now for the first time," Harnack remarks, "there were voices heard in the Church, warning bishops and congregations against the advancing secularization, holding up to the secular Christians those well known sentences about the imitation of Christ in their literal starkness" (Harnack, *Monasticism: Its Ideals and History,* p. 26).

7. Karl Barth, *Church Dogmatics* (Edinburgh: T. & T. Clark, 1956), I, ii, 289-361. See also Daniel Jenkins, *Beyond Religion* (Philadelphia: Westminster, 1962), ch. ii.

8. Will Herberg, *Protestant-Catholic-Jew* (Garden City, N. Y.: Doubleday Anchor Books, 1960), p. 271.

9. Jacques Maritain, *The Range of Reason* (New York: Scribners, 1952), p. 186.

10. Roger Mehl, "La sécularisation de la cité," *Le problème de la civilisation Chrétienne,* ed. Jean Boisset (Paris: Presses Universitaires de France, 1961), p. 14.

11. Although recent studies suggest that the urbanization theory may no longer hold in its original form, it has long been a commonplace that the European working class is lost to the Church (Gerhard Lenski, *The Religious Factor* [Garden City, N. Y.: Doubleday Anchor Books, 1963], pp. 8-12, 322).

12. Mehl, *op. cit.,* p. 20.

13. Dietrich Bonhoeffer, *Letters and Papers from Prison* (New York: Macmillan, 1953), pp. 236-240.

14. Shiner, *op. cit.,* p. 285.

15. Friedrich Gogarten, *The Reality of Faith* (Philadelphia: Westminster, 1959), pp. 208 ff.

16. Augustine, *City of God,* XIX, xxix.

17. See Emmanuel Mounier, "Christian Faith and Civilization," *Cross Currents,* I (1950), 3-23, especially 10-15.

18. Shiner, *op. cit.,* pp. 286-287.

19. H. Richard Niebuhr, *Christ and Culture* (New York: Harper and Row, 1951), pp. 39-44.

20. M.-D. Chenu and Friedrich Heer, "Is the Modern World Atheist?" *Cross Currents,* XI (1961), 13.

21. M.-D. Chenu, *La Parole de Dieu* (Paris: Editions du Cerf, 1964), II, 29.

22. *Ibid.,* p. 33. The danger of a purely sociological Christianity is that it tends to dispense man from committing himself personally to faith. The way to promote a Christianity "for the poor," for example, is not to resign oneself to an easy reliance on Christianity as a "religion for the people," as if it were a matter of historical fate. This would not do justice either to the power of the gospel or to the evangelical resources of the poor. At the same time, we do not want to fall into a view of Christianity that would dispense man from courageously taking responsibility for his human existence. God must be seen at the center of life and not on the boundary where we reach the end of our rope. Faith as the response of man's whole person to the true God creates a genuine relationship with God. And whatever phase our human culture may go through, faith will always demand a trusting surrender to God—a surrender which is never a rejection of responsibility or an alienation. The strange truth is that man can only find himself by losing himself and transcending himself in him who is his life, his freedom and his happiness. (Cf. Claude J. Geffre, O.P., "Desacralization and the Spiritual Life," *Spirituality in the Secular City,* pp. 130-131; also Karl Rahner, *Theological Investigations,* IV, 107-112).

23. Jean Daniélou, however, takes a different position. As he sees it, one danger of the secularizing trend in contemporary theology and spirituality is that Christianity will be so thoroughly cleansed of human and cultural accretions that the Church will become the domain of a tiny elite. This conviction leads him to view the Church as

sent primarily to the disenfranchised—the materially, politically, socially, and intellectually poor. To fulfill such a massive mission the Church must be profoundly rooted in the realities of civilization even on an institutional level. Only in this way can the world—the secular —be re-sacralized; and such re-establishment of the sacred is a necessary condition for the sanctification of the world. It is quite possible, however, that Daniélou and Chenu (together with Maritain and Niebuhr) are not essentially so far apart. All of these men want the faith to penetrate social and political life. Together they reject an oversimplified separation of the spiritual and the temporal, the sacred and the profane, the Christian element and the political element. The quarrel basically comes down to a dispute about the means to be employed in making the faith relevant to modern times. (Cf. Daniélou, *Prayer as a Political Problem* [New York: Sheed and Ward, 1967].) Certainly one can understand Daniélou's concern. But one may also fear that he is providing ammunition for those who long for a return to the past, and one would like to see him just as much haunted by the other "poor," the poor of the modern world who feel themselves more and more alienated from the Church insofar as this Church is still compromised by superstitious practices and out-of-date institutions.

24. Shiner, *op. cit.*, p. 288.

25. Carl Michalson, *The Rationality of Faith* (New York: Scribner's, 1963), p. 188.

26. Paul M. Van Buren, *The Secular Meaning of the Gospel* (New York: Macmillan, 1963), p. 161.

27. Our discussion of Teilhard draws heavily on Christopher Mooney's excellent article, "Teilhard de Chardin and Christian Spirituality," *Thought*, XLII (1967), as well as his *Teilhard de Chardin and the Mystery of Christ* (New York: Harper and Row, 1964). See also the studies by Henri de Lubac, S.J. (*The Religion of Teilhard de Chardin* [New York: Herder and Herder, 1967]) and Robert L. Faricy, S.J. (*Teilhard de Chardin's Theology of the Christian in the World* [New York: Sheed and Ward, 1967]).

28. De Lubac, *op. cit.*, p. 243.

29. Teilhard de Chardin, *The Divine Milieu* (New York: Harper and Row, 1960), p. 91; see also p. 152.

30. Teilhard de Chardin, *Letters from a Traveller* (New York: Harper and Row, 1962), pp. 123, 140.

31. Teilhard de Chardin, "Le Christ dans la matière," *Ecrits du temps de la guerre* (Paris: Grasset, 1965), pp. 98-100.

32. Teilhard de Chardin, "Mon Univers," *Science et Christ* (Paris: Seuil, 1965), p. 96.

33. Chardin, *The Divine Milieu*, p. 82.

34. Cox, *The Secular City*, pp. 83, 265-266.

35. Chardin, *The Divine Milieu*, pp. 113, 23, 42.

36. *Ibid.*, p. 66.

37. Many of our reflections on personalism have been drawn from the work of Robert O. Johann, S.J. See his *The Meaning of Love* (Glen Rock, N. J.: Paulist Press, 1954); "Subjectivity," *The Review of Metaphysics*, XII (1958), 200-234; "Charity and Time," *Cross Currents*, IX (1959), 140-149.

38. See Delbert Brady, "The Organization Principle and the Quality of Human Existence," *Cross Currents*, XVII (1967), 181-195.

39. "The Pastoral Constitution on the Church in the Modern World," *The Documents of Vatican II*, nos. 220, 240, 236, 237.

40. The phrase is Sidney Hook's, *New York Times Magazine*, June 5, 1966.

41. John Macmurray, *Persons in Relation* (New York: Humanities Press, 1961), pp. 127-165.

42. Cf. Besnard, *op. cit.*, pp. 39-44.

43. Chardin, *The Divine Milieu*, p. 71.

44. Chardin, *Letters from a Traveller*, p. 206.

45. Cf. Mooney, "Teilhard de Chardin and Christian Spirituality," *loc. cit.*, p. 395.

46. Johann, "Charity and Time," *loc. cit.*, pp. 140-142.

47. Chardin, *Letters from a Traveller*, p. 104.

48. *Ibid.*, p. 207.

49. Chardin, *The Divine Milieu*, p. 154.

50. Teilhard de Chardin, *Le Coeur de la matière* (an unpublished essay, 1960), p. 2.

51. Mooney, *loc. cit.*, p. 399.

52. Karl Rahner, *The Christian Commitment*, pp. 18-19.

53. Avery Dulles, "The Ignatian Experience as Reflected in the Spiritual Theology of Karl Rahner," *Philippine Studies*, XIII (1965), 190-191.

54. Thomas Merton, "Is the World a Problem?" *Commonweal*, LXXXVI (1966), 305-309. See also John A. T. Robinson, *Honest to God* (Philadelphia: Westminster Press, 1963), pp. 12-28; Paul Til-

lich, *Systematic Theology* (Chicago: University of Chicago Press, 1963), III, 26-101, 244.

CHAPTER XII: THE DESERT AND THE CITY

1. John E. Smith, *Royce's Social Infinite, the Community of Interpretation* (New York: The Liberal Arts Press, 1950), pp. 113-114.
2. Merton, "Is the World a Problem?" pp. 306-307.
3. The following two paragraphs are based on Martin E. Marty, "After the World Doesn't Answer," *The National Catholic Reporter,* November 29, 1967, p. 10.
4. Jürgen Moltmann, *The Theology of Hope* (London: SCM Press, 1967); Johannes B. Metz, "The Church and the World," *The Word and History* (New York: Sheed and Ward, 1966), pp. 69-85; Metz, "Creative Hope," *The Month,* XXXVI (1966), 105-113.
5. Moltmann, *op. cit.,* p. 227.
6. *Ibid.,* p. 225.
7. Metz, "Creative Hope," p. 113.
8. This point is further developed in Rolland F. Smith, "A Theology of Rebellion," *Theology Today,* XXV (1968), 10-22; see also Karl Rahner, "Christianity and the New Earth," *Theology Digest,* XV (1967), 275-282.

Index